Lecture Notes in Artificial Intelligence   6973

Subseries of Lecture Notes in Computer Science

LNAI Series Editors

Randy Goebel
University of Alberta, Edmonton, Canada
Yuzuru Tanaka
Hokkaido University, Sapporo, Japan
Wolfgang Wahlster
DFKI and Saarland University, Saarbrücken, Germany

LNAI Founding Series Editor

Joerg Siekmann
DFKI and Saarland University, Saarbrücken, Germany

Franziska Klügl   Sascha Ossowski (Eds.)

Multiagent System Technologies

9th German Conference, MATES 2011
Berlin, Germany, October 6-7, 2011
Proceedings

 Springer

Series Editors

Randy Goebel, University of Alberta, Edmonton, Canada
Jörg Siekmann, University of Saarland, Saarbrücken, Germany
Wolfgang Wahlster, DFKI and University of Saarland, Saarbrücken, Germany

Volume Editors

Franziska Klügl
Örebro University
Modeling and Simulation Research Center
70182 Örebro, Sweden
E-mail: franziska.klugl@oru.se

Sascha Ossowski
University Rey Juan Carlos
ETSII / CETINIA
Calle Tulipán s/n
28933 Móstoles (Madrid), Spain
E-mail: sascha.ossowski@urjc.es

ISSN 0302-9743   e-ISSN 1611-3349
ISBN 978-3-642-24602-9   ISBN 978-3-642-24603-6 (eBook)
DOI 10.1007/978-3-642-24603-6
Springer Heidelberg Dordrecht London New York

Library of Congress Control Number: 2011937701

CR Subject Classification (1998): I.2, D.2, C.2.4, I.2.11, H.4, F.3

LNCS Sublibrary: SL 7 – Artificial Intelligence

Typesetting: Camera-ready by author, data conversion by Scientific Publishing Services, Chennai, India

Printed on acid-free paper

Springer is part of Springer Science+Business Media (www.springer.com)

Preface

These are the proceedings of the 9th German Conference on Multi-Agent System Technologies (MATES 2011). The MATES conference series provides an interdisciplinary forum for researchers, users, and developers of intelligent agents and multi-agent systems, to present and discuss the latest advances of research in the field, as well as prototyped or fielded systems. It aims at covering the whole range of agent and multi-agent technologies, promoting both theory and applications.

MATES 2011 took place during October 6–7, 2011, in Berlin. Building on the success of the eight previous editions of MATES since 2003, MATES 2011 was co-located with two major events: INFORMATIK 2011, the 41st Annual Conference of the 'Gesellschaft für Informatik e.V.' (GI), and KI 2011, the 34th Annual German Conference on Artificial Intelligence. This was the second time that a co-location with the main German Computer Science conference was sought; yet it turned out to be particularly interesting as the focus theme of INFORMATIK was "communities" – a topic strongly related to multi-agent systems research. The appropriate design of truly open systems as artificial communities constituted one of the core topics of the MATES 2011 conference, with solutions based on the explicit treatment of agreements and agreement processes as well as agent organizations and self-organizing multi-agent systems.

With the support of the International Program Committee of MATES 2011, out of 50 submissions from all over the world, we accepted 12 as full papers and 6 as short papers, yielding an acceptance ratio of 24% for full papers and 36% for all conference papers. To outline the relevance of research into organization and organizational structures for open multi-agent systems, our program included presentations by two distinguished invited speakers, Olivier Boissier and Hartmut Schmeck, covering the range from organization-oriented programming to self-organizing multi-agent systems. Together with the KI 2011 conference, a Doctoral Consortium was organized by René Schumann including a panel on research and quality.

Finally, as Conference Chairs we would like to thank the authors of submitted papers and the invited speakers for their contributions; the members of the Program Committee as well as the additional reviewers for their careful, critical, and thoughtful reviews; and the local conference organizers and their team for their help and support in making MATES 2011 a success.

We hope the attendees enjoyed MATES 2011 and the co-located conferences in Berlin, both scientifically and socially, and will continue to support MATES as a conference series with many more successful events to come in the future.

July 2011

Franziska Klügl
Sascha Ossowski

Organization

Program Committee

Sahin Albayrak	Technical University of Berlin, Germany
Klaus-Dieter Althoff	University of Hildesheim, Germany
Elisabeth Andre	University of Augsburg, Germany
Bernhard Bauer	University of Augsburg, Germany
Ana Bazzan	UFRGS, Brazil
Holger Billhardt	University Rey Juan Carlos, Spain
Vicent Botti	Technical University of Valencia, Spain
Lars Braubach	University of Hamburg, Germany
Frances Brazier	Technical University of Delft, The Netherlands
Jörg Denzinger	University of Calgary, Canada
Jürgen Dix	Technical University of Clausthal, Germany
Torsten Eymann	University of Bayreuth, Germany
Klaus Fischer	DFKI, Germany
Maria Ganzha	University of Gdansk, Poland
Paolo Giorgini	University of Trento, Italy
Christian Guttmann	EBTIC, UAE
Koen Hindriks	Technical University of Delft, The Netherlands
Wiebe van der Hoek	University of Liverpool, UK
Tom Holvoet	KU Leuven, Belgium
Wojtek Jamroga	University of Luxembourg, Luxemburg
Stefan Kirn	University of Hohenheim, Germany
Matthias Klusch	DFKI, Germany
Daniel Kudenko	University of York, UK
Stefano Lodi	University of Bologna, Italy
Beatriz Lopez	University of Girona, Spain
Simon Miles	King's College London, UK
Daniel Moldt	University of Hamburg, Germany
Pavlos Moraitis	University of Paris Descartes, France
Jörg Müller	Technical University of Clausthal, Germany
Eugenio Oliveira	University of Porto, Portugal
Andrea Omicini	University of Bologna, Italy
Julian Padget	University of Bath, UK
Ana Paiva	University of Lisbon, Portugal
Marcin Paprzycki	Polish Academy of Sciences, Poland
Michal Pechoucek	Czech Technical University, Czech Republic
Paolo Petta	OFAI, Austria
Alexander Pokahr	University of Hamburg, Germany
Marko Schorlemmer	CSIC, Spain

Frank Schweitzer	ETH Zürich, Switzerland
Kuldar Taveter	Technical University of Tallinn, Estonia
Ingo Timm	University of Trier, Germany
Denis Trcek	University of Ljubljana, Slovenia
Adelinde Uhrmacher	University of Rostock, Germany
Rainer Unland	University of Duisburg-Essen, Germany
Laszlo Z. Varga	MTA SZTAKI, Hungary
Cees Witteveen	Technical University of Delft, The Netherlands

Additional Reviewers

Bach, Kerstin	Köhler-Bußmeier, Michael
Barakat, Lina	Lopes Cardoso, Henrique
Becker, Marianne	Luetzenberger, Marco
Bernon, Carole	Lujak, Marin
Buck, Christoph	Müller, Marcus
Cabac, Lawrence	Newo, Rgis
Caminada, Martin	Niemann, Christoph
Castro, António	Nunes, Ingrid
Derksen, Christian	Pfitzner, René
Devlin, Sam	Rocha, Ana
Ewald, Roland	Rossetti, Rosaldo
Fricke, Stefan	Savani, Rahul
Gui, Ning	Slavkovik, Marija
Hanif, Shaza	Spanoudakis, Nikolaos
Hermoso, Ramon	Stern, Guillaume
Himmelspach, Jan	Tanase, Dorian
Hudert, Sebastian	Ter Mors, Adriaan
Jacob, Ansger	Vasirani, Matteo
Junges, Robert	Wagner, Thomas
Konnerth, Thomas	Wester-Ebbinghaus, Matthias
Koster, Andrew	Zanetti, Marcelo

Table of Contents

From Organisation Oriented Programming to Multi-agent Oriented Programming

Olivier Boissier

Ecole Nationale Supérieure des Mines
158 Cours Fauriel, 42100 Saint-Etienne, France
Olivier.Boissier@emse.fr

Abstract. Social and organizational aspects of agency have become a major issue in the Multi-Agent Systems (MAS) domain. Recent applications of MAS on Web and Ambient Computing enforce the need of using these dimensions in the programming of MAS. The aim is to ensure the governance of such systems while preserving their decentralization and openness. In this talk, we present how multi-agent organisations provide software abstractions, models and tools that contribute to this aim. We focus on the MOISE framework that we have developped during these last years. This framework proposes an organisation programming language for defining multi-agent organisations, that are managed and supported by organisational artifacts at the system programming level and by organisation-awareness mechanisms at the agent programming level. This framework is included in the JaCaMo platform, integration of Jason Agent Programming Language, CarTaGo environment platform and MOISE. We illustrate different features of Organisation Oriented Programming of MAS using different application examples. We will highlight also how it integrates in a broader perspective of multi-agent oriented programming of decentralized and open systems.

F. Klügl and S. Ossowski (Eds.): MATES 2011, LNAI 6973, p. 1, 2011.

Organic Computing – A Generic Approach to Controlled Self-organization in Adaptive Systems

Hartmut Schmeck

Institute AIFB, Karlsruhe Institute of Technology
Kaiserstr. 89, 76133 Karlsruhe, Germany
hartmut.schmeck@kit.edu

Abstract. Organic Computing is a recent paradigm for the design and management of complex technical systems, addressing the need for adaptive, self-organising systems which are capable of dealing with changing requirements and unanticipated situations in a robust and trustworthy way and which allow an external "observer" or "user" to interfere and influence the system whenever it does not show acceptable behaviour by itself. Research in this area has been supported by a priority program of the German Research Foundation[1]. The talk will present the generic observer/controller architecture of Organic Computing. An essential concept of this architecture is the combined use of online and offline learning. The application of these concepts will be described with respect to our research on organic traffic control and on smart energy systems.

---

[1] http://www.organic-computing.de/SPP

F. Klügl and S. Ossowski (Eds.): MATES 2011, LNAI 6973, p. 2, 2011.

JadexCloud - An Infrastructure for Enterprise Cloud Applications

Lars Braubach, Alexander Pokahr, and Kai Jander

Distributed Systems and Information Systems
Computer Science Department, University of Hamburg
{pokahr,braubach}@informatik.uni-hamburg.de

Abstract. Cloud computing allows business users to scale up or down resource needs according to current demands (utility computing). Infrastructures for cloud computing can be distinguished with respect to the layer they operate on. In case of platform as a service (PAAS) frameworks are provided in order to simplify the construction of cloud applications relying on common base abstractions and tool sets. The focus of current PAAS frameworks is quite narrow and directed towards support for web applications and also visual tools for non-programmers. We envision that cloud computing can also substantially push forward typical enterprise applications if these applications are made to exploit cloud capabilities. In this paper we present an infrastructure for developing, deploying and managing distributed applications with the vision of distribution transparency in mind. The infrastructure is meant to be on PAAS layer but addresses developers instead of end users. It is founded on the active component paradigm for distributed applications, which allows applications being composed of agent-like autonomous entities interacting via services. The model facilitates building scalable and robust enterprise applications due to the high modularity and independently acting modules that can be replaced or restarted if unexpected errors occur. In addition to the infrastructure, a real world scenario of a distributed workflow management systems will be explained.

1   Introduction

Cloud computing [8] is seen as a new approach to IT infrastructure management that facilitates a pay-as-you-go usage model. By making computational resources available on a demand-driven basis instead of statically devoting physical systems to certain applications, the approach minimizes wasted resources. Taking this idea further, it seems reasonable that existing computers in a company network should contribute their spare resources in a company private *enterprise cloud*.

Applications in the cloud can be built on the IAAS (infrastructure as a service) or the PAAS layer. With IAAS, access to the cloud is granted by virtual machines that allow a fine-grained control of the software stack to be used, including low-level aspects like the operating system. On the one hand the level of access does not restrict the application types deployable on the IAAS layer but on the other

F. Klügl and S. Ossowski (Eds.): MATES 2011, LNAI 6973, pp. 3–15, 2011.
© Springer-Verlag Berlin Heidelberg 2011

hand it does not contribute to any of the hard problems of how to develop a complex distributed application. Using PAAS, the cloud operator establishes a new software layer with a dedicated middleware API (application programming interface) and in this way abstracts away lower-level details. This facilitates development of applications on top of the given platform, but on the other hand it firmly restrics the types of applications to those supported by the platform. Today, PAAS platforms are mostly targeted towards typical data-driven web applications with an additional focus on support for non-programmer interfaces.

Summarizing the IAAS and PAAS characteristics, an important gap can be identified for the systematical support for a wide range of enterprise applications in the cloud. This gap is only partially filled by existing enterprise solutions like application servers as these have not been conceived with cloud properties in mind and do not allow transparently exploiting additional resources of the cloud. To achieve the vision of a versatile private enterprise cloud two fundamental challenges remain:

- How to turn a highly dynamic environment consisting of volatile nodes into a robust, manageable cloud infrastructure.
- How to design and implement enterprise applications such that they are able to exploit the cloud characteristics.

These two challenges can be broken down into a number of more concrete requirements. With regard to the first challenge, the cloud middleware should require minimal installation effort and zero administration effort for the single nodes, otherwise it would not be feasible to include the many different types of computers usually found in a company network. Furthermore, the operation of the cloud infrastructure should not affect normal operation of the nodes, e.g. it should not restrict the way, an employee uses her computer. Therefore, the infrastructure has to deal with dynamically appearing and disappearing nodes, as employees turn on and switch off their computers. To support typical enterprise applications, the cloud environment needs to support administration tasks also for applications distributed in the cloud and therefore facilitate a transparent management of distributed applications as a whole. Finally, the deployment of applications should be efficient in terms of resource utilization, which requires monitoring the available resources and reconfiguring the deployment structure based on current application characteristics and infrastructure shape.

For addressing the second challenge, the infrastructure has to provide an intuitive programming model for distributed systems, which facilitates building applications such that they can be transparently partitioned and deployed in the cloud infrastructure. The computing model should also support distribution transparency in the sense of hiding complex distribution and concurrency issues. In summary, this paper aims at developing a distributed computing infrastructure for private enterprise clouds that meets the following requirements:

1. Require minimal installation and administration effort for the infrastructure
2. Support independently operated nodes and dynamic environments
3. Provide an intuitive programming model for distributed applications

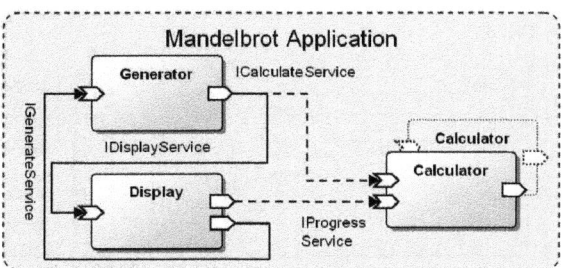

Fig. 1. Architecture of the Mandelbrot example application

4. Allow transparent application administration
5. Perform dynamic reconfiguration

Although all of the above mentioned challenges are vital for a full-fledged private enterprise cloud, the first three are sufficient for an initial solution showing the basic functioning of the cloud. Hence, in this paper mainly the first two questions are tackled and corresponding solutions are presented. An answer to question three with regard to an intuitive programming model for distributed systems has already been given as part of our earlier research work [7] and is only shortly recapped here. The underlying idea consists in using active components, which are software agents with features of components and services. Active components can be seen as extension of SCA (service component architecture) [6], which is a promising new paradigm for enterprise system development superseding traditional approaches like Java EE and has been pushed forward by influential industry players like IBM and Oracle.[1] The last two questions have been addressed only partially so far and are largely subject of future work.

The remainder of this paper is structured as follows. In Section 2 calculating Mandelbrot images will be introduced as a running example. Thereafter, in Section 3 the novel architecture of an agent-inspired cloud middleware will be presented. In Section 4 an extensive real world scenario from the area of distributed workflow management will be described. Section 5 reviews related work and in Section 6 a conclusion and an outlook to planned future work is given.

2   Running Example

Our approach is illustrated by a running example throughout this paper, that provides a complete application scenario but is simple enough to be easily understood. It is called *Mandelbrot* and allows users to render fractal images. To speed up the rendering process, the system should be able to distribute the computation across different hosts in a network.

The application is developed based on the active components paradigm introduced in [7] and the implementation is available as part of the open source

---

[1] http://www.osoa.org

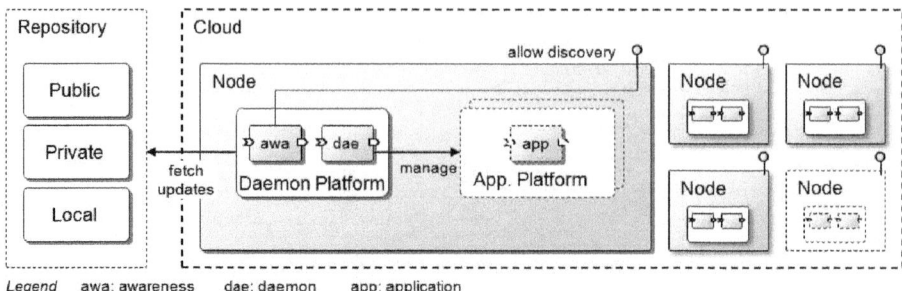

Fig. 2. Daemon layer structure

Jadex active components framework.[2] Each active component represents an independent entity, that serves as unit of concurrency. The decomposition into components thus facilitates a later partitioning and deployment of applications in a distributed infrastructure. The interdependencies between the active components are made explicit by defining appropriate required as well as provided service interfaces, representing functionality that is publicly offered and used by a component. Compositions of an application are designed by specifying concrete bindings for connecting provided and required services at runtime.

Figure 1 shows the Mandelbrot application architecture. The *display* component provides interaction capabilities for a user of the system. It is responsible for presenting rendered images to the user and allowing the user to issue new rendering requests (e.g. by zooming into the picture or by manually entering area values and selecting a fractal type). The *generator* component handles user requests and decomposes them into smaller rendering tasks. It acts as a coordinator responsible for task distribution and result collection. The *calculator* component accepts rendering tasks and returns results of completed tasks to the generator. It implements different fractal algorithms and is thus able to provide the color values for pixels of the image to be rendered. These components are connected by respective required and provided service interfaces. E.g. the display component uses the *IGenerateService* to issue rendering requests to the generator component. The explicit specification of required and provided interfaces allows the application to be dynamically configured and adapted to the available resources in the infrastructure.

3   JadexCloud Architecture

Key concept of the proposed architecture is a layer model that helps separating responsibilities and managing complexity. It is composed of three layers. The *daemon layer* provides a minimal node infrastructure for basic management of cloud resources, e.g. automatically announcing available nodes participating

---

[2] http://jadex-agents.informatik.uni-hamburg.de/

in the network. On top, the *platform layer* supports application related management tasks including e.g. the deployment of application artifacts to different nodes as well as starting and stopping components. Finally, the *application layer* facilitates the application development by providing APIs and debugging tools.

3.1 Daemon Layer

The daemon layer (cf. Fig. 2) consists of different nodes on which a *daemon platform* is running in the background. The daemon platform represents the entry point for a node to the cloud. It has the purpose of facilitating the discovery of the underlying node, which can only be part of the cloud when announced by the awareness agent (*awa*). Depending on the type of network the cloud should span, different announcement protocols have to be used. In case of a local area network, a simple TCP/IP multicast mechanism is sufficient in many cases, whereas more complex network setups also require more elaborated announcement methods.[3] Furthermore, the daemon agent (*dae*) provides a high-level service API for application management from the platform layer. This API allows for starting and stopping application platforms, on which application components (*App*) can be executed. The design is meant to enforce a strict separation between daemon and application execution in order to ensure long-lived manageability of the node even if an application is erroneous. During application execution the daemon can monitor the application platforms and terminate them whenever appropriate. The daemon platform also has access to repositories containing software bundles. Currently the repository is based on flat files, but the idea is to use a chain of Maven repositories to support versioning, etc. In this context it is distinguished between local, private and public repositories. A local repository is located directly on the node of the daemon, whereas a private repository is typically owned by an organization and shared by the member nodes of this organization. Public repositories have global scope and are thus available on Internet scale. The daemon uses these repositories for updating itself by regularly testing if new versions of its library are available.

In the following the role of the daemon layer is illustrated with respect to the running example of the Mandelbrot application. When a user wishes to deploy the Mandelbrot application on, e.g., a pool of workstation computers she has to make sure that all nodes can be discovered by the cloud infrastructure. Therefore, the minimal daemon platform has to be installed on each node. The platform registers itself e.g. as a unix daemon or windows service, such that it is started each time the host operating system is started. Therefore, the daemon has to be installed only once and needs no further attention afterwards. When assuming that the daemon is already present at each of the nodes, e.g. as part of a customized system distribution used for each pool workstation, then no administration tasks are required in the daemon layer for the Mandelbrot application.

---

[3] In ongoing work Internet scale announcement and discovery is analyzed by utilizing existing peer-to-peer mechasims based on registries and superpeers.

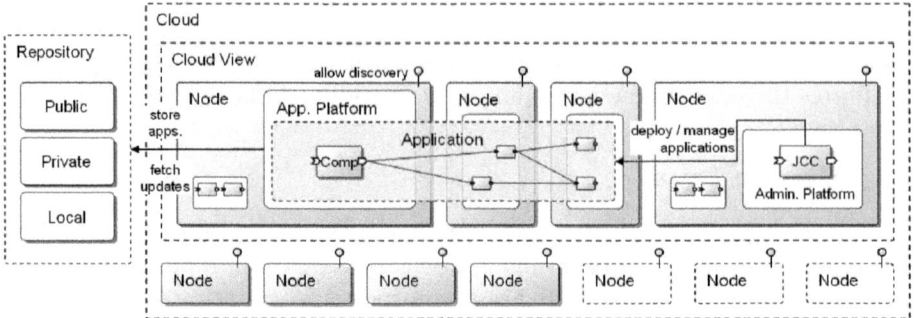

Fig. 3. Platform layer structure

3.2 Platform Layer

The purpose of the platform layer (cf. Figure 3) is to provide a management and execution infrastructure on which applications can be deployed and administered. It can be seen that the layer reuses many of the functionalities of the daemon layer, but introduces a different view. The entry point to the management functionality is an administration tool called *JCC* (Jadex Control Center) on an *administration platform*. To perform administration tasks, a user would typically start a local platform including a JCC. Yet, the choice of the administration platform is unrestricted as the JCC tool can be executed in principle on any platform. Based on local configuration options and user privileges, the JCC provides access to a subset of the existing nodes called the *cloud view*. The administrator can choose, which nodes to include in the deployment of an application, by assigning application components to the platforms running on the different nodes. To start the separate components, each platform will obtain the required component implementations from the local, private, or public repository. Alternatively, e.g. when deploying a new application, the JCC can upload component implementations to the remote platforms, which store them in their local repository. During the runtime of an application, the JCC tool can be used to connect to the platforms hosting the application components. Therefore, an administrator may at any time inspect the running components as well as alter the deployment configuration by starting and stopping components.

The operation of the JCC is further exemplified by illustrating the steps necessary to deploy the Mandelbrot application. The vision is that a user selects an application to deploy and is presented a cloud view of currently available nodes according to her profile. Based on an optional deployment description with requirements of the application components the system generates a deployment plan. By applying the plan the application is started creating components on the selected nodes. This vision as also covered in challenge 4 from the introduction is currently only partially realized. Once the JCC is started by the user, it will discover the available nodes based on the daemon layer awareness and filter them according to user preferences, e.g. a specific IP range. Using the daemon

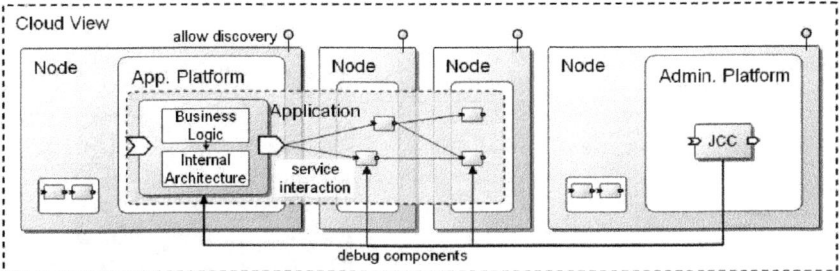

Fig. 4. Application layer structure

service, the user can start new application platforms on each node to host the Mandelbrot components. Afterwards the user can choose, which components to start on which nodes. For the Mandelbrot application the user would typically start calculator components on the remote nodes with the number of components on each node corresponding to the number of available cores.

3.3   Application Layer

The application layer is concerned with how a distributed application can be built based on the active components paradigm as well as providing tools for debugging and testing applications during development. The active component metaphor (cf. Fig. 4) comprises three aspects: a public interface describing provided and required services, an internal autonomous behavior, and service binding specifications. Provided services describe the externally available functionality of the component, while required services explicitly state the dependencies of a component. The active components metaphor supports an agent-oriented view where components do not only passively carry out service requests, but are capable of autonomous behavior. The implementation of such behavior (i.e. *business logic*) is based on one of several supported *internal architectures* allowing to build e.g. BDI (belief desire intention) agents, simple task-based agents or BPMN (business process modeling notation) workflows. To establish a connection for *service interaction*, the active components runtime supports flexible binding mechanisms, which allow statically wiring components together, dynamically searching for available components and even creating new required components on demand. To enable the autonomous behavior of the component, each service request is decoupled from the caller and put into a request queue at the receiver side allowing a component to decide for itself when to react to a request. The active component runtime infrastructure is complemented by a suite of tools, included in the *JCC*, that support common development tasks such as debugging components, monitoring interactions, executing test cases, etc. These tools themselves are also realized using active components and are thus capable of operating transparently on local and remote components. Therefore a developer can debug remote components easily by starting the JCC on her local computer.

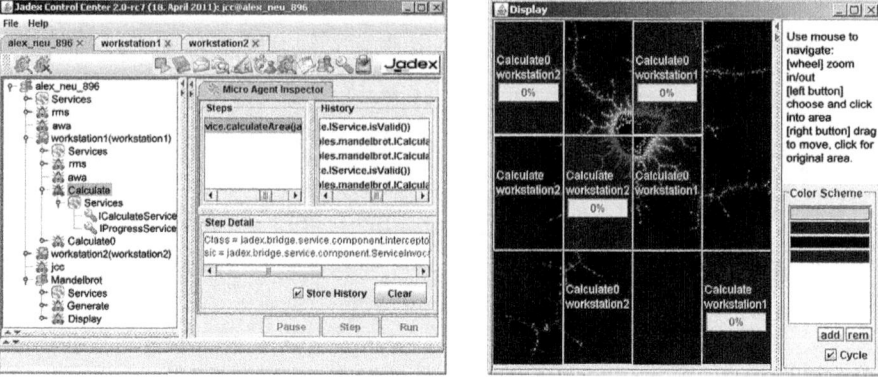

Fig. 5. Screenshot of the JCC (a) and the Mandelbrot user interface (b)

The Mandelbrot design from Section 2 has been implemented using the simple task-based agent kernel. Service interfaces and implementations are realized as plain Java files containing only application functionality, because the infrastructure is capable of adding the required glue for dynamic service binding automatically. The usage of the runtime tools is illustrated in Fig. 5a, showing the JCC while running the Mandelbrot application on three distributed nodes. The tree to the left shows the three platforms on the nodes (*alex_neu_896*, *workstation1*, *workstation2*) and the components on each platform. At the bottom, it can be seen that the main Mandelbrot application including the *display* and *generator* components is running on the local node, while each remote workstation runs two *calculator* components. At the top of the JCC there are tabs allowing to administer the remote platforms directly. To the right of the JCC, the debugger tool is activated for a remote calculator running on workstation1. The tool shows the current step of the agent as well as a history of previously executed steps and furthermore allows a stepwise component execution. In Fig. 5b the user interface of the Mandelbrot application is shown, which illustrates the assignment of completed and ongoing tasks to the four calculator components.

Summary. The previous sections have illustrated our vision and the current state of an infrastructure for a private cloud. The current implementation automatically discovers nodes in local networks and supports manual remote deployment of distributed applications based on the intuitive active components paradigm. In this respect the infrastructure represents a significant improvement for the development and management of complex distributed applications in e.g. company networks. Yet we regard it only as one step towards our ultimate private cloud infrastructure vision, which has to incorporate automatic monitoring and reconfiguration abilities as well as transparent remote application management.

4   Real World Scenario

Business Process Management (BPM) is an important topic for many organizations. *Workflow management systems* are widely deployed to automate and streamline business processes used within an organization. The purpose of such systems consists of managing workflow models, workflow execution, assignment and distributions of tasks (*work items*) and providing monitoring functionality, which allows management and process engineers to review workflow execution, improve the workflow models and intervene if there are problems [9]. Typical workflow management systems consist of centralized software which is deployed on a server and accessed using a web interface. This limits the flexibility regarding system configuration and makes it vulnerable to server breakdowns.

These shortcomings have been partially remedied by a distributed workflow management system implementation shown in Fig. 6, which is based on the cloud infrastructure presented in this paper. The system is partitioned into five components which can be distributed and replicated across multiple platforms and act together to provide the functionality of the system. The *access component* manages access to the system by external clients connecting to it, providing a unified interface to invoke system functions. User authentication and authorization is delegated to the *authentication component*. The access component uses dynamic service discovery to find available authentication services and therefore allows the authentication component to be replaced by an alternative at runtime.

Execution of workflows is handled by the *execution component*, including the workflow model repository and the execution service. The model repository uses the functionality of the platform layer to deploy workflow models which can then be started by the execution service. Executing workflows emit tasks to be performed by system users. Tasks are represented by *work items*, which are processed and distributed to the users by the *work item management component*.

Finally, the *monitoring component* receives events such as work item completion, user authentications and process execution from the other system services and stores them until accessed using the access component. Like the authentication component, this relationship is also dynamic and allows service substitution.

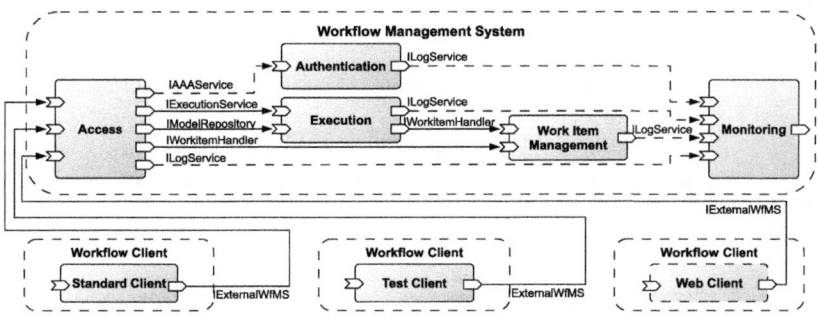

Fig. 6. Architecture of the workflow management system

Moreover, all available monitoring components are notified about events, allowing them to only store a partial set of the events enabling distributed storage.

Two *workflow clients* have been implemented which use the access component to interact with the system. The first is a standard workflow management client with a user interface enabling a workflow participant to process work items, monitor the system and perform administrative tasks, provided they possess the necessary privileges. The second client is an automated client which is used to test process models by repeated execution of test scenarios [4]. A third, web-based client is currently being developed. All of the clients use the service discovery of the infrastructure to find available workflow management systems and allow the user to choose any system available within the enterprise cloud.

As shown, both the workflow management system and the available client software make extensive use of the functionality of the infrastructure. This enables them to distribute the workload across multiple nodes, dynamically replace parts of the system and access remote functionality. Since the infrastructure manages the technical details, the implementation can be relatively simple, requiring little effort to enable a complex application to be distributed.

5   Related Work

The main rationale of the assessment of related approaches, stemming from grid and cloud PAAS, consists in evaluating them with respect to the five challenges from Section 1. In Fig. 7 an overview of the analyzed approaches is given.

The original intent of grid computing approaches is exploiting computing power of other nodes e.g. for high performance computing. This motivation has led to client/server approaches with load being distributed from the server to clients. They perform the assigned tasks and send back the results to the server.

	Platforms	Min. Install and Administration	Ind. Nodes in Dynanmic Env.	Transparent Distributed Apps	Dynamic Reconfiguration	Programming Model
Grid Platforms	GlobusToolkit	no / configurations	yes / registries	no / distributed view	yes / dyn. service discovery	SOA grid/web service
	ProactiveGCM	no / configurations	no / static infrastruc. desc.	no / distributed view	partially / static wires/res.mgmnt	active comps Fractal
	GridGain	yes / normal installer	yes / dyn. node discovery	no / centralized application	yes/ dyn. task assignment	oo & functional Java/grid tasks
	Boinc	yes / client approach	yes / nodes contact server	no / centralized application	yes / dyn. task assignment	oo C++/grid tasks
Cloud PAAS	GoogleApp Engine	yes / centralized access	no / known structure	partially / centralized apps	yes / dyn. resource alloc.	oo web applications
	Run@Cloud CloudBees	yes / centralized access	no / known structure	partially / centralized apps	yes / dyn. resource alloc.	components/oo JEE/Spring
	Paremus	yes / daemon approach	yes / dyn. node discovery	yes / holistic view	partially / rather static deploymnt	components SCA/OSGI
	JadexCloud	yes / daemon approach	yes / dyn. node discovery	partially / man. global view	yes / dyn. services&comps	active comps SCA extension

Fig. 7. Related approaches from cloud and grid computing

The underlying task distribution model with a rather centralized application has inspired several grid approaches like BOINC[4] and GridGain[5]. Other approaches like the GlobusToolkit [3] and Proactive [1] have extended the computational model from client/server to generic distributed applications. The programming model of the approaches directly reflects their application shape assumptions. While GridGain and Boinc use traditional object oriented techniques with tasks as primary abstraction for work distribution, Globus envisions a service oriented world consisting of introspectable and transient grid services, which will be created and terminated on demand. Proactive proposes using a model of components and active objects resembling very much the author's active component approach [7]. Regarding installation and administration complexity GridGain and BOINC address an easy integration of nodes offering installer-based solutions, whereas Globus and Proactive assume that an infrastructure model is explicitly set up, describing e.g. where registries are located and components should be deployed. The dynamics of environments is addressed by very different means. Globus uses service registries, GridGain uses dynamic node discovery based on awareness and BOINC uses a centralized server infrastructure. Proactive is rather focused on the static infrastructure model. Dynamic reconfiguration is supported by all approaches to some extent. GridGain and BOINC allow dynamic distribution of tasks taking into account the current grid structure. Globus allows dynamic binding of services by registry lookups and Proactive components can also be rebound by stopping and restarting them.

Cloud PAAS centers on efficient execution of specific application types, currently dominated by web applications. Typically, cloud PAAS hides distribution and concurrency aspects from developers and enable them to deploy a standard application in the cloud. The application can be scaled by the cloud infrastructure according to the customer demands. The approach is appealing but bounded by the narrow focus of existing PAAS infrastructures. Furthermore, today's applications have to follow vendor specific APIs for characteristics that are subject of scaling, e.g. the storage system. This easily leads to vendor lock-ins and problems in case scaling does not work as expected.

Google App Engine[6] and Run@Cloud from CloudBees[7] are two typical platforms in the direction described above. The first facilitates development of standard web applications while the latter supports Java EE enterprise applications. In contrast Paremus [5] is the only platform similar to JadexCloud targeted at general distributed applications for private clouds. The underlying programming models are object orientation in case of the Google App Engine, component orientation in case of Run@Cloud, and component service orientation (SCA) in case of Paremus. JadexCloud further advances the programming model to active components, which rely on a structural model very similar to SCA. Installation and administration requirements for the first two platforms

---

[4] http://boinc.berkeley.edu/
[5] http://www.gridgain.com/
[6] http://code.google.com/intl/de-DE/appengine/
[7] http://www.cloudbees.com/run.cb

are simplified by centralized web access interfaces to the cloud infrastructure. Paremus and Jadex pursue the idea of a dynamic cloud with a varying number of nodes. For this reason both use a daemon approach, meaning that a minimal bootstrapping software has to be installed on all nodes of the cloud. The cloud structure is rather well known for a typical cloud PAAS like Google App Engine and CloudBees and made fully transparent to the cloud user. Instead, Paremus and JadexCloud are built to deal with dynamic cloud infrastructures allowing nodes to be discovered and dynamically included or excluded to/from the cloud. Thus, the application view is different as well. The first two keep the standard non-distributed application view and use internal logic for scaling, the latter two handle truly distributed applications, meaning that functionally different parts of applications run on different machines. Despite the application distribution both, Paremus and JadexCloud, aim at a high-level view on the distributed application being able to abstract from distribution aspects. All four platforms deal with dynamic reconfiguration of applications. In the Google App Engine and CloudBees, reconfiguration tasks are completely transparent. Paremus and JadexCloud have to deal with more complex situations due to the possibly fine-grained application deployment structure. Relocations of components are difficult to achieve in Paremus due to its reliance on SCA. In JadexCloud, relocations can be achieved, as active components support dynamic service bindings.

Summarizing, most grid toolkits are built for dynamic environments and allow for runtime grid adaptations but suffer from too simple programming models (except Proactive) based on object orientation or services. On the contrary, cloud PAAS infrastructures are typically built to make standard (web) applications scalable and are narrowly focused (except Paremus). They consider applications as being non-distributed and use established programming models like object orientation and components. Approaches like Paremus and JadexCloud go beyond the typical cloud PAAS and facilitate building distributed systems running in a dynamic infrastructure.

6   Summary and Outlook

This paper has argued that enterprises can benefit from private clouds to perform heavy computational tasks allowing a smooth scaling according to current demands. Such a private cloud may not only consist of dedicated servers but may also include normal computers used for daily work. In order to run applications in such a dynamic cloud it is necessary to a) create a robust infrastructure from a varying set of nodes and b) use a programming model allowing applications being assembled of independent components that are dynamically coordinated.

As a solution the JadexCloud infrastructure has been presented, consisting of three layers. The daemon layer is responsible for managing basic cloud resources by e.g. announcing nodes participating in the network. The platform layer is used for application management tasks such as deployment and starting of application components. The application layer supports application development through APIs and tools. Using a workflow management application example it has been shown how a distributed cloud application can be built.

As future work mainly the remaining challenges for allowing transparent application administration and performing dynamic reconfigurations will be tackled. The first requires a conceptual abstraction for distributed applications and their components, possibly inspired by earlier work [2], while the latter has to cope with collecting and evaluating non-functional node data such as performance, utilization and uptime in order to reorganize a running application.

References

1. Baude, F., Caromel, D., Dalmasso, C., Danelutto, M., Getov, V., Henrio, L., Pérez, C.: Gcm: a grid extension to fractal for autonomous distributed components. Annals of Telecommunications 64(1-2), 5 (2009)
2. Braubach, L., Pokahr, A., Bade, D., Krempels, K.-H., Lamersdorf, W.: Deployment of Distributed Multi-Agent Systems. In: Gleizes, M.-P., Omicini, A., Zambonelli, F. (eds.) ESAW 2004, vol. 3451, pp. 261–276. Springer, Heidelberg (2005)
3. Foster, I., Kesselman, C., Nick, J., Tuecke, S.: The physiology of the grid: An open grid services architecture for distributed systems integration. Technical report, Global Grid Forum (2002)
4. Jander, K., Braubach, L., Pokahr, A., Lamersdorf, W.: Validation of agile workflows using simulation. In: Third international Workshop on LAnguages, methodologies and Development tools for multi-agent systemS (LADS 2010). CEUR (2010)
5. Paremus Ltd. The paremus service fabric: A technical overview (2009)
6. Marino, J., Rowley, M.: Understanding SCA. Addison-Wesley, Reading (2009)
7. Pokahr, A., Braubach, L., Jander, K.: Unifying agent and component concepts. In: Dix, J., Witteveen, C. (eds.) MATES 2010. LNCS, vol. 6251, pp. 100–112. Springer, Heidelberg (2010)
8. Sosinsky, B.: Cloud Computing Bible. Wiley, Indiana (2011)
9. Workflow Management Coalition (WfMC). Workflow Reference Model (1995)

Hybrid Multi-agent Planning

Mohamed Elkawkagy and Susanne Biundo

Dept. of Artificial Intelligence
Ulm University, D-89069 Ulm, Germany
firstname.lastname@uni-ulm.de

Abstract. Although several approaches have been constructed for multi-agent planning, solving large planning problems is still quite difficult. In this paper, we present a new approach that integrates landmark preprocessing technique in the context of hierarchical planning with multi-agent planning. Our approach uses Dependent and Independent clustering techniques to break up the planning problem into smaller clusters. These clusters are solved individually according to landmark information, then the obtained individual plans are merged according to the notion of fragments to generate a final solution plan. In hierarchical planning, landmarks are those tasks that occur in the decomposition refinements on every plan development path. Hierarchical landmark technique shows how a preprocessing step that extracts landmarks from a hierarchical planning domain and problem description can be used to prune the search space that is to be explored before actual search is performed. The methodologies in this paper have been implemented successfully, and we will present some experimental results that give evidence for the considerable performance increase gained through our system.

1 Introduction

Multi-agent planning (MAP) has been used to solve large planning problems. It works by splitting the given planning problem into subproblems. Each subproblem is solved individually to produce a solution so-called *subplan*. Then, these subplans have to be combined to construct the solution plan [14]. Furthermore, MAP has been used to interpret the plan coordination process of a set of independent agents. There are three different approaches which discuss the plan coordination process. The first one focuses on the coordination between completed plans such as the work of Tonino et al. [12] that achieves a less costly merging plan by exploiting positive interactions and resolving the conflicts between the generated subplans. In the second one, the processes of coordination and planning are interleaved i.e. the conflicts between subplans are resolved before each agent generates its subplan [13]. The third one is divided into two categories: implicit coordination that propagates general rules to manage agent behavior [15], and explicit coordination that allows for the exchange of information between agents before planning is started and provides additional constraints to the original planning problem to ensure that the generated solution plan is feasible [10].

Many researchers have used hierarchical structure in the MAP approach to improve planning efficiency. NOAH [3] is the first system which was built to interleave the hierarchical planning and merging process by exchanging shared resources. It was developed by focusing on the efficient communication among planner agents [4]. Afterwards,

F. Klügl and S. Ossowski (Eds.): MATES 2011, LNAI 6973, pp. 16–28, 2011.

a new method has been developed to detect the conflicts not only at the primitive levels, but also at abstract levels [2]. Recently, Hisashi [8] presented an HTN planning agent system working in dynamic environments. The set of agents in his approach are arranged in stratified form as parent and children agents which work together to achieve the goal. As opposed to these approaches, integrating MAP with hierarchical preprocessing techniques which prune the search space of a hierarchical planner has not been considered so far. Recently, we have introduced the hierarchical landmark technique for the purpose of domain model reduction [5]. In hierarchical planning, *landmarks* are mandatory abstract or primitive tasks that have to be performed by any solution plan.

In this paper, we present a novel hybrid approach that combines the landmark preprocessing technique in the context of hierarchical planning with multi-agent planning in order to enhance planning efficiency. Our architecture consists of a set of agents. The **pre-processing agent** analyzes a given planning problem by applying a landmark algorithm in hierarchical planning. It does so by systematically inspecting the methods that are eligible to decompose the relevant abstract tasks. Beginning with the (landmark) tasks of the initial plan, the procedure follows the way down the decomposition hierarchy until no further abstract tasks qualify as landmarks. The **master agent** can be divided into two parts: the first part handles a split process and the second handles a merging process. Finally, the **slave agents** are a set of identical agent planners that are executed concurrently, they do not cooperate among each others and each one of them uses HTN-style planning to generate its own individual plan.

Before introducing our approach in section 3, we will review the underlying planning framework in section 2. Section 4 presents the merging technique that combines individual plans to generate a solution plan. Section 5 describes the experimental setting and the evaluation results. The paper ends with some concluding remarks in section 6.

2   Formal Framework

HTN planning relies on the concepts of tasks and methods [7]. Primitive tasks correspond to classical planning operators, while abstract tasks represent complex activities. For each abstract task, a number of methods are available each of which provides a task network, *i.e., a plan that specifies a pre-defined (abstract) solution of the task*. Planning problems are (initial) task networks. They are solved by incrementally decomposing the abstract tasks until the network contains only primitive ones in executable order.

Our planning framework relies on a *hybrid* formalization [1] which combines HTN planning with partial-order causal-link (POCL) planning. For the purpose of this paper, only the HTN shares of the framework are considered, however. A task schema $t(\bar{\tau}) = \langle \text{prec}(t(\bar{\tau})), \text{add}(t(\bar{\tau})), \text{del}(t(\bar{\tau})) \rangle$ specifies the preconditions and effects of a task via conjunctions of literals over the task parameters $\bar{\tau} = \tau_1 \ldots \tau_n$. States are sets of literals. Applicability of tasks and the state transformations caused by their execution are defined as usual. A *plan* $P = \langle S, \prec, V, CL \rangle$ consists of a set S of *plan steps* – (partially) instantiated task schemata that carry a unique label to differentiate between multiple occurrences of the same schema –, a set $\prec$ of *ordering constraints* that impose a partial order on S, a set V of *variable constraints*, and a set CL of *causal links*. V consists of (in)equations that associate variables with other variables or constants; it also reflects the (partial) instantiation of the plan steps in P. We denote by $Ground(S, V)$ the set of ground tasks obtained by equating all parameters of all tasks in P with constants, in a way compatible with V. The causal links are adopted from POCL planning: a causal link $s_i \rightarrow_\varphi s_j$ indicates that φ is implied by the precondition of plan step s_j and at the same time is a consequence of the effects of plan step s_i. Hence, the precondition φ is said to be *supported* this way. Methods $m = \langle t(\bar\tau), P \rangle$ relate an abstract task $t(\bar\tau)$ to a plan P, which is called an *implementation* of $t(\bar\tau)$. In general, multiple methods are provided for each abstract task. Please also note that no application conditions are associated with the methods, as opposed to other representatives of HTN-style planning.

An HTN planning problem $\Pi = \langle D, s_{init}, P_{init} \rangle$ is composed of a domain model $D = \langle T, M \rangle$, where T and M denote sets of task schemata and decomposition methods, an initial state s_{init}, and an initial plan P_{init}. Note, that in our *hybrid* planning framework, one can specify a goal state. However, since we restrict ourselves in this paper to pure HTN planning, the goal state is omitted. A plan $P = \langle S, \prec, V, CL \rangle$ is a solution to Π if and only if: (1) P is a refinement of P_{init} i.e., a successor of the initial plan in the induced search space (see Def. 1 below), (2) each precondition of a plan step in P is supported by a causal link in CL and no such link is threatened, i.e., for each causal link $s_i \rightarrow_\varphi s_j$ the ordering constraints in $\prec$ ensure that no plan step s_k with an effect that implies $\neg\varphi$ can be placed between plan steps s_i and s_j, (3) the ordering and variable constraints are consistent, i.e., $\prec$ does not induce cycles on S and the (in-) equations in V are not contradictory, and (4) all plan steps in S are primitive ground tasks. Please note that we encode the initial state via the effects of an artificial primitive task, as it is usually done in POCL planning. In doing so, the second criterion guarantees that the solution is executable in the initial state.

In order to refine the initial plan into a solution, there are various *refinement steps* (or *plan modifications*) available; in HTN planning, these are: (1) the decomposition of abstract tasks using methods, (2) the insertion of causal links to support open preconditions of plan steps, (3) the insertion of ordering constraints, and (4) the insertion of variable constraints. Given an HTN planning problem Π, its initial plan and the available plan modifications we can define the induced search space as follows.

Definition 1 (Induced Search Space). *The directed graph $\mathcal{P}_\Pi = \langle \mathcal{V}_\Pi, \mathcal{E}_\Pi \rangle$ with vertices $\mathcal{V}_\Pi$ and edges $\mathcal{E}_\Pi$ is called the induced search space of the planning problem Π iff (1) $P_{init} \in \mathcal{V}_\Pi$, (2) if there is a plan modification refining $P \in \mathcal{V}_\Pi$ into a plan P', then $P' \in \mathcal{V}_\Pi$ and $(P, P') \in \mathcal{E}_\Pi$, and (3) $\mathcal{P}_\Pi$ is minimal such that (1) and (2) hold. For $\mathcal{P}_\Pi$, we write $P \in \mathcal{P}_\Pi$ instead of $P \in \mathcal{V}_\Pi$. In general, $\mathcal{P}_\Pi$ is neither acyclic nor finite.*

In order to search for solutions, the induced search space is explored in a heuristically guided manner by our refinement planning algorithm (Alg. 1).

The fringe $\langle P_1 \ldots P_n \rangle$ is a sequence containing all unexplored plans that are direct successors of visited non-solution plans in $\mathcal{P}_\Pi$. It is ordered in a way such that a plan P_i is estimated to lead more quickly to a solution than plan P_j for $j > i$. The current plan is always the first plan of the fringe. The planning algorithm iterates on the fringe as long as no solution is found and there are still plans to refine (line 1). Hence, the flaw detection function f^{FlawDet} in line 1 calculates all flaws of the current plan. A flaw is a set of plan components that are involved in the violation of a solution criterion. The presence of an abstract task raises a flaw that consists of that task, a causal threat consists of a causal link and the threatening plan step, for example. If no flaws can be found, the plan is a solution and returned (line 1). In line 1, the modification generating function f^{ModGen} calculates all plan modifications that address the flaws of the current plan. Afterwards, the modification ordering function f^{ModOrd} orders these modifications according to a given strategy. The fringe is finally updated in two steps. First, the plans resulting from applying the modifications are computed (line 1) and put at the beginning of the fringe (line 1). Second, the plan ordering function f^{PlanOrd} orders the updated fringe. This step can also be used to discard plans, i.e., to delete plans permanently from the fringe. This is useful for plans that contain unresolvable flaws such as an inconsistent ordering of tasks. If the fringe becomes empty, no solution exists and `fail` is returned.

Algorithm 1. Refinement Planning Algorithm

---

input : The sequence `Fringe` $= \langle P_{init} \rangle$.
output: A solution or `fail`.

1 **while** `Fringe` $= \langle P_1 \ldots P_n \rangle \neq \varepsilon$ **do**
2 $\quad F \leftarrow f^{\text{FlawDet}}(P_1)$
3 $\quad$ **if** $F = \emptyset$ **then return** P_1
4 $\quad \langle \mathtt{m}_1 \ldots \mathtt{m}'_n \rangle \leftarrow f^{\text{ModOrd}}(\bigcup_{\mathtt{f} \in F} f^{\text{ModGen}}(\mathtt{f}))$
5 $\quad$ succ $\leftarrow \langle apply(\mathtt{m}_1, P_1) \ldots apply(\mathtt{m}'_n, P_1) \rangle$
6 $\quad$ `Fringe` $\leftarrow f^{\text{PlanOrd}}(\text{succ} \circ \langle P_2 \ldots P_n \rangle)$

7 **return** `fail`

---

3   Hybrid Multi-agent Planning

Figure 1 depicts the components of our architecture. It consists of the pre-processing agent and the planning agents. The planning agents encapsulate the master agent and slave agents as well as a shared constraints set in their context. The shared constraints set (SC) is a shared memory that includes a set of constraints. Note, that all agents have complete knowledge about the initial state of the planning problem. In the following subsections, we will illustrate the key features of our agents.

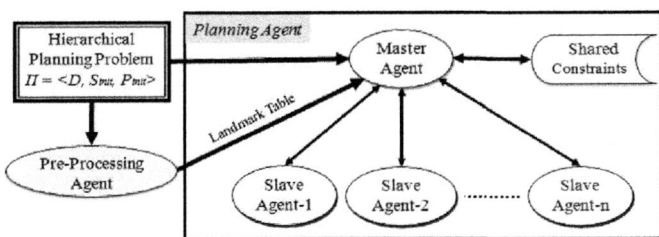

Fig. 1. Hybrid Multi-agent Planning Architecture

3.1   Pre-processing Agent

The pre-processing agent uses a preprocessing technique in order to perform some pruning of the search space before the actual search is performed in order to reduce the planning effort. Recently, we introduced a landmark technique which restricts the domain
and problem description of an HTN to a smaller subset, since some parts of the domain
description might be irrelevant for the given problem at hand [5,6]. Therefore, the pre-
processing agent relies on hierarchical landmarks – ground tasks that occur in the plan
sequences leading from an initial plan to its solution. They are defined as follows.

Definition 2 (Solution Sequences). *Let* $\langle \mathcal{V}_\Pi, \mathcal{E}_\Pi \rangle$ *be the induced search space of plan-
ning problem* Π. *Then,* $SolSeq_\Pi(P) := \{\langle P_1 \ldots P_n \rangle | P_1 = P, (P_i, P_{i+1}) \in \mathcal{E}_\Pi$ *for all*
$1 \leq i < n,$ *and* $P_n \in Sol_\Pi, n \geq 1\}$.

Definition 3 (Landmark). *A ground task* $t(\overline{\tau})$ *is called a* landmark *of planning prob-
lem* Π, *if and only if for each* $\langle P_1 \ldots P_n \rangle \in SolSeq_\Pi(P_{\mathrm{init}})$ *there is an* $1 \leq i \leq n$, *such
that* $t(\overline{\tau}) \in Ground(S_i, V_n)$ *for* $P_i = \langle S_i, \prec_i, V_i, CL_i \rangle$ *and* $P_n = \langle S_n, \prec_n, V_n, CL_n \rangle$.

While a landmark occurs in every plan sequence that is rooted in the initial plan and
leads towards a solution, a *local* landmark occurs merely in each such sequence rooted
in a plan containing a specific abstract ground task $t(\overline{\tau})$.

Definition 4 (Local Landmark of an Abstract Task). *For an abstract ground task*
$t(\overline{\tau})$ *let* $\mathcal{P}_\Pi(t(\overline{\tau})) := \{P \in \mathcal{P}_\Pi | P = \langle S, \prec, V, CL \rangle$ *and* $t(\overline{\tau}) \in Ground(S, V)\}$.
A ground task $t'(\overline{\tau}')$ *is a* local landmark *of* $t(\overline{\tau})$, *if and only if for all* $P \in \mathcal{P}_\Pi(t(\overline{\tau}))$ *and
each* $\langle P_1 \ldots P_n \rangle \in SolSeq_\Pi(P)$ *there is an* $1 \leq i \leq n$, *such that* $t'(\overline{\tau}') \in Ground(S_i, V_n)$
for $P_i = \langle S_i, \prec_i, V_i, CL_i \rangle$ *and* $P_n = \langle S_n, \prec_n, V_n, CL_n \rangle$.

Since there are only finitely many task schemata and we assume only finitely many constants, there is only a finite number of (local) landmarks. Given a planning problem Π,
the relevant landmark information can be extracted in a pre-processing step. The outcomes of the extraction procedure that is introduced by Elkawkagy et al. [5] is stored in
a so-called *landmark table*. Its definition relies on a *Task Decomposition Graph* (TDG).

A TDG is a representation of all possible ways to decompose the initial plan P_{init} of
Π using methods in M. More formally, a TDG of a planning problem Π is a bipartite
graph $\langle V_T, V_M, E \rangle$, where V_T is a set of ground tasks (called *task vertices*), V_M is a set of
methods (called *method vertices*), and E is the set of edges connecting task vertices with
method vertices according to M. Note, that a TDG is finite as there are only finitely many
ground tasks and a finite number of methods. The *landmark table* is a data structure that
represents the TDG plus some additional information about local landmarks.

Definition 5 (Landmark Table). *Let* $\langle V_T, V_M, E \rangle$ *be a* TDG *of the planning problem*
Π. *The* landmark table *of* Π *is the set* $LT = \{\langle t(\overline{\tau}), M(t(\overline{\tau})), O(t(\overline{\tau})) \rangle | t(\overline{\tau}) \in V_T\}$,
where $M(t(\overline{\tau}))$ *and* $O(t(\overline{\tau}))$ *are defined as follows:*
$M(t(\overline{\tau})) = \{t'(\overline{\tau}') \in V_T \mid t'(\overline{\tau}') \in Ground(S, V)$ *for all* $\langle t(\overline{\tau}), \langle S, \prec, V, CL \rangle \rangle \in V_M\}$
$O(t(\overline{\tau})) = \{Ground(S, V) \setminus M(t(\overline{\tau})) \mid \langle t(\overline{\tau}), \langle S, \prec, V, CL \rangle \rangle \in V_M\}$

Each landmark table entry partitions the tasks introduced by decompositions into two
sets. Mandatory tasks $M(t(\overline{\tau}))$ are those ground tasks that are contained in all plans

introduced by some method which decomposes $t(\bar{\tau})$; hence, they are local landmarks of $t(\bar{\tau})$. The optional task set $O(t(\bar{\tau}))$ contains for each method decomposing $t(\bar{\tau})$ the set of ground tasks which are not in the mandatory set.

Once the landmark table has been constructed, the pre-processing agent terminates itself after sending the landmark table to the master agent. Please note that the information about landmarks can be exploited in two ways. The first way is to reduce the domain model by ignoring infeasible method decompositions or, more precisely, to transform a universal domain model into one that includes problem-specific pruning information [5]. The second application of the landmark table is to serve as a reference for the planning strategy to deduce heuristic guidance from the knowledge about which tasks have to be decomposed on refinement paths that lead towards a solution [6]. Each slave agent will use the former way in order to construct its individual solution plan.

3.2 Planning Agents

Our planning scenario includes a set of planning agents. They integrate to generate a final solution for the given planning problem. The set of planning agents is divided into two different types: a master agent and a set of identical agents so-called *slave agents*.

Master Agent: It takes a hierarchical planning problem Π and the computed landmark table LT as input and generates the final solution plan. To this end, the master agent performs two processes: a split process and a merging process.

In the split process, the master agent decomposes a planning problem Π into a set of clusters according to two different techniques: Dependent (Dep) and Independent (Ind). The Dep technique relies on the idea of constructing a set of dependent clusters, while the Ind technique creates a set of independent clusters. A comparison of the respective results will be done in the experimental section (cf. Sec. 5).

In each iteration of the Dep algorithm (Alg. 2), in the current plan, the tasks that are not preceded by other tasks are separated in one cluster. While the set of constraints between tasks in different clusters is inserted in the shared constraints set SC.

The Dep algorithm takes the planning problem Π, a landmark table LT *(i.e., the LT is computed by the pre-processing agent)*, and a set $\Gamma = \langle \Pi_\gamma, SC \rangle$ as input and computes the final set Γ. The set Γ consists of the shared constraints set SC and the set of clusters $\Pi_\gamma = \bigcup_{i=0}^{n} \{\Pi_{\gamma_i}\}$, where n is the number of clusters. Each cluster Π_{γ_i} will be considered as a sub-problem. In order to identify different clusters, the Dep algorithm runs recursively through all tasks in the initial plan P_{init} until all tasks have been traversed. Each cluster $\Pi_\gamma = \langle D, s_{init}, P_{\gamma_{init}}, LT_\gamma \rangle$ includes a domain model D, an initial state s_{init}, a partial plan $P_{\gamma_{init}}$ which represents an initial plan for the cluster Π_γ, and an LT_γ that represents relative landmark information of the tasks in the partial plan $P_{\gamma_{init}}$.

Now, we will have a look at how the set Γ is constructed by our Dep algorithm. First, the set Γ is initialized (line 2). Afterwards, in the current plan P_{init}, the tasks te_i that are pre-request-free are collected (line 2). In lines 2 to 2, a new cluster Π_{γ_i} is created, and the tasks in te_i are added to the task network of the plan $P_{\gamma_{init}}$. Then, the tasks te_i are removed from the task network TE of the plan P_{init}. For the current tasks te_i at hand, lines 2 to 2 illustrate iterative loops to extend the created cluster Π_{γ_i} by adding different constraints and updating SC by inserting new constraints. For each task t in the set of tasks te_i, the preprocessing information in the LT which is relevant to the current task t is added to the field LT_{γ_i} in the cluster Π_{γ_i}. This information in LT_{γ_i} will help the planner (slave) agent to reduce the planning effort necessary to find the individual plan for the cluster Π_{γ_i} (line 2). In lines 2 and 2, the plan $P_{\gamma_{init}}$ in the cluster Π_{γ_i} is extended by adding all variable V, ordering $\prec$ and CL constraints that point to a relation between the current task t and the other tasks in the set te_i. After that, these constraints are removed from the current plan P_{init} in Π. Afterwards, the shared constraints set SC and the current partial plan P_{init} are updated by inserting and removing respectively all constraints that relate task t to other tasks outside the set of tasks te_i (lines 2 and 2). Finally, the current set Γ is updated by adding the current new cluster Π_{γ_i} to the set of cluster Π_γ as well as updating the shared constraints set SC (line 2). Note that SC will play a great role in the merging process. The Dep algorithm is called recursively with the modified plan and the updated Γ to inspect a new cluster (line 2).

On the other hand, in each iteration of the Ind algorithm, in the current plan, the tasks that are dependent are collected in one cluster and consequently SC get empty. Therefore, in order to split the planning problem into a set of clusters according to the Ind algorithm, we will replace line 2 in Algorithm 2 by the following line *"Select tasks te_i **that are dependent"**. Due to this replacement, the set of clusters which are produced are explicitly independent, and the shared constraints set SC will be empty.

Once the set of clusters has been generated either by the Dep or Ind algorithm, the master agent initiates a number of slave agents based on the number of clusters and distributes these clusters among slave agents in order to construct individual solution plans for them. Afterwards, the master agent suspends its activity until all slave agents respond by returning individual solution plans for all clusters, and then wakes up again to perform the merging process in order to generate a general solution plan (cf. sec. 4).

Algorithm 2. *Dependent (Dep) Algorithm*

Input : $\Pi = \langle D, s_{init}, P_{init} \rangle$: Planning problem,
              LT: LandmarkTable, $\Gamma = \langle \Pi_\gamma, SC \rangle$

Output: Γ

1 $\Gamma = \langle \Pi_\gamma, SC \rangle \longleftarrow null$
2 **if** $(TE == \emptyset)$ **then return** Γ
3 Select tasks te_i that are pre-request-free from P_{init}.
4 Create a new cluster $\Pi_{\gamma_i} = \langle D, s_{init}, P_{\gamma_{init}}, LT_{\gamma_i} \rangle$.
5 Add these tasks te_i to the partial plan $P_{\gamma_{init}}$ in cluster Π_{γ_i}.
6 Let $TE \longleftarrow (TE - te_i)$
7 **foreach** *(task $t \in te_i$)* **do**
8 | Attach the relevant information of the task t in the LT to the LT_{γ_i} in the cluster Π_{γ_i}
9 | Add all constraints $(\prec_t, V_t, CL_t)$ that relate task t with the other tasks in te_i to $P_{\gamma_{init}}$
10 | Let $V \longleftarrow (V - V_t); \prec \longleftarrow (\prec - \prec_t); CL \longleftarrow (CL - CL_t)$
11 | Insert all constraints $(\prec_{\bar{t}}, V_{\bar{t}}, CL_{\bar{t}})$ that relate task t with another task $\bar{t} \notin te_i$ into SC.
12 | Let $\prec \longleftarrow (\prec - \prec_{\bar{t}}); V \longleftarrow (V - V_{\bar{t}}); CL \longleftarrow (CL - CL_{\bar{t}})$
13 $\Gamma = \langle \Pi_\gamma, SC \rangle \longleftarrow \langle (\Pi_\gamma \cup \Pi_{\gamma_i}), SC \rangle$
14 **return Dependent**(Π, LT, Γ)

Slave Agents: It is a set of identical agents working concurrently in order to solve the set of clusters which are passed by the master agent. To this end, each slave agent uses our refinement planning algorithm (cf. Alg. 1) to generate its own individual plan. Our refinement algorithm takes the initial plan $P_{\gamma_{init}}$ of the assigned cluster as an input and refines it stepwise until the individual solution plan is found.

Since our approach is based on a *declarative* model of task abstraction, the exploitation of knowledge about hierarchical landmarks can be done *transparently* during the generation of the task expansion modifications: First, the respective modification generation function $f_{AbsTask}^{ModGen}$ is deployed with a reference to the landmark table LT_{γ_i} of the cluster problem Π_{γ_i}. During planning, each time an abstract task flaw indicates an abstract plan step $t(\bar{\tau})$ the function $f_{AbsTask}^{ModGen}$ does not need to consider all methods provided in the domain model for the abstract task $t(\bar{\tau})$. Instead, it operates on a reduced set of applicable methods according to the respective options $O(t(\bar{\tau}))$ in the LT_{γ}.

It is important to see that the overall plan refinement procedure is not affected by this domain model reduction, neither in terms of functionality (*flaw and modification modules do not interfere*) nor in terms of search control (*strategies are defined independently, and completeness of search is preserved*).

Note that if the refinement planning algorithm returns `fail`, the slave agent works as a master agent and performs all functions of the master agent. Finally, each slave agent terminates itself after sending the generated individual solution p_{γ} to the master agent.

4   Merging Methodology

Our merging methodology depends on the notion of *Fragments*. The merging technique proceeds in two processes. Firstly, the set of individual plans $P_{\Gamma} = \{p_{\gamma_1}, p_{\gamma_2}, \cdots, p_{\gamma_n}\}$ (*i.e., which are produced by slave agents*) is divided into a set of *Fragments*. These *Fragments* are constructed according to the ordering constraints in the SC. Each fragment $F = \langle P_{\gamma}, O_{\gamma} \rangle$ consists of a set of individual plans P_{γ} ($P_{\gamma} \subseteq P_{\Gamma}$), and a set of ordering constraints O_{γ} that impose a partial order on P_{γ}. For example, suppose the ordering constraints in SC are $\{s_1 \prec s_2, s_2 \prec s_3, s_4 \prec s_5\}$. Let a set of individual plans $P_{\Gamma} = \{p_{\gamma_1}, \cdots, p_{\gamma_7}\}$ be respectively a solution plan for abstract plan steps $s_1, \cdots, s_7$. Then according to the ordering information in SC, these plans in P_{Γ} constitute three different fragments $F_1 = \langle \{p_{\gamma_1}, p_{\gamma_2}, p_{\gamma_3}\}, \{p_{\gamma_1} \prec p_{\gamma_2}, p_{\gamma_2} \prec p_{\gamma_3}\} \rangle$, $F_2 = \langle \{p_{\gamma_4}, p_{\gamma_5}\}, \{p_{\gamma_4} \prec p_{\gamma_5}\} \rangle$, and $F_0 = \langle \{p_{\gamma_6}, p_{\gamma_7}\}, \{\emptyset\} \rangle$. Note that there are two types of fragments. *Related-Fragment* includes those individual plans that are dependent such as F_1 and F_2, and *Zero-Fragment* which includes those individual plans that do not have explicit dependency such as F_0.

Secondly, the plans in each fragment are merged to produce a plan so-called *Merge-Fragment-Plan (MFPlan)*, and then all *MFPlans* are combined in order to generate a general final solution plan. To this end, we need to identify the implicit dependency between individual plans especially in *Zero-Fragment*. This dependency is identified by matching preconditions and effects of the tasks in individual plans. This means, certain postcondition of plan p_{γ_i} tasks required as preconditions for plan p_{γ_j} tasks.

There are two reasons for determining the plan dependency: canceling the negative interactions (*one task deletes the effect or precondition of another task*), and benefit from the positive interactions *(two different tasks need the same precondition and at least one of them does not remove it, or one task generates precondition of another task)*.

Intuitively, the set of independent plans can be executed concurrently by integrating them into one large plan. Otherwise, if the implicit dependency between individual plans in *Zero-Fragment* is detected, then the master agent updates it by adding ordering constraints between these plans. Despite the order dependency between plans, some tasks in these plans can be performed concurrently. Note that tasks cannot take place concurrently if the pre- or post-conditions of the tasks in the successor plan are inconsistent with the postconditions of the tasks in the predecessor plan [9]. Therefore, in order to determine the concurrent tasks, we will establish a comparison between pre- and post-conditions of tasks in the successor plan with the postconditions of the tasks in the predecessor plan. The comparison process will be started by checking pre- and post-conditions of the first task in the successor plan p_{γ_j} with postconditions of different tasks in the predecessor plan p_{γ_i}. If a pre- or post-condition of the first task in p_{γ_j} is violated, then this task will execute sequentially with plan p_{γ_i} and the procedure of case-1 will be performed. Otherwise, the first task will be executed concurrently with the plan p_{γ_i} and the procedure of case-2 will be performed. The comparison process in case-2 will go further in the successor plan p_{γ_j} in order to repeat the comparison with the next task. At this point, we neither need case-2 nor steps number 4 and 5 in case-1.

Case-1: (1) Create ordering constraint $\langle last\ task\ in\ p_{\gamma_i},\ current\ task\ in\ p_{\gamma_j}\rangle$, (2) Remove ordering constraint $\langle last\ task\ in\ p_{\gamma_i},\ goal()\ task\ in\ p_{\gamma_i}\rangle$, (3) Remove goal() task from p_{γ_i}, (4) Remove ordering constraint $\langle initial()\ task\ in\ p_{\gamma_j},\ current\ task\ in\ p_{\gamma_j}\rangle$, (5) Remove initial() task from p_{γ_j}, (6) Stop comparison process.

Case-2: (1) Remove ordering constraint $\langle initial()\ task\ in\ p_{\gamma_j},\ current\ task\ in\ p_{\gamma_j}\rangle$, (2) Remove initial() task in p_{γ_j}, (3) Create ordering constraint $\langle initial()\ task\ in\ p_{\gamma_i},\ current\ task\ in\ p_{\gamma_j}\rangle$, (4) Continue comparison with the next task in the successor plan p_{γ_j}.

On the other hand, in the merging process, we need to detect possible plan steps that will be merged and to update their constraints. The pair of plan steps in different plans is merged, if their postconditions are matched and there is no other task that is ordered after them that could violate these postconditions. More formally,

Definition 6 (Merging Plan Steps $merge(s_i, s_j)$). $\forall$ *plan steps* $s_i \in P_{\gamma_i}$ *and* $s_j \in P_{\gamma_j}$, $merge(s_i, s_j)\ iff\ ((post(s_i) = post(s_j)) \wedge (\neg \exists s_k \in P_{\gamma_j}\ violate\ post(s_j)\ s.t.\ (s_j \prec s_k)))$

Once a pair of plan steps has been merged, the related constraints of the removed plan step should be modified. This means that the replaced plan step will inherit all constraints of the merged plan steps as well as adding new constraints.

For all merged plan steps $s_j \in P_{\gamma_j}$ and $s_i \in P_{\gamma_i}$: (1) The plan step s_j is replaced by plan step s_i, (2) $\forall s_k, s_l \in P_{\gamma_j}$ and $\exists \langle s_k, s_j\rangle, \langle s_j, s_l\rangle \in \prec$ of plan P_{γ_j} add new order constraint $\langle s_k, s_l\rangle$ to plan P_{γ_j}, (3) Remove $\langle s_k, s_j\rangle, \langle s_j, s_l\rangle$ *from plan* P_{γ_j}. These rules ensure that the whole ordering constraints of the merged plan step are preserved.

On the other hand, the causal link constraints that include the merged plan step in its components should be updated. For all merged plan steps $s_j \in P_{\gamma_j}$ and $s_i \in P_{\gamma_i}$:

$\forall\, s_k, s_l \in P_{\gamma_j}$: (1) $\forall$ causal link $s_j \overset{\Phi}{\to} s_l \in CL$ of plan P_{γ_j} add new causal link $s_i \overset{\Phi}{\to} s_l$ to CL of plan P_{γ_j}, (2) remove causal link $s_j \overset{\Phi}{\to} s_l$ from CL of plan P_{γ_j}, (3) remove causal link $s_k \overset{\Phi}{\to} s_j$ from CL of plan P_{γ_j}.

5   Experimental Results

In order to quantify the practical performance gained by our approach, we conducted a series of experiments with our planning framework. The experiments were run on a machine with a 3 GHz CPU and 256 MB Heap memory for the Java VM. Note that this machine has only one single processor unit. We ran our experiments on two well-established planning domains. The *Satellite* domain is a benchmark for non-hierarchical planning. It is inspired by the problem of managing scientific stellar observations by earth-orbiting instrument platforms. Our encoding of this domain regards the original primitive operators as implementations of abstract observation tasks, which results in a domain model with 3 abstract and 5 primitive tasks, related by 8 methods. The *UM-Translog* is a hierarchical planning domain that supports transportation and logistics. We adopted its type and decomposition structure to our representation which yielded a deep expansion hierarchy in 51 methods for decomposing 21 abstract tasks into 48

Table 1. Results for the *UM-Translog* domain

Problem	PANDA	PLM	HMAP					
			Dependent			Independent		
	Planning Time	Planning Time	Planning Time	Merging Time	Total	Planning Time	Merging Time	Total
Translog-P1	180	104	115	0	115	113	0	113
Translog-P2	155	99	103	0	103	105	0	105
Translog-P3	1450	153	159	0	159	157	0	157
Translog-P4	772	621	630	0	630	625	0	625
Translog-P5	1184	639	358	179	537	512	0	512
Translog-P6	-	3437	476	956	1432	1794	964	2758
Translog-P7	-	-	1413	2397	3810	703	1967	2670
Translog-P8	-	-	4562	6094	10656	1587	6731	8318
Translog-P9	-	-	454	148	602	450	0	450
Translog-P10	1284	583	451	941	1392	627	878	1505
Translog-P11	-	3930	2954	2769	5723	750	2343	3093
Translog-P12	-	-	3335	5981	9316	1218	3622	4840
Translog-P13	-	-	4370	6327	10697	1463	7250	8713
Translog-P14	-	-	770	223	993	673	351	1024
Translog-P15	-	-	1705	1440	3145	2109	1345	3454
Translog-P16	-	-	547	418	965	4785	578	5363
Translog-P17	-	-	3366	5921	9287	1328	4364	5692
Translog-P18	3268	1287	1079	0	1079	698	392	1090
Translog-P19	-	4184	3417	1002	4419	489	835	1324
Translog-P20	-	-	3692	2015	5707	1123	1910	3033
Translog-P21	-	-	4007	3842	7849	1379	4808	6187
Translog-P22	-	-	4705	5841	10546	1777	6370	8147
Translog-P23	5238	1211	832	0	832	383	376	759
Translog-P24	-	10006	3227	1045	4272	537	833	1370
Translog-P25	-	-	3445	2614	6059	686	1939	2625
Translog-P26	-	-	3874	5637	9511	1040	5481	6521
Translog-P27	-	-	4739	6627	11366	1521	5904	7425
Translog-P28	-	2623	1047	0	1047	2045	753	2798
Translog-P29	-	-	6008	697	6705	5069	3471	8540
Translog-P30	-	-	3237	940	4177	540	1014	1554

Table 2. Results for the *Satellite* domain

Problem	PANDA	PLM	HMAP					
			Dependent			Independent		
	Planning Time	Planning Time	Planning Time	Merging Time	Total	Planning Time	Merging Time	Total
Satellite-P1	62	60	65	0	65	69	0	69
Satellite-P2	788	708	14	3	17	272	5	277
Satellite-P3	2035	2027	29	7	36	327	26	353
Satellite-P4	-	-	42	10	52	342	26	369
Satellite-P5	-	-	582	26	608	512	26	539
Satellite-P6	-	-	483	19	502	557	26	582
Satellite-P7	-	-	473	27	501	593	34	627
Satellite-P8	-	-	28	7	35	386	23	409
Satellite-P9	1699	1474	247	0	247	15	0	15
Satellite-P10	3053	3062	356	6	362	26	4	31
Satellite-P11	-	-	364	12	376	30	6	36
Satellite-P12	-	-	529	9	538	37	7	44
Satellite-P13	-	-	820	35	855	52	11	63
Satellite-P14	-	-	643	50	693	70	23	93

different primitive ones. We have chosen these domain models because of the problem characteristics they induce. On the other hand, *Satellite* problems typically become difficult when modeling a repetition of observations, which means that a small number of methods is used multiple times in different contexts of a plan. *UM-Translog* problems, on the other hand, typically differ in terms of the decomposition structure, because specific transportation goods are treated differently, e.g., toxic liquids in trains require completely different methods than transporting regular packages in trucks. We consequently defined our experiments on qualitatively different problems by specifying various transportation means and goods. The number of tasks in the initial plan of these planning problems ranges from one to six tasks.

Tables 1 and 2 show the runtime behavior of our system in terms of the planning and merging time *(in seconds)* consumption for the problems in the *UM-Translog* and *Satellite* domains, respectively. The planning time includes the time of breaking up the planning problem, the time used to solve sub-problems and the preprocessing time. Dashes indicate that the plan generation process did not find a solution within the allowed maximum number of 10, 000 plans and 18, 000 seconds and has therefore been canceled. The column PANDA refers to the reference system behavior [11], the PLM to the version that performs a preprocessing phase and HMAP to the version that performs our hybrid MAP. The column HMAP considers clustering the planning problem by two different clustering techniques Dep and Ind. Our experiments in the *UM-Translog* and *satellite* domains show poor performance (cf. Tables 1 and 2) in PANDA and PLM versions, as it is difficult to solve planning problems which have a large number of abstract tasks in the initial plan. The experiments show that, dividing the planning problem into smaller clusters either by Dep or Ind technique are easier to solve than the original problem. Consequently, we are able to solve the problems for which the competing systems could not find a solution within the given resource bounds. For example, for the *UM-Translog* problems that have a single abstract task in the initial plan *(Translog-P1 to P4)*, the average performance improvement of HMAP is about 59% in comparison with PANDA planner. In those problems, the PLM improves the results by 2%

w. r. t. HMAP. Therefore, it is not a big disadvantage of using HMAP instead of PLM for problems which have a single task in the initial plan. Not surprisingly, the performance improvements will increase dramatically with the number of tasks in the initial plan. Our experiments proved that when there is a causal interaction between tasks in the plan, the Ind decomposition technique is more efficient than the Dep decomposition technique such as in the *UM-Translog* domain, where the Ind technique achieves an average improvement of 22% w. r. t. the Dep technique as documented in table 1.

Although, *satellite* domain does not benefit significantly from the landmark preprocessing technique due to the shallow decomposition hierarchy, it achieves good performance with decomposition techniques *(either Dep or Ind technique)* as depicted in table 2.

6   Conclusion

We have presented a new hybrid approach that integrates the hierarchical landmark preprocessing technique with MAP. Our approach enables us to break up the planning problem into a set of clusters using two different techniques; Dependent and Independent. It guarantees that: (1) the set of agents work independently, (2) the individually constructed plans are merged successfully in order to generate a global plan without additional refinement in any individual plan, and (3) the problems are solved in shorter time. We have performed a number of experiments on our representation framework on exemplary problem specifications for two hierarchical domains in which the HMAP approach competed with a planner "with and without" preprocessing. These results give evidence for the practical relevance of our approach.

Acknowledgements. This work is done within the Transregional Collaborative Research Centre SFB/TRR 62 "Companion-Technology for Cognitive Technical Systems" funded by the German Research Foundation (DFG).

References

1. Biundo, S., Schattenberg, B.: From abstract crisis to concrete relief (a preliminary report on combining state abstraction and HTN planning). In: Proc. of ECP, pp. 157–168 (2001)
2. Bradley, J., Edmund, H.: Theory for coordinating concurrent hierarchical planning agents using summary information. In: Proc. of AAAI, pp. 495–502 (1999)
3. Corkill, D.: Hierarchical planning in a distributed environment. In: Proc. of IJCAI, pp. 168–175 (1979)
4. desJardins, M., Wolverton, M.: Coordinating a distributed planning system. Journal of AI Magazine 20(4), 4553 (1999)
5. Elkawkagy, M., Schattenberg, B., Biundo, S.: Landmarks in hierarchical planning. In: Proc. of ECAI, pp. 229–234 (2010)
6. Elkawkagy, M., Bercher, P., Schattenberg, B., Biundo, S.: Exploiting landmarks for hybrid planning. In: 25th PuK Workshop Planen, Scheduling und Konfigurieren, Entwerfen (2010)
7. Erol, K., Hendler, J., Nau, D.: UMCP: A sound and complete procedure for hierarchical task-network planning. In: Proc. of AIPS, pp. 249–254 (1994)

8. Hayashi, H.: Stratified multi-agent HTN planning in dynamic environments. In: Nguyen, N.T., Grzech, A., Howlett, R.J., Jain, L.C. (eds.) KES-AMSTA 2007. LNCS (LNAI), vol. 4496, pp. 189–198. Springer, Heidelberg (2007)
9. Jeffrey, S., Edmund, D.: An efficient algorithm for multiagent plan coordination. In: Proc. of the AAMAS, pp. 828–835 (2005)
10. Mors, A.W., Valk, J.M., Witteveen, C.: Task coordination and decomposition in multi-actor planning systems. In: Proc. of the Workshop on Software-Agents in Information Systems and Industrial Applications (SAISIA), pp. 83–94 (2006)
11. Schattenberg, B.: Hybrid planning and scheduling. PhD thesis, The University of Ulm, Institute of Artificial Intelligence (2009)
12. Tonino, J., Bos, A., de Weerdt, M.M., Witteveen, C.: Plan coordination by revision in collective agent-based systems. Journal of Artificial Intelligence 142(2), 121–145 (2002)
13. Weerdt, M., Witteveen, C.: A resource logic for multi-agent plan merging. In: Proc. of the 20th Workshop of the UK planning and Scheduling, pp. 244–256 (2003)
14. Wilkins, D.E., Mayers, K.L.: A multi-agent planning architecture. In: Proc. of AIPS 1998, pp. 154–162 (1998)
15. Yang, Q., Nau, D.S., Hendler, J.: Merging separately generated plans with restricted interactions. Journal of Computational Intelligence 8(4), 648–676 (1992)

Social Welfare for Automatic Innovation

Juan A. Garcá-Pardo and C. Carrascosa

Universitat Politácnica de Valéncia
Camino de Vera s/n. 46022 – Valencia (Spain)
{jgarciapardo,carrasco}@dsic.upv.es

Abstract. Individuals inside a society can make organizational changes by modifying their behavior. These changes can be guided by the outcome of the actions of every individual in the society. Should the outcome be worse than expected, they would innovate to find a better solution to adapt the society to the new situation automatically.

Following these ideas, a novel social agent model, based on emotions and social welfare, is proposed in this paper. Also, a learning algorithm based on this model, as well as a case of study to test its validity, are given.

1 Introduction and Motivation

Humans, as social beings, are situated in a society that influences them. In the same way, their actions and opinions may influence their society in a higher or lower degree, depending on their individual position in it; that is, the reputation and the amount of other people who is aware of their actions and opinions. Their opinion will have a relative impact in others: the importance depends on how much their opinion is trusted, and how much of an expert they are. Different personalities will react differently to the same stimulus, which means that different persons will be easier to persuade than others by means of social welfare.

For instance, lets have an individual which is baking bread in the bakery. This baker only knows about what is visible from its position, e.g. flour prices, bread production,. . . Should a problem with wheat production affect flour prices later, it would go unnoticed by the baker, unless the flour providers *express* their opinion of how well the flour production is going. If the baker takes into account that opinion, he would start to innovate in the way he produces bread, for instance, by producing it with less flour, or by baking bagels if they are bought by his customers. Of course, different bakers could have different personalities, which could push them towards innovation more easily or not. The aggregated opinion of the society can be viewed as an indicator of the society's welfare, as all the individuals express their opinion about their situation. We hypothesize that this opinion is useful for adaptation purposes, without the necessity of a change detection mechanism.

Following this idea, in this paper an agent model –based on a well studied psychological model of emotions– is proposed in section 3. Using this model, an algorithm is provided in section 4, as an example of how the model could be used;

F. Klügl and S. Ossowski (Eds.): MATES 2011, LNAI 6973, pp. 29–40, 2011.

the convergence of this algorithm is proven under some assumptions as well. To validate both the model and the example algorithm, two tests on adaptation and optimality were carried out, in section 5. Finally, further discussion about results, model and the example algorithm is done and some future lines of work are enumerated in section 6.

2 Related Work

2.1 Psychological Preliminaries

In the psychology literature the widely adopted *Kirton Adaptor-Innovator* (KAI) index [1] proposes that each individual is located in a continuum between "doing things better" to "doing things differently"; i.e. being "adaptive" or "innovative". This means that each person has, in the cognitive level, a degree of susceptibility or inclination to be innovative in the way they think. A very adaptive person is one which tries to excel at their job, getting the best result out of the known situation. On the contrary a very innovative person would achieve a task by trying different methods, even though some of them would yield dreadful results. We as persons are located somewhere in between the two ends of this continuum.

Also extracted from psychology –and independently of the KAI index– we find a model for emotions, called OCC [2]. This model is widely used because it specifies which actions, events or objects will elicit any of the emotions. It is a cognitive approach to emotions which embraces twenty two of them, in eleven different dimensions (all of the emotions are couples of complementary ones, e.g. *hope* and *fear*). The intensity of the emotions is dependent on four variables: proximity, sense of reality, unexpectedness and arousal. These four variables would modify the weight of the value for each of the 22 emotions.

2.2 Approximations to Adaptive MAS

Different approaches to Multiagent Learning (MAL) are examined here. Some of these approximations make use of an explicit coordination mechanism; some assume certain behavior of the agents –such as that they behave rationally; of course, every algorithm has its limitations, and its advantages.

There are some algorithms which through an explicit coordination mechanism deal with the problem of MAL. One of them is Q-Learning with SSA and ABAP [3] which does not need assumptions on the environment. The core of the algorithm deals with the problem of finding the same Nash equilibrium point out of the many possible equilibria. It assumes the agents will behave rationally to achieve this goal. Some other algorithms based on game theory –just to mention some of the well-known ones– and Nash equilibria are: Nash-Q [4] –which needs the agents to be rational and has some convergence problems–; Nash-DE algorithm [5] –which converges to a stationary Nash equilibrium in the general case, with some assumptions, but still needs the player to behave rationally–. There are some other approximations for the *general sum* games but they all need the agents to behave rationally.

On the other side from rational behavior there are some approaches based in emotion modeling. These have the advantage to behave more human-like than rational agents –property that is sometimes needed–. Furthermore emotions can bias an agent decision, thus emotions can be seen as heuristics as well. The work described in [6], based on *2apl*, is very clarifying. It does not provide a clear mechanism for cooperation, but it doesn't prevent it either. The environment is not restricted here, but since it has a strong basis on psychological models, the agents are supposedly able to observe other agents actions and emotions.

Also in the reinforcement learning (RL) literature we can find an algorithm which explicitly tackles the problem of exploration - exploitation: how much to explore and when should the agent use the gathered information. The algorithm E^3 –or extended version $MDP - E^3$ [7]– does not have strong restrictions on the environment, only that it should be static. That –and the fact that it does not work with multiple agents– renders the algorithm unsuitable for MAL and adaptation. Still it is a very significant approach to the specific treatment of the probability of exploration.

The closest algorithm in spirit to the work presented here is the WoLF algorithm [8] –there is a revision of the algorithm to allow high-dimensionality environments [9]. Both require the agent to know its payoff matrix, and both allow dynamic environments since it *learns faster* when results are not as expected. There is, though, a problem with the convergence of learning: if the agents do not follow stationary strategies the algorithm will not ensure convergence.

Although there is some literature on *Social Reinforcement* [10,11], our approach is completely different. The reinforcement will always and only be given by the environment, and the society will just give its opinion, aiming this opinion towards changing the behavior of the rest of the agents.

3   Agent Modeling

3.1   Psychological Model

The psychological model is based in the OCC [2] emotional model. In human emotional modeling we use emotions –plus some other factors– as the inputs which govern the opinion the individual will give to the society. The opinions of the people –which are in this individual's social network– will influence his KAI index. The KAI index will determine whether to behave innovatively or adaptively. The outcomes of the actions of the individual, again, will be evaluated through his emotional system to produce an emotional response, which is a set of emotions and their intensities. Figure 1(a) summarizes the relationships.

Another important step is the way each individual interprets the outcomes of their actions. In Figure 1(b) a set of 11 functions are shown which transform the *emotional stimuli* to a set of 11 emotions with intensities which is just the *emotional response*. This set of functions is peculiar for each person, so it is part of their *personality* –which is invariant. The functions domains must follow the guidelines described by the OCC model, such as some events should influence some emotions and not others.

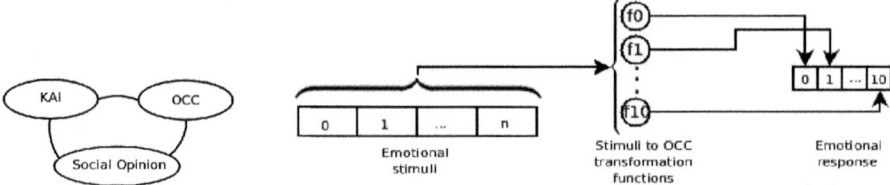

(a) Agent's   Opinion   (b) Emotional response computed for an individual. Each
determinant factors.   of the 11 emotions are *computed* by a different function.

Fig. 1. Bases for the model

3.2   A KAI Based Emotional Social Agent Model

An agent is situated in an environment, but this environment is not only the
physical world ruled by mechanical changes; it also comprehends the social world.
The environment $\mathcal{E}$ is modeled as $< S, A, \delta, r >$, being S the set of states the
environment has; A the analogous set of actions; $\delta : S, A \rightarrow S$ the transition
function, which changes the environment state to another when an action is
performed; and $r : S, A \rightarrow \mathbb{R}$ the observable reward function, that yields a
reward when an action is performed in a state.

The theoretical interest of having *emotions* is double: On the first hand agents
that are modeled with emotions resemble better human behavior –by not showing
a pure rational behavior–, thus the model can be more accurate when simulating
humans. On the second hand, there is psychological and neurological evidence
[12,13,14] that emotions may be *necessary* for a person to behave intelligently,
which arises questions about their necessity in agents.

The transformation between emotional stimuli and emotional responses will
be carried out by a set of 11 functions which output the intensity for each one
of the 11 dimensions. Again, the functions' domains can be composed only by
the set of observable and measurable objects and events of the environment and
perhaps some actions of the agents located there. The emotional response is very
important when emitting each agent's opinion. The Social Opinion will be the
aggregation of every agent's opinion taking into account the trust for each of
them, and the reputation which each agent has in this society.

An agent is modeled as $< \mathcal{P}, \mathcal{S}, R_{\Sigma}, \kappa >$. $\mathcal{P}$ is a set of 11 functions $\mathcal{P}_i : \mathbb{R}^n \rightarrow \mathbb{R}$
which map the emotional stimuli to the emotional response, following the OCC
model; $\mathcal{S} \in \mathbb{R}^n$, is the set of emotional stimuli (observable data); $R_{\Sigma} : \mathbb{R}^{11} \rightarrow \mathbb{R}$
is the social opinion function, used to expose a *public, observable opinion* about
the agent's emotions; and $\kappa : R_{\Sigma}^n \rightarrow \mathbb{R}$ is the KAI index function calculator
that computes how innovative this agent is being given the emotional response.

4   Social-Welfare RL (SoWelL)

The agent is situated in an open environment, thus it needs to learn the functions
which, at a given time, govern this universe. A good method to do so is RL.

Although the agent is learning, it cannot distinguish between what hasn't been learned yet and what has changed. It is desirable to stop learning (or to learn at a slower pace) when the agent has a good approximation for the real functions. The probability of exploration (k) can help if it is a function of the uncertainty about these functions.

Following the previous model (in section 3), the KAI index will represent k, and it has to be computed from the emotional *response* of each agent. The emotional response will have to include means to *feel* (compute) the uncertainty of the learned functions.

Taking into account, also from the model, that the agent should give a negative opinion when its perception of the situation is *bad* –and positive when it is *good*–, the emotional response will also have a way to express these outcomes when executing actions in the environment. To fulfill these two requirements, two of the OCC emotions will be directly linked to the computation of the KAI index k: the joy/distress of the agent, noted by $\mathcal{J}$, and the hope/fear, noted by $\mathcal{H}$. The functions given for $\mathcal{J}$ and $\mathcal{H}$ will define a *pessimistic* agent. I.e. the agent will feel distress *more easily* than joy, when changes occur. That will enable the agent to move faster into different policies, some of which could improve the situation –and thus make the agent feel joy–. The disadvantage is that the agent will need more time to converge to a stable policy. In human terms, the agent's behavior could be identified as *being cautious*.

The functions which compute $\mathcal{J}$ and $\mathcal{H}$ are shown below:

$$\mathcal{J} = \frac{Q_{t+1} - Q_t}{\max(|Q_{t+1}|, |Q_t|) + \epsilon}; \ \mathcal{H} = \frac{Q_{t+1} - M_p}{2\max(|Q_{t+1}|, |M_p|) + \epsilon}; \ M_p = \frac{\sum_1^p Q_{t-p}}{p}$$

Notation: Q_t means the discounted reward the agent[1] has learned so far at timestep t for the given state and the taken action, such as $Q_t \equiv Q_t(s_t, a_t)$. The normalization is done by the maximum in the pair Q_{t+1}, Q_t; then $\mathcal{J} \in\ ]-1, +1[$. M_p is the average of the last p steps. $\mathcal{H} \in\ ]-1, +1[$ is the agent's hope to improve its performance, remembering only p last values. $\epsilon \rightarrow 0$, to avoid division by 0 in $\mathcal{J}$ and $\mathcal{H}$.

The next step is to define the social opinion function. The agent will give its opinion based on the satisfaction it experiences, so it seems logical to describe a function for the representation of the OCC emotion "satisfaction" and use its value as the opinion as well. First, lets define a *prospective happiness* value as $\Psi = \dfrac{\mathcal{J}\mathcal{H} + \mathcal{J}}{2}$. This definition of Ψ allows an agent to give a positive opinion when it *feels* joy and feels no fear ($\mathcal{J} \rightarrow 1, \mathcal{H} \rightarrow 1$). The agent will give a negative opinion when it feels distress and has fear ($\mathcal{J} \rightarrow -1, \mathcal{H} \rightarrow -1$). The limit values of Ψ are shown in table 1 (also, in a static environment, when $t \rightarrow \infty$, it is expected to find $\mathcal{J} \rightarrow 0$ and $\mathcal{H} \rightarrow 0$, by its definitions).

---

[1] Subscripts have been omitted for the sake of clarity; e.g. when it is said $Q(s, a)$ it really means $Q(s, a)_{A_i}$, for the agent A_i. It holds for every parameter in the section.

Table 1. Ψ values in the cases $\{+1, 0, -1\}$ for $\mathcal{J}$ and $\mathcal{H}$

$\mathcal{J}$	+1	+1	+1	0	0	0	-1	-1	-1
$\mathcal{H}$	+1	0	-1	+1	0	-1	+1	0	-1
Ψ	+1	$\pm\frac{1}{2}$	0	0	0	0	-1	$\frac{-1}{2}$	0

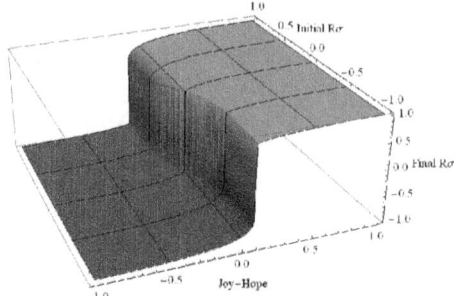

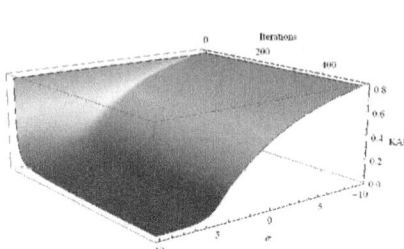

(a) Function $\mathcal{S}$ as a time sequence (interpolated with a degree 1 polynomial).

(b) Function κ as a sequence ($k_0 = 0.8$).

Fig. 2. Two of the most significant SoWelL functions

Using the Ψ function now we define the satisfaction function $\mathcal{S}$ as a sequence which depends on the last value obtained for $\mathcal{S}$ and the evaluation of Ψ:

$$\mathcal{S}_{t+1} = \frac{2}{1 + e^{-e(\Psi + \mathcal{S}_t)}} - 1 \tag{1}$$

Following the OCC model, "satisfaction" is computed taking into account the *temporal proximity* of the emotions "joy" and "hope". The convergence of this sequence cannot be expressed in terms of fundamental algebraic functions, but figure 2(a) shows its behavior.

It is to notice that the sequence at step 500 behaves almost exactly as at 5000, so it can be considered *infinite* at practical means. Some discussion can be made regarding this sequence: the point $(0, 0)$ converges to 0, which means no satisfaction and either no disappointment. This case is peculiar due to the fact that to evaluate $\mathcal{S}$ at that point would mean that the agent had no feeling regarding satisfaction before, and does not experience *joy* (according to the definition of the Ψ function). This is unlikely if the agent has spent some time in the environment and executed actions in there; it can only happen if the Ψ function returns exactly the same opposed value as the "satisfaction" in the step before ($\mathcal{S}_{t-1} = -\Psi_t$). Also there is the fact that the initial value of $\mathcal{S}$ ($\mathcal{S}_0$) makes the sequence very sensitive. This can be adjusted via weighting the exponent $e^{-e(\Psi + \mathcal{S}_{t-1})}$ with an scalar $0 \leq \alpha \leq 2$ in the form $e^{-e(\alpha\Psi + (2-\alpha)\mathcal{S}_{t-1})}$, so the mass of the exponent can be more dependent of Ψ or of the past of the $\mathcal{S}$ sequence.

Recalling the equation for Ψ and table 1 it is observable that this agent is somewhat pessimistic. It will only give positive feedback when it feels joy and hope. As the joy tends to distress, it will start giving negative feedback, accordingly to the hope that it has about the future.

As said before, R_Σ resembles the OCC "satisfaction / fears-confirmed" emotion pair. The resemblance goes into the semantic level as well as into the variables needed to the emotional response. This resemblance induces the definition of R_Σ to be the same as the definition of $\mathcal{S}$ (eq. 1): $R_\Sigma = \mathcal{S}$. This way the personality, which is invariant to an agent, includes how the agent exposes an opinion, without the need for a different function. The model (section 3.2) had R_Σ apart from the personality in case a different function seems more convenient for a different purpose.

The total social opinion will be used by κ function to compute the KAI index. The total social welfare –noted as σ for short– is computed as:

$$\sigma = \sum_{A_i} R_{\Sigma A_i} \tag{2}$$

for every agent A_i, including itself.

For the KAI index calculation, carried out by the κ function, we propose a time sequence in which both the last value of κ and the total social welfare σ from eq. 2 are used:

$$\kappa \equiv k_{t+1} = \frac{k_t}{k_t + 2^{k_t(\sigma-2)}} \tag{3}$$

The sequence is similar to a sigmoid when centered around $\sigma = 0$, but converges differently (see figure 2(b) for the κ sequence with $t = 500$). κ is not very sensitive to the initial value k_0, as long as $k_0 \in]0,1]$ (with $k_0 = 0$ it holds that $k_i = 0$, $\forall i$, regardless of the values of σ).

4.1   Convergence of Learning

Convergence of the learning process is proven under some assumptions:

- The agent represents the universe without taking into account other agents. At least the agent has a function of representation which can represent the universe with no ambiguity with a high probability that increases with time.

- The agent knows the set of actions available at time t.

- The agent observes the response of the system to its actions.

To prove that the algorithm converges, the k_t sequence (eq. 3) has to converge as well –necessary condition. If it is so, the Q-learning algorithm will behave as usual, thus converging to the optimal policies (under the former assumptions) if all the states are visited enough. It is proven in [15] that:

$$\lim_{k \to \infty} k_t = 1 - \frac{W(ln(2)2^{\sigma-2}(\sigma-2))}{(\sigma-2)ln(2)} \tag{4}$$

In (4) the $W(x)$ stands for the Lambert-W function such that for every number $x \in \mathbb{R}$, $x = W(x)e^{W(x)}$.

The proof of the convergence of the learning algorithm follows intuitively from the proof of Q-learning convergence [16]: The agents will learn a policy converging to Q^* while exploring. With enough time, the Q values will converge (eq. 1); thus their opinion will be positive, making them explore less and less. It is possible, though, that the values obtained are optimal only locally, when the exploration time wasn't enough to make them visit other states very often.

5 Tests and Validation

5.1 Study Case

To study the effects of social learning on a practical level we have proposed a simple collaborative game: a market economy in which the production line has different types of units, and the agents should build some or consume certain products for their survival. The agent enters the system with certain amount of money and life points; these values hold for every agent entering the system. In this scenario the agent competes with other for survival, or by obtaining as many points as possible. But it can collaborate to build some of the intermediate products, and earn money to use it later. Agents with life below 0 disappear: it is considered by the system that the agent is unable to produce more than what it consumes. This is called a *failure* of an agent –it failed to be productive–. In the event of a player disappearance, the market automatically removes all products which were unsold and belong to that player. If the agent reenters the market, it spawns with the initial values of *life* and *money*. The market hosts the products that the agents build. Any product may have n dependencies of n_i, $i \in [0, p]$ units of m different products, and need some specific time to be built.

Finally, the price of the products is fixed by each one of the agents.

To get a product from the market the player must pay in advance. Negative balances are not allowed, but agents are able to modify the price of the products they built even when they are already on the market.

In this environment the actions of other players are not observable, but its results may be: they cannot tell if an agent is making a product, but they notice –if they are willing to– that that agent built something when it puts the product on sale on the market.

The system –the market– may change the production rules of the system at any time. The variations allowed are the creation and deletion of product types, changes on the dependencies –both the amount and the type– and the modification of the base time needed for production. Other changes involve the possibility of agents entering and leaving the market at any time.

The environment can simulate supply chain processes, where demand can vary and rules can be altered. This way, a good agent would innovate and adapt to the variations automatically, and –with some time– come back with a good behavior competing and collaborating with other agents inside the environment.

5.2 Simulation

Reinforcement learning in a continuous domain environment cannot be applied unless some conditions are given. For the simulation the agents use a well-known technique for grouping states (Soft State Aggregation, or SSA) which allow them to represent an infinite space of continuous values, with D dimensions, in a D-dimensional finite space (clusters) [17]. For the study case the environment state space is seen as a D-dimensional matrix, grouping the states ($\in \mathbb{R}^D$) in an exponential way. The discrete position (or index of the cluster) i for the continuous variable x is computed as:

$$i = \lfloor \min(log_2(x+1), \omega) \rfloor$$

Bounding i on some number (ω) which is to be considered near to the maximum that is to be seen for that variable, for D dimensions that are taken into account for the environment representation. Therefore the total set of states which every agent must represent is $\omega^D \times |A|$. The number of actions $|A|$ is known by every agent (although it may change with time).

Two different types of agents will be differentiated; those who can receive and understand social opinions –executing Social-Welfare RL– and those which not –using standard Q-learning.

Learning of the Q-table was done individually for both the social-aware agents and the non-social. Parameter ω was fixed at 5, which means that the last state for each dimension will represent values of $x \in [15, +\infty[$. The dimensions (or variables) taken into account to represent the environment are the number of products of each kind in the market plus agent's *life* and *balance*.

Three types of products where loaded: *Wheat*, with no dependencies and needing 1 cycle. *Flour*, requiring 2 units of *flour* and 2 cycles. And *Bread*, eatable, providing 10 units of life, requiring 2 units of *flour* and 2 cycles.

The actions available to the agents are the creation of any kind of the products, plus another one called *eating*. The total space of representation needed by each agent is only of $(5)^{(3+2)} \times 4 = 12500$ states. Learning stage has taken $1,000,000$ cycles, with a probability of exploration $k = 1$, hopping to explore as many states as possible, as many times they could. Every agent starts with exactly the same Q-matrix at the beginning of the simulation. The experiment includes three different scenarios, thus there are two significant changes. The scenarios are:

1. No changes in the environment.
2. Relaxing the production rules: *Flour* needs 1 unit of time and 1 unit of *Wheat*; *Bread* needs 1 unit of time and 1 unit of *Flour*.
3. Hardening the production rules: *Wheat* needs 2 units of time; *Flour* needs 2 units of time and 3 units of *Wheat*; *Bread* stays as originally, needing 2 units of time and 2 units of *Flour*.

As a remark, it is important to control the value of κ such that never reaches 0. For that matter, the computation of κ is corrected by a $\epsilon \to 0$ which is representable by a machine so that $\epsilon \leq \kappa \leq 1$.

It is expected to observe a better adaptation of the social-aware agents compared to the non-social ones which use traditional reinforcement learning (SSA Q-learning).

5.3 Results

Two different experiments were carried out: the first one with 4 agents in the system, and the second one with 32. Two rounds per experiment were done: one with classic Q-learning agents (using SSA to represent the environment), and another round with social aware RL agents (also using SSA). In both experiments we mesured the number of failures and the welfare of the society, for the two types of agents. Both values are normalized per number of agents. In each figure the two vertical lines represent the moment in time when a change in the environment was made.

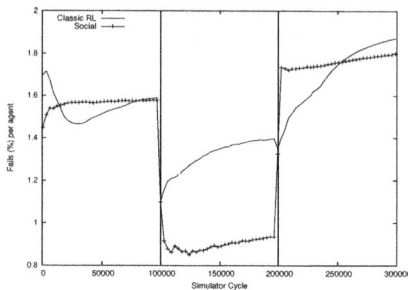   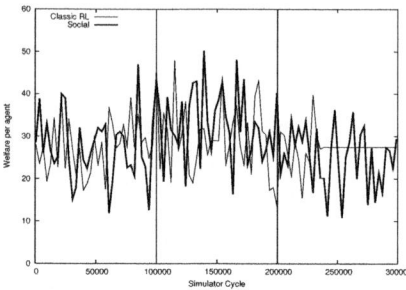

(a) Failures per agent comparison.   (b) Welfare per agent comparison.

Fig. 3. System with two significant changes. Results using 4 agents in the system.

The *failures* represent agents which were in the system yielding loses –for a given time– instead of producing welfare. It is the equivalent of business having loses in the economy: they start with an initial amount of resources but they have a limited time until they start yielding benefits. Otherwise they would confront bankruptcy. The lower the number of failures, the better the system behaves as a whole –it means the system has coped with many different agents and few of them had problems with their policies.

The *welfare* represent the wealth of the society. The higher, the better. The final aim of the system is, actually, to produce as much wealth as possible. The agents –which do not cooperate explicitly, but through their learned policies– face the problem of concurrency in the environment, hence the fact that the double the number of agents does not mean the double of wealth.

From the data in figure 3(a) we see that social aware agents are able to cope with the changes better than the others. The algorithm keeps agents innovative until they reach a (local) maximum; after this, the agents start adapting their behavior to the new conditions. Nevertheless, we see in figure 3(b) that the welfare per agent in the social-welfare society is not much higher than the one in the non-social. The agents have not found a good policy. Despite the fact that the number of failures is low, their achievements are not too good. We will talk about this in a moment after examining the other experiment.

In figure 4(a) it is shown[2] that social agents have fewer failures than non-social ones. As expected in the theory, the more agents the system has, the easier is to

---

[2] The Y-axis is in logarithmic scale.

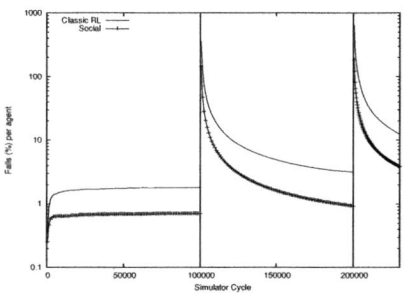

(a) Failures per agent comparison.

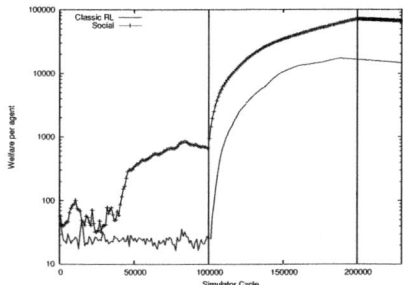

(b) Welfare per agent comparison.

Fig. 4. System with two significant changes. Results using 32 agents in the system.

notice changes; but also when there are many agents, it is more probable that they interfere with each other, which would make harder to find a policy in a short period of time –policies get more complicated as agents are added in the society–. That explains also the data shown in figure 4(b), where a big difference between the two types of agents appear. When having more agents in the system it is easier to have them spread out of the different states, so when the majority agree that they should behave adaptively, it is more probable that the different states of the environment have been already explored by some agent inside the organization.

6   Conclusions and Future Work

This paper has presented a new agent model based on three main topics: the KAI index, emotions and the opinion of the society in which it is immersed. The communication of the opinion inside the society is a good mechanism to trigger innovation when a change requires it. The mechanism works better when the number of agents increases which is very promising in terms of scalability of MAS using SoWelL as the learning algorithm.

The convergence of SoWelL has been proven, but the agents can converge towards a non-global optimum. Where this may be a problem for some environments, it can be alleviated with agents which are even more pessimistic than the one showed in this paper –being more pessimistic would move the KAI index towards innovation faster, thus exploring the environment longer–.

Some further work should be carried out to integrate the social welfare mechanism in algorithms such as WoLF or one of its variants. Also tests in zero-sum games would clarify whether this mechanism works well in pure competitive games. Some scenarios –rock, paper, scissors; matching pennies; etc.– are a good benchmark in zero-sum games. Related to this line of research is the possibility of computing the similarity of goals of two agents given their social opinions. Intuitively we can say that when two agents have similar opinions, their goals are similar, with increasing probability as time increases. This similarity would be semantically equivalent to a composition between trust and reputation between both agents, and will allow to *distinguish* cooperative and competitive agents among themselves.

Acknowledgements. This work has been partially funded by TIN2009-13839-C03-01, TIN2008-04446, PROMETEO/2008/051, GVPRE/2008/070 projects, CONSOLIDER-INGENIO 2010 under grant CSD2007-00022.

References

1. Kirton, M.: Adaptors and innovators: A description and measure. Journal of Applied Psychology 61(5), 622–629 (1976)
2. Ortony, A., Clore, G.L., Collins, A.: The Cognitive Structure of Emotions. Cambridge University Press, Cambridge (1988)
3. Melo, F.S., Ribeiro, M.I.: Coordinated learning in multiagent MDPs with infinite state-space. In: Autonomous Agents and Multi-Agent Systems, pp. 1–47 (2010)
4. Hu, J., Wellman, M.P.: Nash Q-learning for general-sum stochastic games. The Journal of Machine Learning Research 4, 1039–1069 (2003)
5. Akchurina, N.: Multiagent reinforcement learning: algorithm converging to nash equilibrium in general-sum discounted stochastic games. In: AAMAS 2009: Proceedings of The 8th International Conference on Autonomous Agents and Multiagent Systems, pp. 725–732 (2009)
6. Steunebrink, B.R., Dastani, M., Meyer, J.-J.C.: A logic of emotions for intelligent agents. In: AAAI 2007: Proceedings of the 22nd National Conference on Artificial Intelligence, pp. 142–147. AAAI Press, Menlo Park (2007)
7. Kearns, M., Koller, D.: Efficient reinforcement learning in factored MDPs. In: International Joint Conference on Artificial Intelligence, vol. 16, pp. 740–747. Citeseer (1999)
8. Bowling, M., Veloso, M.: Multiagent learning using a variable learning rate. Artificial Intelligence 136(2), 215–250 (2002)
9. Bowling, M., Veloso, M.: Scalable learning in stochastic games. In: AAAI Workshop on Game Theoretic and Decision Theoretic Agents, pp. 11–18 (2002)
10. Mataric, M.: Learning to behave socially. In: From Animals to Animats: International Conference on Simulation of Adaptive Behavior, pp. 453–462. MIT Press, Cambridge (1994)
11. Fabregat, J., Carrascosa, C., Botti, V.: A social reinforcement teaching approach to social rules. Communications of SIWN 4, 153–157 (2008)
12. Martinez-Miranda, J., Aldea, A.: Emotions in human and artificial intelligence. Computers in Human Behavior 21(2), 323–341 (2005)
13. Oatley, K., Keltner, D., Jenkins, J.M.: Understanding Emotions. Wiley-Blackwell (2006)
14. Damasio, A.R., Sutherland, S.: Descartes' error: Emotion, reason, and the human brain. Picador (1995)
15. García-Pardo, J.A., Soler, J., Carrascosa, C.: Social Conformity and Its Convergence for Reinforcement Learning. In: Dix, J., Witteveen, C. (eds.) MATES 2010. LNCS, vol. 6251, pp. 150–161. Springer, Heidelberg (2010)
16. Watkins, C.J.C.H., Dayan, P.: Q-learning. Machine learning 8(3), 279–292 (1992)
17. Singh, S.P., Jaakkola, T., Jordan, M.I.: Reinforcement learning with soft state aggregation. In: Advances in Neural Information Processing Systems, vol. 7, pp. 361–368. MIT Press, Cambridge (1995)

An Agent-Based Simulation of Payment Behavior in E-Commerce

Axel Hummel[1], Heiko Kern[1], and Arndt Döhler[2]

[1] Business Information Systems, University of Leipzig
Johannisgasse 26, 04103 Leipzig, Germany
{hummel,kern}@informatik.uni-leipzig.de
[2] Intershop Communication AG
Intershop Tower, 07745 Jena, Germany
a.doehler@intershop.de

Abstract. The optimal configuration of an online store is a challenging task. Nowadays store managers decide on basis of their expert knowledge. This decision making is insufficient because their choices are often non-transparent and the effects of their decisions are difficult to predict. An example of this problem is the optimal configuration of payment methods that should be offered in an online store. In this paper, we focus on the problem of payment method configuration. We present an agent-based simulation that enables the simulation of the customer's payment behavior in order to support the decision-making process of store managers. We validate this simulation model by using data from real online stores and discuss the simulation results.

Keywords: Agent-Based Simulation, E-Commerce, Payment Behavior.

1 Introduction

The electronic commerce (e-commerce) on the Internet is for many enterprises an important channel of distribution in order to sell their products or to provide their services. Regarding the e-commerce between business and consumers (B2C), business transactions are typical realized by online stores (e-shops). The success of an online store depends among other on an optimal configuration of different aspects such as the shop layout, business processes, marketing activities, available payment methods, or the integration of third-party service providers.

The optimal configuration of an online store is a challenging task. The configuration requires precise knowledge about the interdependency between configuration parameters and the impact of these parameters within the e-commerce ecosystem. This interdependency is often multidimensional nature and includes dimensions such as technical, economics or social aspects. Today, store managers are responsibility for an online store and decide on basis of their expert knowledge about a configuration. Store managers have to configure in their (daily) business the store on basis of current trends or business objectives. Hence, they have to make decisions which might cause changes of the e-commerce system like pricing or marketing actions. These modifications directly influence the consumer

F. Klügl and S. Ossowski (Eds.): MATES 2011, LNAI 6973, pp. 41–52, 2011.

behavior and are reflected in key performance indicators such as conversion rate, business volume, or clickthrough rate. Due to numerous network effects, the store manager cannot forecast the consequences of his decisions. This is insufficient because their decisions are often non-transparent and the effects of their decisions are difficult to predict.

The shop configuration includes many aspects. Hence, we focus in a first step on the configuration of payment methods that should be offered in an online store. Today, there are a numerous payment methods. Out of these, a store manager has to identify the relevant ones that are accepted by the customers and suited for the business. Assuming the following scenario, a store manager wants to offer the possibility to pay with credit card. On the one hand, the credit card payment will attract new customers and thus, the sales volume will rise. On the other hand, regular customers will switch to the new payment method. This may have negative effects for other offered payment methods as they are mostly transaction-based. Hence, a lower number of transactions results in higher costs per transaction. After all, is it beneficial to integrate the credit card as an additional payment method?

An approach for the decision support is simulation. The simulation model represents the fundamental attributes of a system. This model is used to study the behavior of the system over time in order to draw conclusions about the behavior of the real system. As a result, different scenarios can be tested without changing the real system [1]. Since the customer acceptance is one of the critical factors for optimizing the payment methods, we want to develop a simulation model that forecasts the consumers' payment behavior according to the specific payment configuration. Typical question that we want to answer are, for instance: Does the integration of additional payment methods always result in new consumers? Are there payment methods that have a very high or very low consumer acceptance? Which is the configuration with the lowest dropout rate?

The paper is structured as follows. In the subsequent section, we describe our simulation model. We give first an overview of the entire simulation and present afterwards our agent-based payment simulation in detail. In Section 3 we calibrate and run our simulation in order to validate and evaluate the simulation results. In Section 4 we compare our simulation with other simulation approaches. Finally, we conclude in Section 5 with a discussion of our simulation approach and describe future work.

2   Simulation Model

2.1   Overview of the Shopping Simulation

The simulation of the payment behavior is part of a larger simulation chain. Before presenting the payment simulation in detail, we give a general overview of this simulation chain. We can essentially differentiate two parts: the customer group and the e-commerce system (see Fig. 1). The customer group represents people participating in online business as consumers. They have specific properties and a certain behavior. These customers can interact with the e-commerce

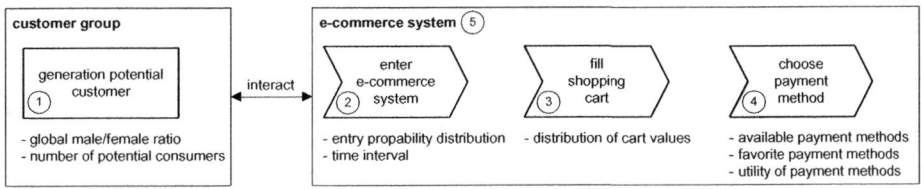

Fig. 1. Overview of the simulation components

system. The e-commerce system has also a specific behavior and is also described by abstract properties. The system behavior is defined by a process consisting of different activities. Each activity represents a point of interaction between the customers and the e-commerce system. Thus, each interaction point can be realized by an encapsulated simulation. This encapsulation enables the reuse or replace of individual simulations.

The complete simulation chain consists of five parts. (1) The first part generates the set of potential customers with a specific gender (female or male). Input parameters are the share ratio of gender and the number of customers who can participate in online business. (2) The second part simulates the shop entry of customers. Since from the potential customers, only a small number visits the shop. The entrance mainly depends on the gender and the time of entrance. Thus, we can define as input parameter the probability in dependency of the gender and time. This time differentiation enables the simulation of typical seasons such as Christmas or Easter. (3) The third part simulates the filling of the cart with a customer-specific cart value. The distribution of the cart values serves as input for the simulation and differentiates between male and female consumers. The cart values can be used to calculate economic key data according to the offered payment types. Moreover, it is possible to model a dependency between the cart value and the available payment methods. (4) The fourth part simulates the payment behavior of the customers. Input parameters are the preferred payment method of the customers, the available payment types, and the utility of the available payment methods. We provide a more detailed presentation of this simulation in the next section. (5) The fifth part of the simulation is the e-commerce system that serves as container for the aforementioned simulations two, three and four.

2.2   Simulation of the Payment Behavior

The objective of this simulation is to reproduce the payment behavior of customers in an online store in order to find the optimal payment configuration. The input of this simulation is a set of customers with a gender and a cart value. The output is customers with a certain payment method or a cancel of buying.

The assumed behavior of a typical customer is shown in Figure 2 as an UML activity diagram. A customer prefers to pay with her/his favored payment method and checks for the availability of this method. If the method is

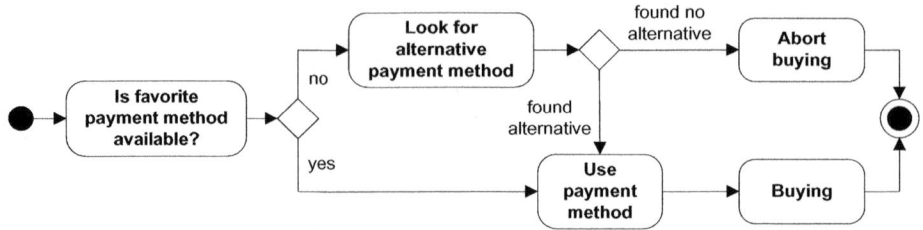

Fig. 2. Model of the payment behavior

available, then the customer will use this method and the payment process is finished. Otherwise the customer will cancel the buying or look for an alternative payment method in the shop. We define the function fav that yields the probability for a certain payment method Z_i (e.g. invoice, credit card, prepayment or cash on delivery) to be the favorite type of payment

$$fav : Z \rightarrow [0,1] \in \mathbb{R} \ . \tag{1}$$

Based on studies [2,3] and the evaluation of real payment data, we identify a dependency between the favorite payment method and the gender. For instance, credit card is preferably used by men and invoice is preferably used by women. Hence, we distinguish between the functions fav_m and fav_f for men and female, respectively. As the two functions fav_m and fav_f cannot be determine directly from the shop data, we have to derive these functions from the gender-neutral function fav. We assume the following two conditions. First, the gender-neutral favored payment method is the male-specific favored payment method times the probability that a consumer is male $P(male)$ plus the female-specific favored payment method times the probability that a consumer is female $P(female)$. Formally, this is defined as:

$$fav(Z_i) = fav_m(Z_i) \cdot P(male) + fav_f(Z_i) \cdot P(female) \ . \tag{2}$$

Second, the ratio $r(Z_i)$ of the payment method Z_i is specified as the quotient of $fav_f(Z_i)$ and $fav_m(Z_i)$, formaly defined as:

$$r(Z_i) = \frac{fav_f(Z_i)}{fav_m(Z_i)} \ . \tag{3}$$

Based on equation (2) and (3), we derive the favorite payment method for men and women as follows:

$$fav_m(Z_i) = \frac{fav(Z_i)}{P(male) + r(Z_i) \cdot P(female)} \tag{4}$$

$$fav_f(Z_i) = fav_m(Z_i) \cdot r(Z_i) \ . \tag{5}$$

If the favored payment method is not available, then the customer will look for an alternative payment method in the shop or cancel the buying. The customer decides on basis of a certain probability for an alternative payment method. This decision essentially depends on the utility of a payment method which is gender-neutral and described by the following function:

$$utility : Z \rightarrow \mathbb{R} \ . \tag{6}$$

In the literature, there are different approaches for modeling the consumer specific decision process using a utility for each alternative. We use the so-called Luce model [4] which is defined as follows:

$$P(Z_i) = \frac{utility(Z_i)}{\sum_{i=1}^{n} utility(Z_i)} \ . \tag{7}$$

Finally, if the customer finds one or more alternative types of payment, then he will choose those alternatives with the specific probability and the purchase process will end. In case she/he does not find an appropriate alternative, this will lead to the abort of the purchase and the termination of the payment process.

2.3   Agent-Based Implementation of the Shopping Simulation

In the course of time, several simulation techniques have been developed. A relatively new method is multi-agent simulation which has become a common approach for simulation in social science [5]. This technique uses intelligent agents for the modeling of complex systems. Agents are entities in a certain environment with a limited perception of their environment. They are capable of doing autonomous actions and interactions with other agents in order to delegate their objectives [6].

Multi-agent systems are widely-used in the field of retailing. The heterogeneous behavior of the customers and their several interactions are well supported by the agent-based paradigm. The underlying bottom-up approach allows for a realistic modeling of consumer behavior. Furthermore, the approach enables the usage of user-specific information collected from real systems such as Customer Relationship Management (CRM) or e-commerce systems.

We apply the agent-based approach for modeling the heterogeneous payment behavior depending on specific attributes. The implementation of a multi-agent system is usually done by means of agent-based modeling platforms. Today, there is a large number of such platforms available, see [7] or [8] for an overview of various toolkits. We use SeSAm (Shell for Simulated Agent Systems) to implement the different parts of our shopping model. This open source tool supports a visual programming of the implementation. The behavior of the agents is specified using an activity graph derived from UML [9].

The customers are modeled as agents. We specify the general class customer and derive two special classes thereof. One represents male consumers, the other characterizes the female consumers. The e-commerce system and its relevant attributes are modeled as the environment of the agents. Resources are not used within the model. The information exchange between the different parts of the shopping simulation is realized via comma-separated files.

3   Validation of the Payment Simulation

3.1   Calibration

In order to run and validate the payment simulation, we have to calibrate the input parameters with initial values. These values based mainly on German studies about the payment behavoir and real data from available online stores.

First, our model contains the four payment methods: invoice (Z_1), prepayment (Z_2), credit card (Z_3), and cash on delivery (Z_4). These types of payment are widely-used in Germany. Furthermore, we set the number of customers to 100.000. In order to study the gender-specific payment behavior, we use the following gender ratio female/male: 23/77 and 77/23. Next, we define the function fav by the co-domain shown in Table 1. The values are adopted from the study [2]. Based on these gender-unspecific values, we calculate the function values for men (fav_m) and women (fav_f). For calculating these values, we need the ratio r of the favored payment methods in dependency of the gender. The ratio is shown in Table 2 as the result of an analysis of real shop data. Further, we need the *utility* function as an input parameter. The values of the distinct payment types are defined in Table 3. These values are derived from a study [3]. In this study customers evaluated different payment methods with the grade 1 (very well) till 5 (bad). The utility value is the percentage rate of the customers who gave a grade better than average grade 2.6.

3.2   Simulation Run and Validation

We run the simulation experiment 30 times with the input parameters described in the section above, ten with a gender ratio of 23/77, ten with 50/50, and ten with 77/23. Due to the lack of space, we only show the simulation results produced with a gender ratio 23% female and 77% male. In our evaluation (see Sec. 3.3), we also include the inverse and fifty-fifty gender ratio and. The average of the simulation results is shown in Table 4. We validate the results by using the values from this study [2] and real store data. The study includes seven configurations of payment methods that are shown in Table 5. If we compare the results of the study with the results of the proposed simulation model, then four configurations exactly coincide and only three configurations have differences. A detailed comparison shows in Table 6 the absolute and relative errors.

Table 1. Probability distribution of the favorite payment method depending on the gender

Gender	Invoice (Z_1)	Prepayment (Z_2)	Credit Card (Z_3)	Cash on Delivery (Z_4)	Cancel
neuter	0.65	0.04	0.23	0.03	0.05
male	0.62	0.04	0.26	0.03	0.05
female	0.77	0.03	0.13	0.02	0.05

Table 2. Ratio r between $fav_f(Z_i)$ and $fav_m(Z_i)$ of the several payment methods

Invoice (Z_1)	Prepayment (Z_2)	Credit Card (Z_3)	Cash on Delivery (Z_4)	Cancel
1.20	0.66	0.52	0.53	1

Table 3. Utility of payment methods ($utility(Z_i)$) based on [3]

Invoice (Z_1)	Prepayment (Z_2)	Credit Card (Z_3)	Cash on Delivery (Z_4)	Cancel
0.96	0.09	0.29	0.12	0.3

The maximum of all absolute errors is three percentage points (see Tab. 6, Z_2, Config. 3) and the maximum of all relative errors is 18% (see Tab. 6, Z_2, Config. 9). The payment method with the biggest relative errors is prepayment with three relative errors more than ten percent (see Tab. 6, Z_2, Config. 3, 9, and 13). All other types of payment have a relative error that is less than five percent. In summary, one can state that the presented simulation has a high conformity with the results of [3]. If we involve the rounding error, then we can substantiate this statement. The values of the study are rounded on two decimal places and the absolute error can be as minimum 0.01. For instance, this can be in the case of payment Z_2 a reason for the high relative error. In general, we conclude that our model is correct.

3.3 Evaluation of the Simulation Results

In this section, we analyze the simulation results of Table 4 with regard to the questions of Section 1. First, the results show, if more payment methods are offered, then the dropout rate is lower. On average, if only one payment type is available, then 50% (see Tab. 4, Config. 2–5) of the consumers cancel the payment process. If two payment methods are offered, the average dropout rate is 26% (see Tab. 4, Config. 6–11). For three offered types the value is 13% (see Tab. 4, Config. 12–15) and if all payment methods are available the dropout rate is only 5% (see Tab. 4, Config. 16). The values remain constant if the rate of female customers is raised. Moreover, the table shows that every payment method is accepted by at least 24% if it is the only one offered.

Furthermore, the results indicate that the purchase on invoice has the highest rate of acceptance. More precisely, if purchase on invoice is offered, then the dropout rate is with less than 15% small (see Tab. 4, Config. 2, 6, 7, 8, 12, 13, 14, and 16). The other types of payment cannot replace purchasing on invoice, even if all alternatives are available the dropout rate is 29% (see Tab. 4, Config. 15). If the rate of female consumers is increased, then this observation is strengthening. If 77% of the customers is female, then the dropout rate for purchase on invoice is only 10%. The dropout rate in case that all other alternatives are available is 32%.

Table 4. Simulation results of the several configurations of payment methods (payment methods: Z_1=Invoice, Z_2=Prepayment, Z_3=Credit Card, Z_4=Cash on Delivery; payment configuration: 0=off, 1=on)

Config.	Z_1	Z_2	Z_3	Z_4	Z_1	Z_2	Z_3	Z_4	Cancel
1	0	0	0	0	-	-	-	-	1.00
2	1	0	0	0	0.88	-	-	-	0.12
3	0	1	0	0	-	0.24	-	-	0.76
4	0	0	1	0	-	-	0.59	-	0.41
5	0	0	0	1	-	-	-	0.28	0.72
6	1	1	0	0	0.84	0.06	-	-	0.10
7	1	0	1	0	0.69	-	0.24	-	0.07
8	1	0	0	1	0.84	-	-	0.05	0.11
9	0	1	1	0	-	0.13	0.52	-	0.35
10	0	1	0	1	-	0.19	-	0.23	0.58
11	0	0	1	1	-	-	0.52	0.14	0.34
12	1	1	1	0	0.67	0.04	0.23	-	0.06
13	1	1	0	1	0.81	0.05	-	0.04	0.10
14	1	0	1	1	0.67	-	0.24	0.03	0.06
15	0	1	1	1	-	0.11	0.47	0.13	0.29
16	1	1	1	1	0.65	0.04	0.23	0.03	0.05

Finally, we close the evaluation with the following observations. The results of Config. 6 and Config. 13 illustrate that the adding of additional payment methods does not always lead to new consumers. In this case the type cash on delivery is added but the dropout rate remains with 10% constant. The configurations 12 and 14 show that one payment method can substitute another. In this example, prepayment and cash on delivery are able to replace each other. Similar effects appear if the rate of male and female consumers is changed. If half of all consumers is female and purchase on invoice and credit card are offered, then cash on delivery can be omitted without raising the dropout rate. Furthermore, prepayment and cash on delivery will replace each other if purchase on invoice

Table 5. Reference values [2] (payment methods: Z_1=invoice, Z_2=prepayment, Z_3=credit card, Z_4=cash on delivery; payment configuration: 0=off, 1=on)

Config.	Z_1	Z_2	Z_3	Z_4	Z_1	Z_2	Z_3	Z_4	Cancel
1	0	0	0	0	-	-	-	-	1.00
3	0	1	0	0	-	0.21	-	-	0.79
6	1	1	0	0	0.84	0.06	-	-	0.10
9	0	1	1	0	-	0.11	0.53	-	0.36
10	0	1	0	1	-	0.19	-	0.23	0.58
13	1	1	0	1	0.80	0.06	-	0.04	0.10
16	1	1	1	1	0.65	0.04	0.23	0.03	0.05

Table 6. Absolute and relative error of the several configurations (payment methods: Z_1=invoice, Z_2=prepayment, Z_3=credit card, Z_4=cash on delivery; payment configuration: 0=off, 1=on; error: Δ=absolute error, δ=relative error; direction: $\downarrow$=simulation value < reference value, $\uparrow$=simulation value > reference value)

Config. $Z_1\ Z_2\ Z_3\ Z_4$	Z_1 Δ	δ	Z_2 Δ	δ	Z_3 Δ	δ	Z_4 Δ	δ	Cancel Δ	δ
1 0 0 0 0	-	-	-	-	-	-	-	-	0	0%
3 0 1 0 0	-	-	0.03	14% ↑	-	-	-	-	0.03	4% ↓
6 1 1 0 0	0	0%	0	0%	-	-	-	-	0	0%
9 0 1 1 0	-	-	0.02	18% ↑	0.01	2% ↓	-	-	0.01	3% ↓
10 0 1 0 1	-	-	0	0%	-	-	0	0%	0	0%
13 1 1 0 1	0.01	1% ↑	0.01	17% ↓	-	-	0	0%	0	0%
16 1 1 1 1	0	0%	0	0%	0	0%	0	0%	0	0%

is the only alternative. If 77% of all consumers is female, then similar effects can be observed.

4　Related Work

Multi-agent models are widely-used to simulate customer behavior. Moreover, agent-based computational economics is a separate research field which uses agent-based systems to study economies that are emerge from individual decisions of autonomous agents and their interactions [10]. In the following, we discuss four approaches for model consumer behavior.

A relevant contribution to our work has come from Rigopoulos et al [11]. The authors describe a multi-agent system for the acceptance of payment systems. The customer decision process of choosing a payment method is also simulated using the utility theory. The consumer calculates the utility of each available payment method resulting in a probability vector including an adopting probability for each payment method. In opposition to our model, the utility of a payment method depends on several consumer-specific attributes. Another difference is the application area. Rigopoulos et al. focus on digital retail payments in general, whereas our model addresses the payment process in online stores. Since the model described in [11] is developed to support the strategic decisions of banks and other payment service providers, it is also possible to forecast the success of new payment methods. Our model considers the most widely-used payment methods of the German market.

The agent-based simulation technique is also used to model the behavior of customers in a supermarket [12]. In conformity with our approach, the authors characterize every customer agent with specific attributes such as gender. Additionally, each consumer is characterized by a set of feature agents. Every feature agent represents a single parameter of the consumer's behavior and is modeled as an autonomous agent. The interaction of the feature agents yields the shopping behavior of the customer. Consequently, the utility theory is not used within this model. Another difference is in the modeling of the shopping process. The model presented in [12] addresses the purchasing behavior in general, whereas we primarily focus on the payment process.

A multi-agent system for optimization of promotional activities is described in [13]. Using this simulation, the effects of different points in time and target groups can be studied for the market penetration of new products. Each consumer is represented by an agent. Furthermore, the decision of adopting a new product is modeled by using the utility theory, analogous to the simulation model presented in this paper. In [13] the utility of a new product consists of an individual preference and a social influence whereas the second factor is not considered for choosing the preferred payment method.

Another example of modeling consumers as autonomous agents within a multi-agent system is described in [14]. The authors propose a model which can be used by sellers to determine the optimal mail-in rebate for different products depending on their prices. In contrast to our model, the model in [14] does not include the payment process. A special feature of their work is the fact that the agents gain experience about the used mail-in rebates and take this into account for future decisions. Such learning effects are currently not implemented in our approach.

5   Conclusion and Future Work

5.1   Summary

Multi-agent simulation is a technique that uses the bottom-up approach to model complex systems. Hence, multi-agent simulations are widely used to model customer behavior. We propose an agent-based model for the simulation of the shopping process in online stores. The developement of the model based on the expert knowledge from shop managers, past payment data from real online stores, and several studies. Our description focus on the forecasts of the consumers payment behavior in order to support store managers in their decision making process. We use five parts to model the shopping process. This modularity simplifies the adaptability to other e-commerce systems. For instance it is possible to add additional components that are relevant for modeling the consumer behavior. In some cases the customers have to register in the e-commerce system in order to use additional types of payment.

Further, we have validated the simulation results and have shown the correctness of this simulation. Only the method prepayment shows a high relative error in some configurations. From the viewpoint of a shop manager, we evaluated the simulation results and derived some regularity in the payment behavior. We point out that the behavior of the consumers is based on data of the German market. Since the payment behavior differs greatly between countries, the applicableness of e-commerce systems outside the German market has to be checked.

5.2   Future Work

The proposed simulation focuses on the consumers' payment behavior. Nevertheless it is possible to calculate the business volume of a certain time interval according to different payment configurations because the entering in the online store and the filling of the shopping cart are also parts of the model. In order to forecasts the profit of different scenarios the shopping simulation has to be extended. Hence, one of our next steps is the integration of the specific costs (fixed costs and transaction costs) of each payment method. We intend, further, to develop an additional module that simulates the customer-specific risk of non-payment.

The presented model considers only four payment methods namely purchase on invoice, prepayment, credit card and cash on delivery. Thus, the adding of further payment methods is an essential task for future modeling. Moreover, there are various aspects that need refinement of the consumer behavior. Our initial model differentiates between male and female customers. The distinction with respect to additional attributes like age, salary or order frequency is future work. Moreover, modeling the experience of customers and the influence of selecting a payment method is also a future task.

We model the process of choosing an alternative payment method by using a general utility for every type of payment. We intend for every attribute that affects the decision process of a consumer (e.g. security, speed or consumer-specific costs) to use several utility functions. The refinement of the utility function belongs also to our future work.

Acknowledgments. The work presented in this paper is undertaken as a part of the SimProgno project (01IS10042C). SimProgno is funded by the German Federal Ministry of Education and Research.

References

1. Banks, J., Carson, J.S., Nelson, B.L., Nicol, D.M.: Discrete-Event System Simulation (International Edition), 5th edn. Pearson, London (2010)
2. Krabichler, T., Wittmann, G., Stahl, E., Breitschaft, M.: Erfolgsfaktor Payment—Der Einfluss der Zahlungsverfahren auf Ihren Umsatz (German). ibi research an der Universität Regensburg GmbH (2008)
3. Rodenkirchen, S., Krüger, M.: Ausgewählte Studien des ECC Handel—Der Internet-Zahlungsverkehr aus Sicht der Verbraucher: Ergebnisse der Umfrage IZV10 (German) 25 (2011)
4. Matsatsinis, N.F., Samaras, A.P.: Brand choice model selection based on consumers' multicriteria preferences and experts' knowledge. Computers & Operations Research 27, 689–707 (2000)
5. Gilbert, N., Troitzsch, K.G.: Simulation for the Social Scientist, 2nd edn. Open University Press, McGraw Hill Education (2005)
6. Wooldridge, M.: An Introduction to MultiAgent Systems, 2nd edn. John Wiley & Sons, Chichester (2009)

7. Nikolai, C., Madey, G.: Tools of the Trade: A Survey of Various Agent Based Modeling Platforms. Journal of Artificial Societies and Social Simulation 12 (2009)
8. Allan, R.: Survey of Agent Based Modelling and Simulation Tools. Technical report, Science and Technology Facilities Council (2010)
9. Klügl, F., Herrler, R., Fehler, M.: SeSAm: implementation of agent-based simulation using visual programming. In: Nakashima, H., Wellman, M.P., Weiss, G., Stone, P. (eds.) Proceedings of the 5th International Joint Conference on Autonomous Agents and Multiagent Systems (AAMAS 2006), Hakodate, Japan, pp. 1439–1440. ACM, New York (2006)
10. Tesfatsion, L., Judd, K.L. (eds.): Handbook of Computational Economics: Agent-Based Computational Economics. Handbooks in Economics, vol. 2. Elsevier, Amsterdam (2006)
11. Rigopoulos, G., Psarras, J., Karadimas, N.V.: Multi-Agent Modeling and Simulation of Consumer Behaviour Towards Payment System Selection. In: Proceedings of the 20th European Conference on Modelling and Simulation (ECMS 2006), Bonn, Germany, May 28-31 (2006)
12. Schwaiger, A., Stahmer, B.: SimMarket: Multiagent-based customer simulation and decision support for category management. In: Schillo, M., Klusch, M., Müller, J., Tianfield, H. (eds.) MATES 2003. LNCS (LNAI), vol. 2831, pp. 74–84. Springer, Heidelberg (2003)
13. Delre, S.A., Jager, W., Bijmolt, T.H.A., Janssen, M.A.: Targeting and timing promotional activities: An agent-based model for the takeoff of new products. Journal of Business Research 60(8), 826–835 (2007)
14. Khouja, M., Hadzikadic, M., Zaffar, M.A.: An agent based modeling approach for determining optimal price-rebate schemes. Simulation Modelling Practice and Theory 16(1), 111–126 (2008)

On the Power of Global Reward Signals in Reinforcement Learning

Thomas Kemmerich[1] and Hans Kleine Büning[2]

[1] International Graduate School Dynamic Intelligent Systems
University of Paderborn,
33095 Paderborn, Germany
[2] Department of Computer Science
University of Paderborn,
33095 Paderborn, Germany
{kemmerich,kbcsl}@uni-paderborn.de

Abstract. Reinforcement learning is investigated in various models, involving single and multiagent settings as well as fully or partially observable domains. Although such models differ in several aspects, their basic approach is identical: agents obtain a state observation and a global reward signal from an environment and execute actions which in turn influence the environment state. In this work, we discuss the role of such global reward signals. We present a concept that does not provide a visible environment state but only offers a numerical engineered reward. It will be proven that this approach has the same computational complexity and expressive power as ordinary fully observable models, but allows to infringe assumptions in models with partial observability. To avoid such infringements, we then argue that rewards, besides a true reward value, shall never contain additional polynomial time decodable information.

Keywords: reinforcement learning, global reward, conceptual models, partial observability.

1 Introduction

Reinforcement learning in single and multiagent systems (MAS) can be realized based on different formal models. The model choice depends on the assumed agent abilities or on the requirements of the underlying problem domain. A large amount of work deals with Markov decision processes (MDP) or stochastic games (SG), where agents are supposed to observe the entire environment state as well as the actions of other agents (see e.g. [19] and [4] for introductions). In contrast, in partially observable MDPs [9] or partially observable SGs [3], it is assumed that agents are unable to observe everything but only perceive (small) excerpts. These models are also used for planing and learning under uncertainty. Despite different assumptions, e.g. on observability, the basic approach is the same in all models: agents make an observation, decide to execute a specific action that changes the state of the environment, and finally obtain a reward

F. Klügl and S. Ossowski (Eds.): MATES 2011, LNAI 6973, pp. 53–64, 2011.

from the environment. To put it simply, such a reward rates the quality of the performed action with respect to reaching a certain goal.

In this work, we will concentrate on the power of such environment-based rewards that play the same role in all models. Note that we assume anything that is not controllable by the agent as being part of the environment. Basically, there are two different possibilities for calculating the reward [14]. First, a reward function can be build into the agent, i.e. an agent itself calculates rewards based on the observed state and its action. This approach is usually followed in literature, for instance in robotic teams [18]. The second option, in which we are particularly interested, is to let the environment calculate and give rewards to the agent [2]. In this setting, the environment can be considered as a central instance or an entity like a teacher that gives the rewards. Consider, for example, a telecommunication system involving large numbers of mobile devices with local view on the system and several radio base stations which are connected through a backbone network. In this scenario, a central computer would be able to measure a global performance measure like a load factor that should be optimized by the mobile devices. Thus, the computer could realize the entity which calculates the rewards that are given to the agents (mobile devices). We will show how such a setting could be exploited by engineered reward signals that do not only represent a numerical reward, but also encode additional information which should not be available locally. It is then proven that engineered rewards do not add additional expressiveness in fully observable domains. However,they enable agents in partially observable domains like the above introduced telecommunication setting, to obtain information which the agents are not supposed to get. In order to formally avoid this, we then argue that existing models should demand rewards that do not contain polynomial time decodable information. Note, that this work thus does not claim to present novel engineered reward-based algorithms which deal with well known problems of reinforcement learning, e.g. coordination or convergence issues, but investigates the power of global rewards.

The next section briefly presents related work. Then, in Sect. 3 we review the state of the art concept used in reinforcement learning and introduce the engineered reward-based concept. In Sect. 4, the latter is shown to be equivalent to the ordinary fully observable model in terms of complexity and expressiveness. Next, in Sect. 5 we consider partially observable domains in conjunction with engineered rewards and show that an additional assumption on reward signals is necessary to avoid exploitation by encoded informations. Then, in Sect. 6, we provide a clarifying example and discuss how engineered rewards can be used beneficially in problems with special structures. Finally, we conclude in Sect. 7.

2   Related Work

First of all, note that we assume the readers to be familiar with reinforcement learning (RL). Thus, for an introduction, we refer to [10,14,19] for single agent RL, and to [4,16,17] for multiagent RL.

A key assumption of most models used in reinforcement learning is that the environment has to be Markovian. This means that transition probabilities do not depend on the state and action history but only on the current state and action. Various models for RL that are based on the Markov property have been investigated in the past, see e.g. [2,3,4,9,16,17] and its references for introductory descriptions. Notably, in all these models, agents obtain a numerical global reward signal which they use to learn a policy. Thus, the results of this paper might also be extended to and investigated in other models.

A technique that is related to the approach followed in this work is known as *reward shaping*. This technique tries to fasten the learning process by supplying an agent with additional rewards that guide it towards the learning goal. Such rewards must be designed carefully so as to avoid learning undesired policies and to avoid including non-observable information. A work of Melo and Ribeiro [13], for instance, encodes entropy information of a fully observable MDP into the rewards to solve a robotic navigation task that is modeled as POMDP. Ng et al. [15] investigate the requirements under which shaped rewards maintain optimal policies. While the goal of reward shaping is to guide the learning process, our concept allows to transmit probably non-observable information through the engineered reward. Thus, agents in our approach might use such additional knowledge but will rely on original rewards for learning. Recent work also deals with reward shaping in multiagent systems [7].

Another aspect of global rewards deals with the question of how well it can support learning in general. Particularly, learning from a common global reward in large MAS is hard, as this often involves several problems like coordination or credit assignment questions. For MAS, Bagnell and Ng [1] prove a worst-case lower bound indicating that learning from a global rewards requires roughly as many examples as there are agents in the system. They show that learning from local rewards can be faster, requiring only logarithmically many trajectories.

Chang et al. [5] consider the role of global rewards in MAS. From an individual agent's point of view, they consider the global reward as a sum of the agent's true reward and a random Markov process that describes the influence of other factors or agents to the global reward. Using Kalman filtering, they develop a simple approach to estimate local rewards from a single global reward signal.

3 Concepts

Next, we briefly review the current state of the art concept for reinforcement learning. It is used in the aforementioned models and provides a state and a reward signal. Thereafter, a novel concept is given that gets along with a single engineered reward signal. Since this concept can easily be extended to MAS, we will concentrate on single agent settings and refer to the multiagent case if necessary. Note that throughout this text, we make common assumptions like bounded rewards, finite state sets, and finite state representations.

3.1 State of the Art

Reinforcement learning problems are mostly modeled as Markov decision processes (single agent systems) resp. as stochastic games (multiagent systems) [4],

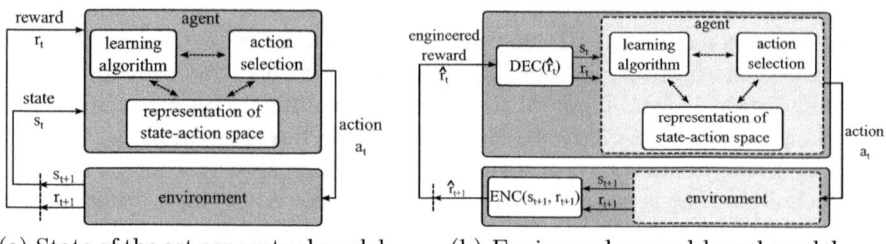

(a) State of the art conceptual model.   (b) Engineered reward-based model.

Fig. 1. Concepts considered in this work

or as variants thereof [17]. Although existing models differ in some aspects, they all share one commonality: the environment has to offer a state as well as a distinguished reward signal to the agent(s). Figure 1(a), based on the illustration of Sutton and Barto [19], visualizes these signals in an agent system modeled as Markov decision process (MDP, introduced later in Sect. 4).

To emphasize the inherent importance of both signals in the general case consider the agent-internal components shown in Fig. 1(a). The components, without being exhaustive, interact with each other in order to form a learning agent. Here, the state signal is required for an appropriate state-action space representation, e.g. in the form of a Q-Table [19]. It is also required to select actions depending on the current state of the environment. The reward signal constitutes an inherent feature of reinforcement-based learning algorithms in the sense that agents aim at maximizing the expected return over time. Accordingly, agents are required to be able to observe and to distinguish both signals.

3.2   Engineered Reward-Based Model

We will now propose an alternative conceptual model for reinforcement learning. In this model, state features are not visible and the agent only observes one signal—an engineered reward. Figure 1(b) visualizes this approach.

Starting from an MDP, the core idea is to design an engineered reward which encodes original state and reward signals into a single value. The encoding happens on environment level either at runtime or during the process of designing the engineered MDP. Then, the engineered reward is the only signal submitted to or observed by the agent. Accordingly, the environment does not need to offer any visible state feature to the agent and the agent itself is not required to sense anything else but the engineered reward. Due to the encoding, however, the agent is still able to obtain non-visible state information and the original reward. Therefore, the used decoding (DEC)/encoding (ENC) approach needs to run in polynomial time and formally has to ensure that $\text{DEC}(\text{ENC}(R(s, a), s)) = (R(s, a), s)$ holds, where s is an environment state from a set of states $\mathcal{S}$, a is an action from a set of actions A, and $R : \mathcal{S} \times A \rightarrow \mathbb{R}$ is a reward function.

At the end of this section will present a concrete coding approach. For the moment, however, we want to concentrate on the role of this concept in the remainder of this article. First, we will show that the engineered reward-based approach has the same computational complexity and expressive power as the state of the art approach in fully observable games, i.e. in MDPs and their multi-agent counterparts named stochastic games (SG). Having this in mind, we then will consider partially observable domains. Engineered reward signals in such domains augment the expressive power compared to ordinary partially observable models. However, time complexity remains and constructing an engineered reward signal is not forbidden in state of the art models. From this it follows that one could easily—accidentally or intentionally—supply agents with knowledge they are not supposed to obtain, e.g. on states or joint actions. Based on this observation, we then propose to add an additional requirement on reward signals in existing models that formally prevents such exploitation. The engineered reward-based model in this work, thus, should mainly be understood as a means to investigate the power of global rewards. However, as described in the context of an example in Sect. 6, it is also useful in problems with a special structure.

A Polynomial Time Coding Approach. A general encoding function ENC is presented in Alg. 1. Its basic idea is to create a string $code(s)\#code(r)$ that combines codes of state s and reward r separated by a special character ($\#$). This string is then converted to a bit string, whereas each character is encoded with the same number of bits b (e.g. $b = 8$ bits as in ASCII encoding). A single '1' is added at the head of the resulting bit string for decoding reasons as explained below. The resulting bit string is then interpreted as a number. Note that the constructed bit strings are bounded, since rewards and state representations are bounded, too. This approach requires time linear in the length of the bit string. Note that states may also contain information about executed (joint) actions. A corresponding decoding function DEC is straightforward. The idea is to interpret a received reward as bit string. By construction, the string starts with a '1', which is removed. The remaining bit string, that might start with zeros now, is split into substrings, each of length b, where b equals the value of b in the encoding procedure (e.g. $b = 8$ for ASCII encoding, cf. Alg. 1, line 7). Then, these substrings can be interpreted as characters, from which we can

---

Algorithm 1. (Encoding algorithm)

Input: state $s \in \mathcal{S}$, reward $r \in \mathbb{R}$
Output: engineered reward $\hat{r} \in \mathbb{R}$
1: **procedure** ENCODING(s, r)
2:     $cs \leftarrow$ convert state s to character array $(cs_1, cs_2, \ldots, cs_n)$
3:     $cr \leftarrow$ convert reward r to character array $(cr_1, cr_2, \ldots, cr_m)$
4:     codeword $\leftarrow$ CONCATENATE($cs, \#, cr$)   ▷ create code word $code(s)\#code(r)$
5:     bitstream $\leftarrow 1$ ▷ initialize new bit stream with 1
6:     **for** $i = 1, \ldots, |$codeword$|$ **do**
7:         bitstream $\leftarrow$ CONCATENATE(bitstream, bitcode(codeword$[i], b$))   ▷ use b bits
    to encode codeword$[i]$
8:     **return** TONUMBER(bitstream)   ▷ interpret bitstream as number and return it

---

easily reconstruct the code word code(s)#code(r). Finally, this word is split at the separator (#) and the resulting parts represent the original state resp. reward. Obviously, this decoding also runs in polynomial time. By construction it holds that DEC(ENC($R(s,a), s$)) = ($R(s,a), s$). Clearly, other polynomial time approaches exist and can be used if they obey the requirements stated above.

4   Complexity Results and Expressiveness

Based on [6] and [8], we first briefly recall some theoretical foundations. Complexity theory classifies computational problems into complexity classes. For convenience, important techniques are often designed for decision problems, i.e. problems whose solution is either *yes* or *no*. Reinforcement learning, however, is not a decision problem but an optimization problem, as agents seek to maximize the expected return. Hence, to investigate RL problems using complexity theory, we have to convert them into decision problems. A simple and common technique is to add a bound B to an optimization problem O and to ask if O can be solved such that the optimization objective is at least (or at most) B. Clearly, such a converted problem is at most as hard as the original problem.

Different complexity classes exist, among which $\mathcal{P}$ and $\mathcal{NP}$ are fundamental. Decision problems that belong to the class $\mathcal{P}$ are solvable in polynomial time, while those belonging to $\mathcal{NP}$ can be solved using nondeterministic polynomial time algorithms. It is known that $\mathcal{P} \subseteq \mathcal{NP}$ and widely believed that $\mathcal{P} \neq \mathcal{NP}$. To show that two problems fall into the same complexity class, a technique called polynomial time reduction is used. Therefore, one needs a polynomial time reduction function $f : O \to O'$ that i) transforms any instance $o \in O$ of a decision problem into an instance $f(o) \in O'$, and which ii) ensures that if and only if o evaluates to *yes* then also $f(o)$ evaluates to *yes*. We write $O \leq_p O'$ to denote that a problem O is polynomial time reducible to a problem O'.

In the remainder of this section, we will show that the proposed conceptual model is equivalent to the state of the art model that provides both, state and reward signals to the agent. To do so, we first have to formally define our understanding of equivalent models. Therefore, we adopt the same notion and approach as Seuken and Zilberstein [17] and use polynomial time reductions:

Definition 1. *Two models M_1 and M_2 are said to be* polynomial time equivalent *if and only if $M_1 \leq_p M_2$ and $M_2 \leq_p M_1$.*

By this definition, two models are polynomial time equivalent if they can express the same problems and belong to the same complexity class.

Next, we formally define the models that were illustrated in the previous section. There, Fig. 1(a) basically illustrates a Markov decision process (MDP) which, based on [9], can be defined as follows:

Definition 2. *(Markov Decision Process) A Markov decision process (MDP) is defined as a tuple $\langle S, A, \delta, R \rangle$, where S is a finite set of world states and A is a finite set of possible actions. The state-transition function $\delta : S \times A \to \Pi(S)$*

gives a probability distribution to be in state $s' \in S$ after action $a \in A$ in state $s \in S$ was executed. The reward function $R : S \times A \to \mathbb{R}$ returns an immediate reward for executing action $a \in A$ in state $s \in S$. The agent executes actions from A and is able to observe the current state of the environment and the reward.

As mentioned above, an MDP $M = \langle S, A, \delta, R \rangle$ can be formulated as decision problem by adding a bound B. Thus for an MDP $M' = \langle S, A, \delta, R, B \rangle$ the question is whether or not there is a policy that results in a return of at least B starting from the initial state $s_0 \in S$.

The engineered reward-based approach for single agent systems visualized in Fig. 1(b) formally is defined as follows:

Definition 3. *(Engineered Reward-Based Markov Decision Process) An engineered reward-based Markov decision process (ERBMDP) is defined by a tuple $E = \langle S, A, \delta, R, \text{ENC}, \text{DEC} \rangle$, where S, A, δ, R are defined as in an MDP. $\text{ENC} : \mathbb{R} \times S \to \mathbb{R}$ is a polynomial time function that calculates an engineered reward which encodes original rewards and states into a single real value. Agents can only observe the engineered reward, and are able to decode these rewards using a polynomial time decoding function $\text{DEC} : \mathbb{R} \to \mathbb{R} \times S$. It holds that $\text{DEC}(\text{ENC}(R(s,a),s)) = (R(s,a),s)$.*

Using these definitions and the general coding approach presented in the previous section, we can now show the following equivalence result:

Theorem 1. *Engineered reward-based Markov decision processes (ERBMDP) and Markov decision processes (MDP) are equivalent.*

Proof. We have to show that the decision problem variants are mutually reducible in polynomial time, i.e. ERBMDP $\leq_p$ MDP and MDP $\leq_p$ ERBMDP. To construct a decision problem, we add bounds B/B' to the respective tuples.

1. ERBMDP $\leq_p$ MDP: An arbitrary ERBMDP $E = \langle S, A, \delta, R, \text{ENC}, \text{DEC}, B \rangle$ can be transformed into an MDP $M = \langle S', A', \delta', R', B' \rangle$ in polynomial time by setting $S' = S, A' = A, \delta' = \delta, R' = R$, and $B' = B$. The agents also have to be allowed to observe the state signal. Since the encoding and decoding function, ENC and DEC, are only required to construct the engineered reward and because $\text{DEC}(\text{ENC}(R(s,a),s)) = (R(s,a),s)$ holds by definition, these functions have no influence on the expected return. Thus, whenever a policy in E results in a return of at least B, this also holds for the MDP M.

2. MDP $\leq_p$ ERBMDP: Let $M = \langle S, A, \delta, R, B \rangle$ be an arbitrary MDP. Then, an ERBMDP $E = \langle S', A', \delta', R', \text{ENC}, \text{DEC}, B' \rangle$ can be obtained by forbidding the agent to observe the state signal and by setting $S' = S, A' = A, \delta' = \delta, R' = R$, and $B' = B$. It remains to show that there are polynomial time algorithms for encoding and decoding such that $\text{DEC}(\text{ENC}(R(s,a),s)) = (R(s,a),s)$ holds—this was done in Sect. 3.2. Finally, as before, a policy for M that results in a return of at least B will result in the same return in E.

It is easy to see that the same result also holds for fully observable multiagent settings, i.e. stochastic games and engineered reward-based stochastic games, as they are constructed analogously to the single agent case using joint actions.

5   Partial Observability

The theoretical results concerning equivalence of MDPs/SGs and its engineered reward-based counterparts are not surprising as, by definition, agents are able to observe the state and the actions of other agents (see e.g. [19,4]). Accordingly, no additional information can be added by using engineered rewards. In the area of planing and learning, so-called *partially observable Markov decision processes* (POMDP)[9], *decentralized POMDPs* (Dec-POMDP) [2,17,16], and *partially observable stochastic games* (POSG) [3] are used to model systems where agents are unable to observe the full state of the environment, or obtain noisy, probably erroneous information. Like in MDPs/SGs, these models also supply agents with a *global* reward and a sort of state information in the form of observations. We now investigate such settings and, like before, concentrate on single agent settings by considering POMDPs, which formally can be defined as follows [9]:

Definition 4 (POMDP). *A partially observable Markov decision process can be described as a tuple $\langle S, A, \delta, R, \Omega, O \rangle$, where S, A, δ, R are defined as in a Markov decision process and*

- *Ω is a finite set of observations the agent can make from the environment.*
- *$O : S \times A \rightarrow \Pi(\Omega)$ is an observation function that returns a probability distribution over possible observations. Let $O(s, a, o)$ denote the probability that observation $o \in \Omega$ is observed after action a was executed in state s.*

Although an agent in this domain can only make observations on the current environment state, it still aims at maximizing the return based on the rewards it receives. Figure 2 visualizes a general POMDP. The agent percepts an observation based on the current state of the environment and estimates the actual environment state using its own history of observations and actions. This estimation is called *belief state* and is calculated in the state estimation (SE) element shown in the figure. More details on partially observable domains and solution techniques can be found in e.g. [2,3,9,16,17].

As can be seen in Fig. 2, an agent obtains a *global* reward that is calculated within the environment. Note that in order to formally define a reward function, states and actions have to be known. For partially observable domains with more than one agent (e.g. Dec-POMDPs or POSGs), this also implies knowledge about joint actions. Please note that all this knowledge hence has to be available at the (central) environment level in order to define an ordinary reward function. Since these information are available and because an engineered reward function does not require more information, it is formally allowed and — according to Sect. 3.2 — possible to use polynomial time engineered rewards in state of the art models. Thus, a reward signal that encodes all information available at the central environment level can be constructed.

Since a POMDP with engineered rewards can be constructed in polynomial time, the computational complexity of this extension is equal to the ordinary POMDP model. However, as engineered reward signals can encode arbitrary additional information, an agent in an engineered reward-based POMDP can

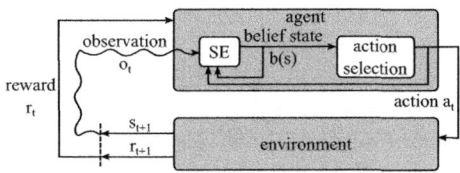

Fig. 2. Visualization of a POMDP(based on Kaelbling et al. [9])

benefit from information that are not observable in an ordinary POMDP. Accordingly, engineered reward-based partially observable Markov decision processes (ERBPOMDP) establish a richer concept compared to ordinary POMDPs. Despite the intended partial observability, an agent in an ERBPOMDP is able to obtain additional information and, thus, can easily exploit the framework.

Obviously, encoding additional information into an engineered reward is explicitly not desired in a model based on the partial observability assumption. In order to (formally) prevent exploitation by engineered rewards, we propose to slightly adjust existing models. As stated in the preceding sections, the key requirement which enables agents to work with additional information is that it must be possible to efficiently decode engineered rewards. More formally, it is required that agents are able to decompose an engineered reward into its components in polynomial time. To prevent exploitation of partially observable models by agents that obtain global information from a global engineered reward, we shall demand one additional property on the reward function in existing models:

Property 1. *Besides the true reward, reward signals in partially observable domains are not allowed to carry additional polynomial time decodable information.*

Note that this property intensionally does not explicitly define what "additional information" are, as this depends on the considered model. We will come back to this issue later in Sect. 7.

6   Example

Next, we consider an example application modeled as decentralized partially observable Markov decision process, which, based on [2], is defined as follows:

Definition 5 (Dec-POMDP). *A decentralized partially-observable Markov decision process (Dec-POMDP) is defined by a tuple $\langle \mathcal{S}, \boldsymbol{A}, \delta, R, \boldsymbol{\Omega}, O \rangle$, where*

- *$\mathcal{S}$ is a finite set of states with distinguished initial state s_0.*
- *$\boldsymbol{A} = \times_{i \in \mathcal{AG}} A_i$ is a joint action set, where A_i denotes actions of agent i.*
- *δ is a state transition function, where $\delta(s, \boldsymbol{a}, s')$ denotes the probability of transitioning from state s to state s' when joint action $\boldsymbol{a} \in \boldsymbol{A}$ is executed.*
- *R is a reward function. $R(s, \boldsymbol{a}, s')$ is the reward obtained from executing joint action $\boldsymbol{a}$ in state s and transitioning to state s'.*

- $\Omega = \times_{i \in \mathcal{AG}} \Omega_i$ *is a finite set of observations, where o_i denotes the set of observations agent i can make.*
- *O is a table of observation probabilities. $O(s, \boldsymbol{a}, s', \boldsymbol{o})$ is the probability of observing joint-observation $\boldsymbol{o} = \langle o_1, \ldots o_n \rangle$ when executing joint action $\boldsymbol{a}$ in state s and transitioning to state s'. Each agent i only perceives element o_i from the joint-observation $\boldsymbol{o}$.*

Figure 3 illustrates the considered partitioning problem, which basically is a cooperative game. In this application, a set of mobile devices should distribute equally onto a set of base stations. This has to be accomplished in a decentralized manner and it is assumed that mobile devices can only communicate with base stations within their communication range. The system state is described by a list of tuples $\langle d_i, b_j \rangle$, that defines for each mobile device d_i a currently selected base station b_j. States are evaluated according to optimization criteria, which are i) to assign the same number of agents to each base station and ii) to minimize the sum over all radio distances between a mobile device and its selected base station. The actual assignment quality is calculated by a central computer that is connected to all base stations via a backbone network. Since, from a multiagent perspective mobile devices represent agents of the system, we will use the two terms interchangeably. Formal details on this multi-objective optimization problem can be found in [12].

Based on the description, the conversion to a Dec-POMDP is straightforward:

- the state set $\mathcal{S}$ contains all assignments of mobile devices to base stations; a start state s_0 can be chosen arbitrarily from $\mathcal{S}$.
- a mobile device has one distinct selection action for each base station.
- the state transition function is deterministic, as a joint action immediately leads to a new state defined by the joint action.
- the reward equals the solution quality.
- devices only observe elements located within the communication radius.
- the table of observation probabilities O is constructed such that with high probability agents observe the correct system state.

The mainframe, as central instance of the environment, is able to calculate a reward which can be submitted to agents via the base stations. Note that the Dec-POMDP has no assumptions on the reward function. Accordingly, because the mainframe knows the current assignment of agents to base stations, it could

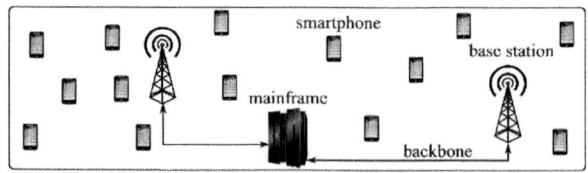

Fig. 3. Partitioning problem: mobile devices such as smartphones should distribute equally to a set of base stations while minimizing the sum of communication distances

construct an engineered reward which encodes these information. Therefore, the previously stressed coding approach can be used. Since we deal with a cooperative game and each agent then would obtain full state information, it could simply consider the game as a MDP where actions are joint actions and solve the problem using Q-Learning (see e.g. [14]). Using the engineered reward-based concept, agents then could easily exploit the system which certainly leads to undesired system properties. For instance privacy issues as agents would be able to identify and track a particular other mobile device. As soon as we use rewards that fulfill Prop. 1, the system can no longer be exploited in this way.

Although in this work, the engineered reward-based concept is used to emphasize the risks that stem from such rewards, the concept also allows to efficiently solve games with a special structure. An example can be found in [11], where a novel game class called *sequential stage games* and a near optimal MARL approach were introduced. That algorithm benefits from engineered rewards as it can solely rely on the order of magnitude of the reward values to distinguish between different "states" of the game, which leads to a space-efficient approach.

7 Discussion and Conclusion

We investigated the expressive power of global rewards in reinforcement learning. Particularly, we focused on rewards that are calculated by the environment, i.e. by that entity which by definition has full information about states and joint actions. Using a polynomial time coding we showed how engineered rewards containing full information can be constructed. Though this technique does not add more expressiveness to models with full observability, it offers a way to provide agents with full information in partially observable domains. To prevent this undesired knowledge transfer, we argue that reward signals should only contain *true* rewards but never additional polynomial time decodable information.

Note that equivalence results for fully observable models hold only if, as assumed in this work, engineered rewards solely encode state information which possibly include information on (joint) actions. In general, however, the concept allows to encode arbitrary information, e.g. state transition probabilities, observation functions, etc., into a single numerical reward. Under such conditions, the engineered reward-based concept basically can reduce agent and environment to a single unit where all information are accessible. Clearly, the entity that gives (and calculates) rewards then is very powerful and should be handled with care. In that context, the contribution of this work is to point out that rewards should be designed carefully to avoid infringement of model assumptions.

For the future, it remains to investigate the influence of engineered rewards in other models. In addition, it should be investigated how engineered rewards can be used to solve problems with special structures as shown in the example.

References

1. Bagnell, J.A., Ng, A.Y.: On local rewards and scaling distributed reinforcement learning. In: Advances in Neural Information Processing Systems, NIPS 2005 (2005)
2. Bernstein, D.S., Givan, R., Immerman, N., Zilberstein, S.: The complexity of decentralized control of markov decision processes. Math. Oper. Res. 27, 819–840 (2002)
3. Bernstein, D.S., Hansen, E.A., Zilberstein, S.: Dynamic programming for partially observable stochastic games. In: AAAI, pp. 709–715. AAAI Press / The MIT Press (2004)
4. Buşoniu, L., Babuška, R., De Schutter, B.: Multi-agent reinforcement learning: An overview. In: Srinivasan, D., Jain, L.C. (eds.) Innovations in Multi-Agent Systems and Applications - 1. SCI, vol. 310, pp. 183–221. Springer, Heidelberg (2010)
5. Chang, Y.H., Ho, T., Kaelbling, L.P.: All learning is local: Multi-agent learning in global reward games. In: Thrun, S., Saul, L.K., Schölkopf, B. (eds.) NIPS. MIT Press, Cambridge (2003)
6. Cormen, T.H., Leiserson, C.E., Rivest, R.L., Stein, C.: Introduction to Algorithms, 2nd edn. MIT Press, Cambridge (2001)
7. Devlin, S., Kudenko, D.: Theoretical considerations of potential-based reward shaping for multi-agent systems. In: Proc. of 10th Intl. Conf. on Autonomous Agents and Multiagent Systems (AAMAS 2011), pp. 225–232 (2011)
8. Garey, M.R., Johnson, D.S.: Computers and Intractability: A Guide to the Theory of NP-Completeness. W. H. Freeman and Company, New York (1979)
9. Kaelbling, L.P., Littman, M.L., Cassandra, A.R.: Planning and acting in partially observable stochastic domains. J. Artif. Intell. Res. 101(1-2), 99–134 (1998)
10. Kaelbling, L.P., Littman, M.L., Moore, A.P.: Reinforcement learning: A survey. J. Artif. Intell. Res. 4, 237–285 (1996)
11. Kemmerich, T., Kleine Büning, H.: A convergent multiagent reinforcement learning approach for a subclass of cooperative stochastic games. In: Proc. of the Adaptive Learning Agents Workshop @ AAMAS 2011, pp. 75–82 (2011)
12. Kemmerich, T., Kleine Büning, H.: Region-based heuristics for an iterative partitioning problem in multiagent systems. In: Proc. 3rd Intl. Conf. on Agents and Artificial Intelligence (ICAART 2011), vol. 2, pp. 200–205. SciTePress (2011)
13. Melo, F.S., Ribeiro, I.: Transition entropy in partially observable markov decision processes. In: Arai, T., Pfeifer, R., Balch, T.R., Yokoi, H. (eds.) IAS, pp. 282–289. IOS Press, Amsterdam (2006)
14. Mitchell, T.M.: Machine Learning. McGraw-Hill, New York (1997)
15. Ng, A.Y., Harada, D., Russell, S.J.: Policy invariance under reward transformations: Theory and application to reward shaping. In: Bratko, I., Dzeroski, S. (eds.) ICML, pp. 278–287. Morgan Kaufmann, San Francisco (1999)
16. Oliehoek, F.A., Spaan, M.T.J., Vlassis, N.A.: Optimal and approximate Q-value functions for decentralized POMDPs. J. Artif. Intell. Res. 32, 289–353 (2008)
17. Seuken, S., Zilberstein, S.: Formal models and algorithms for decentralized decision making under uncertainty. Autonomous Agents and Multi-Agent Systems 17(2), 190–250 (2008)
18. Stone, P., Sutton, R.S., Kuhlmann, G.: Reinforcement learning for robocup-soccer keepaway. Adaptive Behavior 13(3), 165–188 (2005)
19. Sutton, R.S., Barto, A.G.: Reinforcement Learning: An Introduction. The MIT Press, Cambridge (1998)

Motivating Agents in Unreliable Environments: A Computational Model

Patrick Krümpelmann, Matthias Thimm, Gabriele Kern-Isberner, and Regina Fritsch

Information Engineering Group, Department of Computer Science,
Technische Universität Dortmund, Germany

Abstract. The development of formal models for rational agents is mainly driven by the well-established BDI approach which divides an agent's mental state into beliefs, desires, and intentions. In this paper, we argue that motivation as well has to be taken into account in order to allow for a flexible and proactive behavior of intelligent agents in unreliable environments. In our approach, *motives* take the role of describing an agent's personality and are the driving force for creating desires and abandoning previously selected goals. We investigate the relationships between motives and their associated desires as well as the impact brought about by the uncertainty and unreliability of the environment.

1 Introduction

Today, formal approaches for representing the mental state of an intelligent agent mostly employ the BDI model, a framework that originated in psychology and describes intelligent behavior such as decision making, deliberation, and means-end reasoning in rational beings. This model divides a mental state into *beliefs*, *desires*, and *intentions* and gives a formal account for their interactions. Beginning with the work [1] many researchers in the field of artificial intelligence and intelligent agents applied this (informal) framework to formalize autonomous intelligent behavior [10].

However, the BDI model is an abstraction of a mental model of an intelligent being and given some sufficiently complex scenario it is not enough to represent proper decision making adequately. In the area of intelligent agents specifically the *desires* of an agent are oversimplified and often assumed to be initially given. A desire represents some state of the world such as *"I want to be rich"* or *"I want to get a professorship"* that the agent wishes to achieve. In contrast to *intentions* which represent a currently pursued course of action the set of desires does not need to be consistent, i. e. completely achievable, as the previously mentioned statements have shown. Furthermore, a single desire might be unachievable in general or unachievable in some specific context, e. g. due to some physical (*"I want to fly"*) or mental (*"I want to learn all languages of the world"*) limiting factors. Formal models employing the BDI model assume the desires of an agent to be given as agents are typically situated in some constrained environment with limited capabilities and tasks. Looking at the well-known cleaner robot the two desires *"I want to clean the room"* and *"I want to have a high battery level"* are completely sufficient to describe its world. Generally, however, assuming desires to be given inhibits real autonomous behavior. Bringing agents into more complex environments demands for mechanisms that allow an agent to set its desires by itself. Looking

F. Klügl and S. Ossowski (Eds.): MATES 2011, LNAI 6973, pp. 65–76, 2011.

at how humans handle their desires, motivation theory [6] bridges the gap between a being's personality and its desires it wishes to satisfy. A *motive* such as *"benevolence"* or *"greed"* is a basic marker of an agent's personality that can be used to create (or abandon) some desire. We illustrate this intuition with a simple example.

Example 1. Given an agent competes with other agents for food, the motive *"greed"* would generate the desire of acquiring as much food as possible, while motive *"benevolence"* would generate the desire of acquiring just as much food as really needed and to ensure that other agents acquire as much food as they need. Both motives might very well be present in the agent's personality but with differing strengths.

In this paper, we develop a formal account for incorporating motivation into the BDI approach. Instead of assuming desires to be given we assume that an agent comprises of some set of basic motives that drives its behavior. Each motive of the agent is equipped with some weight and each motive is coupled with a set of desires that can be positively or negatively influenced by the motive. We give a formal account on the aggregation of the weights of the motives and these couplings in order to determine the desires the agent is motivated to follow. Furthermore, using the notion of *reliability* [4] we investigate how beliefs about actions (*know-how*) and beliefs about the world might influence the deliberation on motivation. More precisely, the motivation to follow some desire is strongly influenced by the uncertainty of the world and the knowledge of the agent that some course of action might not be reliable achievable.

The rest of this paper is organized as follows. In Section 2 we begin by giving some background on BDI agents and a formal account on representing motives and motivation that derives from psychology. In Section 3 we elaborate a simple agent model that integrates handling of motivation. We go on in Section 4 by giving a formal account on the dynamics of motivation and in Section 5 we consider the unreliability of the environment and discuss its influence on the motivational model of the agent. In Section 6 we review related work in Section 7 we conclude.

2   Agents and Motives

The BDI approach is a well-established approach to model rational agents. This model distinguishes between *beliefs*, *desires*, and *intentions* in order to represent human-like reasoning and behavior. In this model, beliefs represent the agent's (subjective) knowledge about itself, the world, and other agents. Desires describe what the agent is longing for in its environment and intentions account for its currently pursued goals and the intended course of action. Given some percept from the environment the agents usually employs some form of belief revision or update in order to incorporate the new information into its own beliefs. Afterwards, by taking the current state of the world into account, the agent considers its desires and selects some desire to be pursued as a *goal*. It appropriately updates its intentions using means-end reasoning and planning techniques [3], selects some course of action, and eventually performs some action in the environment. In general, this process is repeated indefinitely.

While most formalizations of the BDI model [10] assume the agent's desires to be given, a more natural as well as flexible and powerful approach, demands for the possibility to generate desires. The research in psychology describes how desires are created by an agent's motivation [5,6]. In what follows, we formalize the notion of motivation in order to incorporate it into a formal agent architecture. This allows for a more rational representation of an intelligent agent.

The theory of motivation is concerned with the question of how an agent determines its desires. Motivation is driven by *motives* which describe reasons for some specific behavior and are meant to be as basic as possible, e.g. hunger or love. A classification of basic motives is provided by *Maslow's hierarchy of needs* [5] that distinguishes between five levels of motives. From top to bottom motives in the corresponding levels are ordered by their importance and motives in higher levels are only *active* if some appropriate portion of lower level motives are *satisfied*. In its bottom level are the most basic motives, those for *physiological needs* such as health and food followed by *safety needs* (law and order), *love and belonging* (family, friends, love), followed by *esteem* (independence, respect) and finally *self-actualization* such as individuality. Motives of different levels have different susceptibilities to deficiency, in general more basic motives are more prone to deficiency, while top level motives may not be satisfiable. There are critical claims on the applicability of the hierarchy of needs for the human reasoning process due to the simplification of a strict hierarchy [9]. Nonetheless, we choose this conceptual framework to be used within our model as it provides a sufficient abstraction for the relationships of motives.

Let $(\mathcal{L}, \succ)$ be a totally ordered set of *motive levels* such that $L \succ L'$ with $L, L' \in \mathcal{L}$ means that motives on level L are more basic than motives on level L'. In the following we use $\mathcal{L}^M = (\{\mathsf{sa}, \mathsf{es}, \mathsf{lb}, \mathsf{sn}, \mathsf{pn}\}, \succ)$ with $\mathsf{pn} \succ \mathsf{sn} \succ \mathsf{lb} \succ \mathsf{es} \succ \mathsf{sa}$ (pn stands for *physiological needs*, sn for *safety needs*, etc. as listed above), thus using *Maslow's hierarchy of needs* to represent importance of basic motives. Our framework, however, is open to other types or quantities of motive levels. We also adapt the notion of deficiency needs by partitioning the set of motive levels into deficiency and non-deficiency levels. For $\mathcal{L}^M$ we define the deficiency levels as $\mathsf{d}(\mathcal{L}^M) = \{\mathsf{pn}, \mathsf{sn}, \mathsf{lb}\}$. This simplification of the above mentioned susceptibilities of motives might be generalized to a more granular or continuos representation. But it will be sufficient to enable the agent to focus on the deficiency needs in unreliable situations.

For our agents we assume some (finite) set Mot of basic motives. For every motive $m \in$ Mot let $\mathsf{L}(m) \in \mathcal{L}$ denote the motive level of m.

The importance of individual motives and motive levels for an agent constitutes its personality. To measure importance of motives we employ the unit interval as the general range for weights[1]. In general, a smaller weight indicates a less important motive level.

Definition 1. *A level weight range function wr on $\mathcal{L}$ maps a motive level $L \in \mathcal{L}$ onto a continuous subset of the unit interval, i.e. $wr(L) = [l_L, u_L]$ with a lower and upper bound $l_L, u_L \in [0, 1]$ and $l_L \leq u_L$. We abbreviate $\delta_L = u_L - l_L$.*

For a motive level $L \in \mathcal{L}$ the value $wr(L) = [l_L, u_L]$ indicates that each motive belonging to L has at least an importance of l_L and at most an importance of u_L.

---

[1] Note, that our approach can be generalized to ranges represented by any totally ordered set; we choose to use the unit interval only for reasons of simplicity of presentation.

Example 2. For $\mathcal{L}^M$ an adequate level weight range function wr can be given by

$$wr(\mathsf{pn}) = [0.75, 1] \qquad\qquad (\delta_{\mathsf{pn}} = 0.25)$$
$$wr(\mathsf{sn}) = [0.55, 0.85] \qquad\quad (\delta_{\mathsf{sn}} = 0.3)$$
$$wr(\mathsf{lb}) = [0.35, 0.65] \qquad\quad (\delta_{\mathsf{lb}} = 0.3)$$
$$wr(\mathsf{es}) = [0.15, 0.45] \qquad\quad (\delta_{\mathsf{es}} = 0.3)$$
$$wr(\mathsf{sa}) = [0, 0.25] \qquad\qquad (\delta_{\mathsf{sa}} = 0.25)$$

Notice, that the weight ranges of motive levels might overlap in order to allow for situations where some less basic motive has a stronger influence than some more basic motive. We come back to this issue when taking the reliability of the environment into account.

These ranges describe the general importance of a motive level. The actual importance of a motive level at some point in time, called *level weight*, is given by a function $w : \mathcal{L} \to [0, 1]$ which maps a motive level $L \in \mathcal{L}$ to an element of its level weight range, i. e. $w(L) \in wr(L)$ for all $L \in \mathcal{L}$. Let W denote the set of all such functions w. While weight ranges are assumed to be fixed, level weights are subject to change when an agent acts in some environment and perceives new information about the world.

The weights of motive levels control how desires are created. The links between motives and desires are provided by *motive couplings*.

Definition 2. *A motive coupling mc is a tuple (m, D, cs, ϕ) with $m \in$ Mot, a desire D, $cs \in [-1, 1]$, and ϕ some sentence in the language of the beliefs of the agent. Let $\mathcal{MC}$ denote the set of all motive couplings. For a motive coupling $mc = (m, D, cs, \phi)$ we abbreviate $D(mc) = D$, $\mathsf{L}(mc) = \mathsf{L}(m)$ and $\phi(mc) = \phi$.*

A motive coupling (m, D, cs, ϕ) denotes some tendency of a motive m to influence the creation of a desire D positively ($cs > 0$) or negatively ($cs < 0$) with *coupling strength* cs if some statement ϕ can be verified in the beliefs of the agent. There, ϕ represents a condition that may trigger the coupling according to the given situation. That is, if for the current beliefs B, we find that $B \models \phi$, then the coupling between motive m and desire D is activated to the degree cs. Let $\mathcal{D}$ denote the set of desires that appear in some motive coupling.

Example 3. Let us consider the motive "*environmental awareness*". This motive is a strong influence on the desire "*save the whales*" with e. g. a coupling strength of 0.9 and a relatively weak influence for the desire "*buy fruits from your own country*" with e. g. a coupling strength of 0.3. Furthermore, it exhibits a negative influence on the desire "*buy a sports car*" with e. g. a coupling strength of -0.9.

Definition 3. *A motive state M is a tuple $M = (\mathcal{M}, MC, wr, w)$ with $\mathcal{M} \subseteq$ Mot, $MC \subseteq \mathcal{MC}$, wr is a level weight function on $\mathcal{L}$, and $w : \mathcal{L} \to wr(\mathcal{L})$ denotes the actual weight of each motive level. Let Ω denote the set of all motive states.*

We assume the beliefs of an agent to be represented in some logic. Let B be the belief state of an agent at some point in time with $B \in \mathcal{B}$ and $\mathcal{B}$ denotes the set of all possible belief states an agent may have. We assume that the agent maintains some form of structural knowledge on actions or *know-how* within its logical beliefs which is able to assess the reliability of achieving some desire $D \in \mathcal{D}$ in the given situation. We denote by $B \models reliable(D)$ that the current state of beliefs B gives reasonable grounds to believe that the desire D is reliably achievable, cf. [4]. For example, in a situation where the agent is rich the desire "*buy a Ferrari*" is reliably achievable whereas in a situation where the agent is poor it is not.

Definition 4. *Let* $D_1, \ldots, D_n \in \mathcal{D}$ *and* $\mu_1, \ldots, \mu_n \in [-1, 1]$. *Then the set of tuples* $\gamma = \{(D_1, \mu_1), \ldots, (D_n, \mu_n)\}$ *is called a* motivational structure. *Let* Γ *denote the set of all motivational structures.*

A motivational structure γ describes the motivation to follow the desires of an agent in some specific situation. For a tuple $(D, \mu) \in \gamma$ the value μ is called *motivational value* for D and represents the strength of the motivation. In general, a positive value of μ represents a positive motivation to follow D while a negative value represents motivations to not follow D. A zero value of μ describes a neutral motivation to follow the desire D.

3   An Abstract Model for Motivated Agents

As in the standard BDI approach the inner cycle of our formal agent model starts with incorporating newly received percepts into the belief using some belief revision function. As the world might have changed the motive state of an agent might change as well. In order to adapt to a changed world the agent has to reconsider the current weights and weight ranges of its motives.

Example 4. We continue Example 3. There, the motive "*environmental awareness*" lies in level 5 of Maslow's hierarchy of needs: self-actualization. The motive "*food*" lies in the lowest level of physiological needs. If the agent is low on food and low on money there are usually stronger grounds to prefer desires generated by motives in the lower levels. But if the situation changes, e. g. if the agents becomes wealthy, then the weights of the levels might change. Consider some generous level weight ranges, e. g $wr(\mathsf{pn}) = [0.4, 1]$ and $wr(\mathsf{sa}) = [0, 0.6]$. As the situation has become very *reliable* and the agent is not frightened about fulfilling its physiological needs the weights of the higher levels decrease and therefore motives for self-actualization can become even more motivated than motives for physiological needs.

The adjustment of the agent's motive state is performed by some *weight adjustment function* which determines a new level weight for the motives of the agent.

Definition 5. *Let* Δ *be a function* $\Delta : \Omega \times \mathcal{B} \to W$ *that determines for the motive state* M *in a situation described by beliefs* B *a new level weight function* $\Delta(M, B)$.

After adjusting the motive state of the agent with a new level function the motivational structure might be subject to change as well.

Example 5. We continue Example 4 and consider the desires *"buy cheap food"* and *"buy fruits from your own country"*. Usually, in resource-bounded situations the first desire is preferred to the latter one. If the agent becomes wealthy the situation is secure enough to give *"buy fruits from your own country"* a higher motivation.

Definition 6. *Let Λ be a function $\Lambda : \Omega \times \mathcal{B} \to \Gamma$ that creates a new motivational structure $\Lambda(M, B)$ for some motive state M and beliefs B.*

Having adjusted the motivational structure the agent now has to decide which desires to follow. In general, the agent is best off in selecting its maximally motivated desires as goals, i.e. desires D with $(D, \mu) \in \gamma$ such that μ is maximal in γ. This is true for situations where the agent does not currently pursue any intention or the world has changed drastically and the agent has to reconsider its course of action completely. Usually, the agent is currently pursuing some intentions and switching to a new desire—because it is slightly more motivated as the current ones—does normally not make sense. The agent might start alternating between desires and switching to a new desire likely has further ramifications as it can be incompatible with currently pursued intentions which would need to be dropped. It is crucial to carefully deliberate on this decision as dropping an intention that has been pursued for some time may imply a considerable waste of resources. At this point we do not go into more details on the selection of desires but assume there is some mechanism to either select zero or more desires from the current motivational structure for pursuit. Figure 1 gives a rough overview on the agent model we developed in this section. In the figure, solid lines indicate action flow and dashed lines indicate information flow.

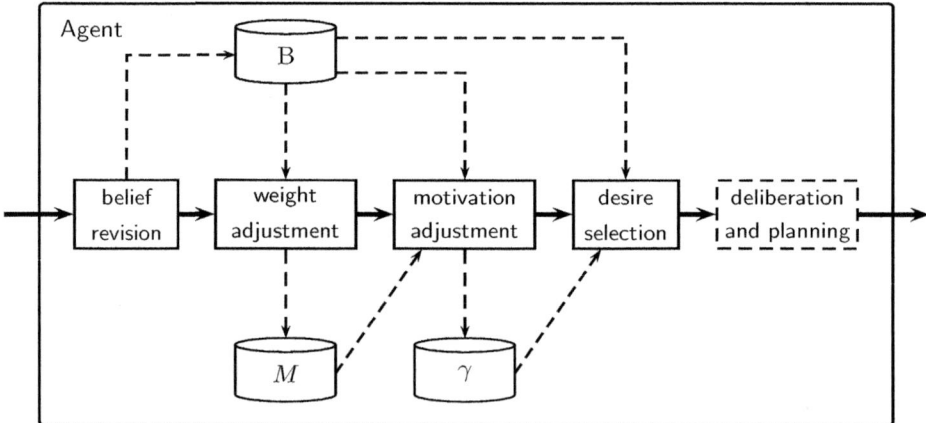

Fig. 1. A simple model of a motivated agent

4   Adjusting Motivation

In this section we elaborate on how the motivation adjustment function Λ of our agent model (see Definition 6) can be realized. In particular we present functions to combine components of the motive state and the belief of the agent to compute the motivational values of desires.

For the computation of the motivational value of a desire we have to combine the coupling strengths with the level weights for each motive coupling. Based on these basic motivations we need to consider the interaction of motivations by combining the basic motivations for the same desire from different motive couplings to determine the resulting motivational value.

For the computation of the basic motivations we introduce a function that combines coupling strengths with the level weights for a motive coupling. For this function from $[0, 1] \times [-1, 1]$ to $[-1, 1]$ we demand the properties associativity, commutativity, monotony and having 1 as its neutral element. Hence, this function should be some kind of a t-norm (appropriately extended to the interval $[-1, 1]$) and we picked the product as a sufficient candidate for the following definition.

Definition 7. *Given a motive coupling mc, its coupling strength $cs(mc)$ and level weight $w(mc)$ we define a function $\beta : [0, 1] \times [-1, 1] \to [-1, 1]$ representing a* basic motivation *as: $\beta(w(mc), cs(mc)) = w(mc) \cdot cs(mc)$.*

Assuming positive values of the coupling strength, the influence of the level weight and the coupling strength is symmetric, for a level weight or coupling strength of 0 the resulting basic motivation will be 0. For a level weight of 1 the basic motivation is limited by the coupling strength and vice versa. For values of the level weight and coupling strength other than 0 and 1 the basic motivation is smaller than both, e. g., $0.5 \cdot 0.5 = 0.25$. For negative values of the coupling strength the behavior of the absolute value is the same but the resulting basic motivation is negative, thus acting against the realization of the associated desire.

For each desire there might exist several motive couplings and hence a set of basic motivations results for each desire. In order to determine the motivation value of a desire we combine the basic motivations for it. This combination function has to account for the nature of interaction of different motives for the same desire. In order to realize an adequate combination method, we base our approach for the combination of basic motivations on the parallel combination initially used for certainty factors in the MYCIN expert system [2] and using the commutative and associative aggregation function f: $(-1, 1) \times (-1, 1) \to (-1, 1)$ defined as

$$f(x, y) = \begin{cases} x + y - x \cdot y, & \text{if } x, y > 0 \\ x + y + x \cdot y, & \text{if } x, y < 0 \\ \frac{x+y}{1-\min\{|x|, |y|\}}, & \text{else} \end{cases}$$

we define the motivation value $\mu(D)$ of a desire D as follows.

Definition 8. *Let $D \in \mathcal{D}$, let $mc_1, \ldots, mc_l$ be all motive couplings with $D(mc_i) = D$ for $i = 1, \ldots, l$, and let $m_i = \beta(w(mc_i), cs(mc_i))$. Then the* motivation value $\mu(D)$ *for a desire D is defined as*

$$\mu(D) = f(m_1, f(m_2, \ldots, f(m_{l-1}, m_l) \ldots))$$

for $l > 1$ and $\mu(D) = m_1$ otherwise.

The function $\mu(D)$ computes the motivation value for the desire D. For adjusting the motivational structure γ of the agent we compute the motivational value for each desire for which exists at least one active motive coupling.

Definition 9. *For a motive state $MS = (\mathcal{M}, MC, wr, w)$ and a belief state B we set*

$$\Lambda(MS, B) = \{(d, \mu(d)) \mid \exists mc \in MC : d = D(mc),$$
$$B \nvDash d, B \vDash \phi(mc)\}$$

The motivation structure γ contains the set of desires that are not satisfied and for whose there exists at least one active motive coupling, i.e., the condition of the coupling is satisfied together with their respective current motivational value.

Example 6. We continue Example 3 and instantiate the level weights according to the ranges given in Example 2 assuming a very reliable situation of the agent.

$$w(\mathsf{sa}) = 0.25 \in wr(\mathsf{sa}),$$
$$w(\mathsf{pn}) = 0.75 \in wr(\mathsf{pn}),$$
$$w(\mathsf{es}) = 0.45 \in wr(\mathsf{es})$$

For the motive couplings we formalize those of Example 3 and add the motive "*prestige*" with a positive coupling for "*buy a sports car*".

$$(env\_awareness, save\_whales, 0.9, endangered\_whales),$$
$$(env\_awareness, buy\_local\_fruits, 0.3, true),$$
$$(evn\_awareness, buy\_sports\_car, -0.9, true),$$
$$(prestige, buy\_sports\_car, 1, true)$$

The beliefs of the agent shall be given by $B = \emptyset$. Given the motive state described above we can compute the corresponding motivational structure as follows. The desire "*save_whales*" is contained in a motive coupling but as the agent is ignorant it does not believe that whales are endangered and consequently does not have a motivation for saving the whales. The desire "*buy_local_fruits*" has a motive coupling with level weight 0.25 and coupling strength 0.3. The resulting basic motivation is $\beta(0.25, 0.3) = 0.075$. As there are no other motive couplings for the desire the motivation value is equal to the basic motivation. The desire "*buy_sports_car*" has two motive couplings from different motives, one positive coupling and one negative. The resulting basic motivations are $\beta(0.25, -0.9) = -0.225$ and $\beta(0.45, 1) = 0.45$. From these we get the motivation value:

$$\mu(buy\_sports\_car) = f(-0.225, 0.45) = \frac{-0.225 + 0.45}{1 - 0.225}$$
$$= \frac{0.225}{0.775} \approx 0.29$$

Thus, the resulting motivation value for "*buy_sports_car*" is positive such that the motive coupling from the motive "*prestige*" is dominating the coupling from "*environmental awareness*", as expected. The resulting motivational structure of the agent is given by

$$\gamma = \Lambda(MS, B)$$
$$= \{(buy\_local\_fruits, 0.075), (buy\_sports\_car, 0.29)\}.$$

The motivational structure, whose creation is explained in this section, changes if the motive state is adjusted. The following section elaborates the computation of the motive state adjustment.

5   Taking Reliability into Account

Agents usually behave differently in reliable vs. unreliable situations. Reliability makes the agent feel safe, whereas unreliability may signalize harassment, even danger. The degree of reliability of the current situation has direct impact on the motivational structure of the agent in our approach. As said before for every desire D we assume that the beliefs B of the agent is able to derive whether the desire is reliably achievable $B \models reliable(D)$. This means that the agent has the means (in form of plans and actions) to achieve the desire D in the current situation, cf. [4]. The belief on the reliability of all desires enables the agent to assess the reliability of the whole situation and gives an idea whether more basic motives, respectively desires, should be pursued instead of more higher motives, respectively desires. For example, if the agent is situated in some resource-bound location, say a desert, then usually a very small portion of the agent's desires is reliably achievable. In unreliable environments the agent should stick to desires that derive from more low-level motives, i. e. from motives that are in deficiency levels.

Definition 10. *Let m be a motive and let $K = \{(m, D_1, cs_1, \phi_1), \ldots, (m, D_l, cs_l, \phi_l)\}$ be the set of motive couplings for m with $cs_i > 0$ for $i = 1, \ldots, l$. Then m is called satisfiable wrt. beliefs B, denoted by $B \models sat(m)$, if there exists an $k \in \{1, \ldots, l\}$ desire D with*

$$cs_k \geq \frac{1}{l} \sum_{i=1}^{l} cs_i \quad and \quad B \models reliable(D).$$

The above definition says that a motive m is satisfiable if there is a desire D that is coupled to m above average and that is reliable. Given the information on satisfiability of motives in a given situation the agent has to compare its set of motives with the set of motives that are satisfiable. In general, the more motives of an agent are satisfiable the more reliable the current situation is. In this comparison one has to consider the different motive levels as especially the deficiency motives have more weight in assessing the situation as reliable. Therefore, for a motive state $M = (\mathcal{M}, MC, wr, w)$ and beliefs B the reliability of the current situation with respect to the reliability of desires and hence the satisfiability of motives, denoted by rel_sit, is assessed by

$$rel\_sit = Z \cdot \sum_{L \in \mathcal{L}} \frac{l_L + u_L}{2} \frac{|ST_L|}{|S_L|} \tag{1}$$

with (remember that $\mathsf{L}(m) \in \mathcal{L}$ denotes the motive level of m)

$$ST_L = \{m \in \mathcal{M} \mid \mathsf{L}(m) = L \wedge B \models sat(m)\}$$
$$S_L = \{m \in \mathcal{M} \mid \mathsf{L}(m) = L\}$$
$$Z = \frac{1}{\sum_{L \in \mathcal{L}} \frac{l_L + u_L}{2}} \quad .$$

In Equation (1) the reliability of the situation is determined as a weighted sum over the proportions of satisfiable motives to the set of all motives in a given level. The weight of the proportions is defined to be the center of the level range which amounts to an average weight for the level. The term rel_sit is normalized by the factor Z and hence we have $0 \leq rel\_sit \leq 1$.

We modeled motivations according to Maslow's hierarchy in Section 2 distinguishing five types of motives of decreasing importance, i.e. the motives on the first level are the most basic ones. In order to implement Maslow's hierarchy, in Definition 1 we defined an interval of weights for each motive level L, assessing a lower bound l_L and an upper bound u_L for the importance of motives of level L, with δ_L denoting the width of the respective weight interval.

As a special feature of our approach, the current weight of the motive levels will depend on the reliability of the current situation: The more reliable the situation is, the more safe will the agent feel, and the less important are the motives of the motive levels that are deficiency needs. Consequently, the non-deficiency motives might obtain more influence. In unreliable situations, the basic motives are more important to sustain the agent's vital functionality. This is realized by adjusting the level weights $w(L)$ in the following way:

$$\begin{aligned} w(L) &= u_L + \delta_L f_\downarrow(rel\_sit), \quad L \in \mathsf{d}(\mathcal{L}^M), \\ w(L) &= u_L + \delta_L f_\uparrow(rel\_sit), \quad L \notin \mathsf{d}(\mathcal{L}^M), \end{aligned} \tag{2}$$

with a monotonically decreasing function $f_\downarrow : [0,1] \to [0,1]$ and a monotonically increasing function $f_\uparrow : [0,1] \to [0,1]$. Here, we set $f_\downarrow(y) = 1 - y$ and $f_\uparrow(y) = y$. Equations (2) realize a level weight adjustment function Δ as specified in Definition 5 and used in Definition 8 for computing the motivational values of desires. The influence of the reliability of the current situation might be modeled by families of more complex functions, even going beyond the dichotomy of deficiency vs. non-deficiency. We demonstrate the adjustment of level weights in the following example.

Example 7. We continue Example 5 and consider the two motives $m_1 =$"*environmental awareness*" and $m_2 =$ "*food*". As in Example 4 let the level weight ranges of the motive levels "*physiological needs*" and "*self-actualization*" be given by $wr(\mathsf{pn}) = [0.4, 1]$ and $wr(\mathsf{sa}) = [0, 0.6]$ and let $w(\mathsf{pn}) = 0.8$ and $w(\mathsf{sa}) = 0.4$. Consider the desires $d_1 =$"*buy fruits from your own country*" and $d_2 =$"*buy cheap food*" and the motive couplings $(m_1, d_1, 0.3, true)$ and $(m_2, d_2, 0.3, true)$. In this situation the motivational structure amounts to $\gamma = \{(d_1, 0.12), (d_2, 0.24)\}$. Imagine the above motivational structure derives from the situation that the agent is poor and he knows of no reliable way to acquire fruits from its own country. In that situation only the motive "*food*" is satisfied but not the motive "*environmental awareness*". Consider now the situation that the agent becomes wealthy and does not have to worry the price of local fruits. Therefore, let the current beliefs B of the agent be of a form such that both $B \models reliable(d_1)$ and $B \models reliable(d_2)$. Therefore, both motives *"food"* and *"environmental awareness"* are satisfiable which amounts to

$$rel\_sit = \frac{1}{1} \left(\frac{0.4 + 1}{2} 1 + \frac{0 + 0.6}{2} 1 \right) = 1$$

and it follows

$$w(\mathsf{pn}) = u_{\mathsf{pn}} + \delta_{\mathsf{pn}} f_{\downarrow}(rel\_sit) = 0.4 + 0.6(1 - 1) = 0.4$$
$$w(\mathsf{sa}) = u_{\mathsf{sa}} + \delta_{\mathsf{sa}} f_{\uparrow}(rel\_sit) = 0.0 + 0.6(1 - 0) = 0.6\,.$$

Computing the new motivational structure for the new level weights yields $\gamma = \{(d_1, 0.18), (d_2, 0.12)\}$. Therefore, in a reliable situation the desire *"buy fruits from your own country"* is more motivated than *"buy cheap food"*.

6   Related Work

There is a large body of established literature on motivation in the field of psychology and philosophy, see e. g. [6], while the literature in artificial intelligence and intelligent agents is rather limited. Nonetheless, on the conceptional level Norman and Long [8] also use motives and motivation. However, our approach goes further than theirs by adapting levels of motives and ideas from Maslow's hierarchy for the BDI model. We also take the reliability of the environment for the agents motivational state under consideration. The implementation of the motivational model of [8] defines a new agent architecture called *motivated agency* that allows for the generation of motivated goals that are active if a threshold is met. The aim of their model is to limit the number of goals pursued by the agent and stands in parallel to the BDI model whereas our approach is fitted neatly into it [4] and complemented by other extensions such as explicit representation of structural knowledge. We also use a far more structured approach giving a framework of motive levels, their weights and couplings to desires that are used for goal selection.

Other work towards a computational model has been done by Luck and colleagues with in the publication [7]. The approach presented there works with one single structure of motivations. This structure updates the intensity of a given motivation that is aggregated over time until a predefined threshold is met which triggers a goal selection for this motivation and the mitigation of the motivation. The model we present here is far richer, more modular and flexible. We differentiate the concepts of motives, motivation and goal selection, add the levels of motives and consider the reliability of the environment.

7   Summary and Conclusion

The ability to generate desires and goals is a crucial feature of autonomous agents. In this paper, we presented a fully elaborated computational model that allows agents to be driven by motivations which are linked to their needs and desires and the influence of which depends on their current beliefs as well as on their self-evaluation. In summary, our model of a motivated BDI agent is based on the following principal ideas: 1.) we make use of a flexible hierarchy of motive types that roughly follows Maslow's model [5] and distinguishes between deficiency and non-deficiency needs, 2.) desires are linked to motives by couplings that are assigned some degrees of strength (positive or negative) and that can be triggered by conditions found to be true in the agent's belief about the world, and 3.) the interactions between motives on different levels of the hierarchy are processed by use of an aggregation function and give rise to the motivational structure of the agent that guides its current behavior.

In spite of the richness and complexity of our approach, the motives of the agent are clearly seen to be the basic driving component for the agents behavior. This enables the agent to act autonomously and on intrinsic incitement.

References

1. Bratman, M.E.: Intention, Plans, and Practical Reason. CSLI Publications (1987)
2. Buchanan, B.G., Shortliffe, E.H.: Rule-Based Expert Systems: The MYCIN Experiments of the Stanford Heuristic Programming Project. Addison-Wesley, Reading (1984)
3. Ghallab, M., Nau, D., Travers, P.: Automated Planning: Theory and Practice. Morgan Kaufmann, San Francisco (2004)
4. Krümpelmann, P., Thimm, M.: A Logic Programming Framework for Reasoning about Know-How. In: Proc. of the 14th Int. Workshop NMR (2010)
5. Maslow, A.H.: Motivation and personality. Harper and Row, Cambridge (1970)
6. Mele, A.R.: Motivation and Agency. Oxford University Press, Oxford (2003)
7. Meneguzzi, F., Luck, M.: Motivations as an Abstraction of Meta-level Reasoning. In: Burkhard, H.-D., Lindemann, G., Verbrugge, R., Varga, L.Z. (eds.) CEEMAS 2007. LNCS (LNAI), vol. 4696, pp. 204–214. Springer, Heidelberg (2007)
8. Norman, T.J., Long, D.: Alarms: An implementation of motivated agency. In: Tambe, M., Müller, J., Wooldridge, M.J. (eds.) IJCAI-WS 1995 and ATAL 1995. LNCS, vol. 1037, pp. 219–234. Springer, Heidelberg (1996)
9. Wahba, A., Bridgewell, L.: Maslow reconsidered: A review of research on the need hierarchy theory. Organizational Behavior and Human Performance 15, 212–240 (1976)
10. Weiss, G. (ed.): Multiagent systems. MIT Press, Cambridge (1999)

Learning Dynamic Adaptation Strategies in Agent-Based Traffic Simulation Experiments

Andreas D. Lattner[1], Jörg Dallmeyer[1], and Ingo J. Timm[2]

[1] Information Systems and Simulation, Institute of Computer Science
Goethe University Frankfurt, P.O. Box 11 19 32, 60054 Frankfurt, Germany
[2] Business Informatics I, University of Trier, D-54286 Trier, Germany

Abstract. The increase of road users and traffic load has lead to the situation that in some regions road capacities appear to be exceeded regularly. Although there is natural capacity limit of roads, there exist potentials for a dynamic adaptation of road usage. Finding out about useful rules for dynamic adaptations of traffic rules is a costly and time consuming effort if performed in the real world. In this paper, we introduce an agent-based traffic simulation model and present an approach to learning dynamic adaptation rules in traffic scenarios based on supervised learning from simulation data. For evaluation, we apply our approach to synthetic traffic scenarios. Initial results show the feasibility of the approach and indicate that learned dynamic adaptation strategies can lead to an improvement w.r.t. the average velocity in our scenarios.

Keywords: Agent-based traffic simulation, supervised learning, adaptation strategies.

1 Introduction

In the past decades, the number of road users and traffic load has constantly increased. This has lead to the situation that road capacities in some areas seem to be exceeded and congestions occur regularly. Although there exists a natural limit of road users, a road infrastructure can deal with, there are still potentials for optimization of road usage and activities to prevent or reduce traffic jams, e.g., by re-routing of road users or by introducing traffic regulations aiming to avoid risky situations. Current solutions provide already means in order to dynamically reroute road users with GPS-based navigation systems utilizing traffic information as well as to adapt traffic regulations by setting a speed limit if high traffic load is present or if congestions have already occurred in the subsequent course of the road. Different measurement techniques are used to get online information about the current traffic status at certain control points [11].

Finding out about useful rules for dynamic adaptations of traffic rules or traffic rerouting is a costly and time consuming effort if performed in the real world. Although certain general experiences about traffic can be utilized in order to set up such rules, emergent effects of changes are not obvious in all

F. Klügl and S. Ossowski (Eds.): MATES 2011, LNAI 6973, pp. 77–88, 2011.

cases. This can lead to the situation that improving the situation at one point in the road network will worsen the situation somewhere else. Simulation provides a useful instrument in order to investigate different strategies and to find out about effects in different settings. Nevertheless, it should be at least mentioned that simulation does not come for free as a certain modeling effort has to be considered and that simulation results are not always trusted.

We present an approach to learning dynamic adaptation strategies for simulated traffic scenarios. The basic idea is to extract features of the current traffic situation and to investigate the effects of various activities. The desired outcome of this process is to identify a strategy which can dynamically adapt the behavior of certain infrastructure elements (e.g., road segments) or to provide suggestions to road users how they should behave in order to improve the situation. We apply supervised symbolic machine learning algorithms in order to find out about useful rules. Having in mind situation descriptions and potential actions with the aim to learn a successful strategy, reinforcement learning techniques seem to be very well suited. However, in this work we have the additional requirement that comprehensible rules should be generated which can be understood and maybe even manually adapted by experts. We apply the approach to two scenarios. In the first scenario, it is learned what speed limit should be set on a road depending on the actual situation. In the second scenario, a variable-message sign (VMS) can force road users to change the lane in order to let cars enter the motorway. A classifier is learned in which situations the VMS should be active. Although it would also be possible to learn dynamic adaptation strategies for road users by using their individual or even joint experiences for learning, we focus on a central infrastructure-based setting in this paper.

2   Related Work

The combination of data mining and agent-based systems is discussed in recent work. Baqueiro et al. present a study where they discuss two different approaches for a combination of the two fields [1]: 1) Using data mining techniques for investigation of agent-based modeling and simulation (ABMS) and 2) Utilizing ABMS results in data mining. Many works have also been done in the field of Adaptive Traffic Control Systems (ATCS). For instance, Bull et al. [4] discuss learning classifiers in order to improve traffic-responsive signal control systems. A review of ATCS is provided, e.g., in [16].

Gehrke and Wojtusiak [7] present an approach to react online on influences from the environment (for example weather) in the context of route planning. The approach tries to identify the best routes by taking into account the wetness and the speed limits of the roads. Every truck is represented by an agent and can dynamically react to new events. The (propositional) rule induction system AQ21 has been used to learn prediction rules.

Bazzan et al. have investigated the adaptation of driver behavior and traffic light agents [3]. The motivation for their approach is an integrated consideration of traffic light control and route choices for drivers. The adaptation of both types of behaviors is carried out locally, i.e., without central control. In the cases where no fixed or greedy settings are used, the traffic light agent adaptation is based on Q-Learning and for the routing decision a probabilistic selection is performed in dependence of previous experience. The authors report an improvement in travel time and occupancy for the combined adaptation in comparison to situations where only drivers or traffic lights are adapted. In another article, Bazzan [2] discusses opportunities for multiagent systems and learning in the context of traffic control with a focus on reinforcement learning approaches.

The approach of Fiosins et al. [6] addresses the detection of change points for intelligent agents in city traffic. They apply a bootstrapped cumulative sum charts (CUSUM) test and a pairwise resampling test in order to detect change points. In a case study, the approach is applied to a vehicle routing problem. The authors report that the change point detection and re-routing decision could reduce the travel times of the vehicles.

In our work, we decided to use a supervised learning setting especially taking into account decision rule or decision tree induction in order to meet the requirement of getting comprehensible and manually adaptable results. In our approach we investigate different behaviors in a "concurrent" setting to decide how to behave in different situations utilizing the learned strategy.

3 Traffic Simulation

The traffic simulation used here is based on an underlying geographic information system (GIS), built on the toolkit *GeoTools*[1] and implemented in JAVA. The simulation system is designed to simulate urban traffic scenarios with different kinds of road user, e.g., cars, trucks and bicycles on up-to-date cartographical material. Traffic rules like the way of right are implemented, giving the car coming from the right side the higher priority if the corresponding road is equal righted as the other road. In this section we provide a brief summary of the simulation system. A more detailed description can be found in [5]. The use of this particular simulation system is not mandatory for this approach. However, having available the source code allows for direct integration of control behavior and coupling of the machine learning component.

The road map is modeled by means of a graph datastructure. Each road is represented by a data structure *EdgeInformation* (EI). Multiple EIs can be connected with help of a *NodeInformation* (NI). EIs store information about the corresponding road (e.g. attributes like "roadname", "maximum velocity", "number of lanes", "priority for the right of way", ...) and administrate the simulated road users. Each NI stores information about the connected EIs like, e.g. rotation directions between each two connected EIs, etc.

The behavior of the simulated road users is based on the well known Nagel-Schreckenberg model (NaSch) [13]. The NaSch model partitions a road in cells with length of 7.5m, what is not sufficient for urban scenarios. Therefore, we adapted the model by removing the cells and enabling simulated road users to

---

[1] http://www.geotools.org

Algorithm 1. Traffic model

1: **if** *attentive* **then**
2:     $v_{t+\frac{1}{3}} \leftarrow \min\left(v_t + a^{\oplus}\left(v_t\right), v\text{max}, v_{\text{max}}^{\text{EI}}\right)$
3:     $v_{t+\frac{2}{3}} \leftarrow \min\left(v_{t+\frac{1}{3}}, dist - sd\left(v_{t+\frac{1}{3}}\right)\right)$
4:     **if** $random \leq prob\left(v_{t+\frac{2}{3}}\right)$ **then**
5:         $v_{t+1} \leftarrow \max\left(v_{t+\frac{2}{3}} - a^{\ominus}\left(v_{t+\frac{2}{3}}\right), 0\right)$
6:     **else**
7:         $v_{t+1} \leftarrow v_{t+\frac{2}{3}}$
8: **else**
9:     $v_{t+1} \leftarrow v_t$
10: $position_{t+1} \leftarrow position_t + v_{t+1}$

---

drive with continuous velocities. The basic behavior of a simulated car was described in [5]. Algorithm 1 shows an extended version, which notices brake lights of the preceding car [8] and a slow start rule [10]. Each simulated car performs Algorithm 1 in parallel in order to update its velocity. One time step in the simulation correlates to one second real-time. In line 2, the car will accelerate from its velocity v_t at time t with a velocity dependant amount $a^{\oplus}\left(v_t\right)$, if it is slower than its own maximum velocity $v\text{max}$ and the maximum allowed velocity on the road $v_{\text{max}}^{\text{EI}}$. Afterwards, it will brake in line 3, if it is not able to hold the safety distance to the preceding car under usage of the current velocity $v_{t+\frac{1}{3}}$. Line 3 avoids collisions. Line 4 lets the car dally with a probability, $prob\left(v_{t+\frac{2}{3}}\right)$, which is dependent on the current velocity (slow start rule) and on the brake light of the preceding car. We also assume, that a car on the left lane will dally less than a car on the right lane, in order to overtake cars on the right lane. Each car has a standard probability for dallying $\perp$, which is a normally distributed factor ($\mu = 0.3$, $\sigma = 0.1$) as basis for $prob\left(v_{t+\frac{2}{3}}\right)$. If $v_{t+\frac{2}{3}} = 0$ and the car "sees" brake lights, $\perp$ will be multiplied with 2. Afterwards, the probability is divided by the lane used by the simulated car (counting from right to left where the right lane is lane 1). Dallying is done by decelerating with an amount of $a^{\ominus}\left(v_{t+\frac{2}{3}}\right)$. If a car has $v_{t+\frac{2}{3}} = 0$, dallying will result in a negative velocity. The resulting velocity v_{t+1} thus is limited to 0 as lower bound. The braking without deeper reason was first described in [13]. It has been widely examined and enables the simulation model to produce traffic jams without external influences.

Lane changing is done w.r.t. an incentive criterion "Do I want to change lane?" and a security criterion "Is it possible to change without accident?", according to [14]. Ways to simulate the occurrence of accidents in microsimulation models for traffic simulation were studied in literature (e.g., [12]). The main idea in these works is the integration of inattentiveness leading to rear-end collision accidents. Each car is inattentive with a probability $\perp'$ and does not change its velocity in this iteration (see line 9). This may lead to an accident, if the driver in front was braking harshly. Huge differences in speed lead to a higher probability of accidents and therefore a slower forthcoming because of a lane blockage where the accident took place.

We parallelized the simulation in order to run the evaluation for our scenarios. In our implementation, a server controls a set of simulation clients.

4   Learning Dynamic Adaptation Strategies

In this section, we describe the approach to learning dynamic adaptation strategies. The underlying goal is to identify patterns from experimental results of simulation runs and to utilize this information to dynamically adapt a system's behavior. The following sections address the used representation for situations and actions, the learning process, and the utilization of a learned strategy. As the intention is to develop a generic approach that can be used in different simulations and settings, the description is on a rather abstract level in this section.

4.1   Representation

In this work, we have chosen a rather simple, straight-forward representation for situations and actions. The selected representation allows for a direct application of supervised propositional learning approaches like decision tree and decision rule learning. Situations are described by a set of attributes whose values for an actual situation are extracted from the simulation system. Each attribute can be either numeric or symbolic. Domains – i.e., possible values for a certain attribute – of symbolic attributes are defined by a set of different symbolic values. The domain of a symbolic attribute $F_{i,symb}$ is defined as $dom(F_{i,symb}) = \{v_{i,1}, \ldots, v_{i,n}\}$. Domains of numeric attributes $F_{i,cont}$ are defined by an interval: $dom(F_{i,cont}) = [v_{l,i}, v_{u,i}]$ with $v_{l,i}, v_{u,i} \in \mathbb{R}$.

A list of attributes $(F_1, \ldots, F_n)$ is used for the representation of a situation. A specific situation is represented by a list of corresponding values of the attributes $(f_1, \ldots, f_n)$ with $f_i \in dom(F_i)$ for $1 \leq i \leq n$. Potential actions (behaviors) to be performed in a specific situation are represented by a set of identifiers $A = \{a_1, \ldots, a_m\}$, e.g., different speed limits that can be imposed on a road or the decision if a variable-message sign is turned on or off.

4.2   Learning Strategies

Figure 1 illustrates the principal pattern learning process. The simulations we are addressing in our work consist of a set of parameters (e.g., number of cars in the simulation and fraction of trucks) and underly certain random effects which effect the simulation. In dependence of the seed value of the random number generator, different simulation results might be generated even if identical parameter settings are used (cf. aforementioned probabilistic behaviors in Sect. 3, e.g., dallying). Thus, multiple runs of identical parameters lead to different results (in the general case). After performance of a set of simulation runs and

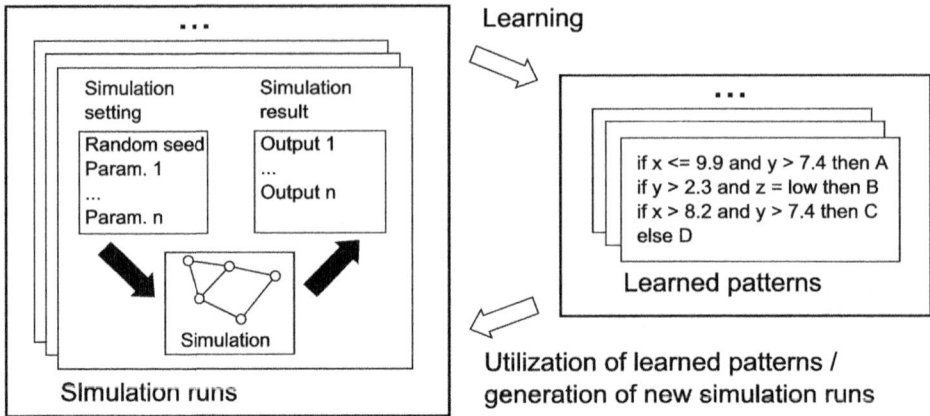

Fig. 1. Pattern learning

capturing of simulation outputs, a learning phase is initiated which leads to a set of patterns which are extracted from simulation. Having identified these patterns, it is possible to use the generated information for an adapted behavior in the simulation or for the decision which simulation runs should be performed next (i.e., what parameter sets to use in upcoming experiments). This general pattern learning approach is not restricted to strategy learning but could also be used in order to identify patterns about future events which are likely to be happen if a certain situation is present. However, in this work we focus on action selection for a current situation.

The goal of learning is to identify a strategy how to behave in certain situations. A *strategy* is defined by a function mapping a current situation to an action to be performed: $strategy : dom(F_1) \times \ldots \times dom(F_n) \longrightarrow A$.

In order to find out which action might be the best to encounter a certain situation, we apply a "concurrent" execution from identical simulation situations applying all potential actions. This procedure is illustrated in Figure 2. At a certain time step t_n in simulation, a situation description is computed resulting in the j attributes' values $(f_1, \ldots, f_j)$. From this time step on, the different actions (elements of the set A) are applied and executed in different simulation runs. All these runs start from the same situation at t_n. After some time at time step t_{n+k}, the situation is assessed for the different runs and the action a_{best} leading to the best situation is stored in combination with the situation description: $(f_1, \ldots, f_j, a_{best})$. The training input for learning a classifier is a set of such situation descriptions.

4.3   Utilization of Learned Strategies

In order to dynamically adapt the behavior to the current situation, the same feature computation procedure as for generating the training data is used. Whenever a dynamic strategy decision should be performed, a tuple $(f_1, \ldots, f_j)$ with

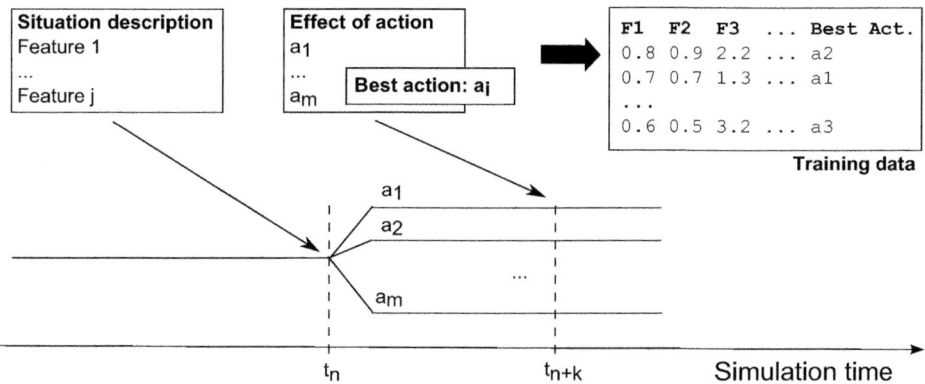

Fig. 2. Generation of training examples

the feature values is generated. These values are passed to the learned (or manually specified) strategy *strategy* leading to the proposed behavior $a \in A$.

Depending on the set of actions, it might not be useful to continuously initiate the strategy decision as it might take some time until an effect of the newly selected strategy can be seen. It might even be disadvantageous to switch behaviors too often as a transition could lead to additional costs (e.g., changing the route of a vehicle) and oscillating behavior could occur in borderline situations. For our first investigations in the traffic simulation domain, we invoke the strategy decision in fixed intervals, e.g., every 60s of simulated time.

5 Evaluation

The evaluation scenarios for this work are located on a motorway. Simulated cars vary in driving behavior w.r.t. different acceleration potentials $a^{\oplus}(v_t)$, maximum velocities v_{max}, dallying behavior $prob\left(v_{t+\frac{2}{3}}\right)$ and car lengths. For each simulation run, a uniformly distributed probability p_{truck} smaller than 0.1 is determined. A road user is generated as a truck with probability p_{truck} and as a car otherwise. Trucks can be seen as a special case of cars. They have a lower maximum velocity, accelerate slower, and have a greater length.

The evaluation is divided into two parts: At first, a static scenario with one traffic situation per simulation run is used to learn a classifier. Afterwards, a dynamic scenario with time-dependent heterogeneous traffic situations is used to check the coherence of the approach for more realistic problems.

5.1 Static Scenario: Imposing a Speed Limit

Our first evaluation scenario is placed on a rather simple road map representing a circle with 24 km length. The road has two lanes. In traffic theory, it is useful to homogenize the traffic (e.g., by speed limits) in order to prevent from disturbances that could lead to a traffic jam. It is clear that on low traffic densities this

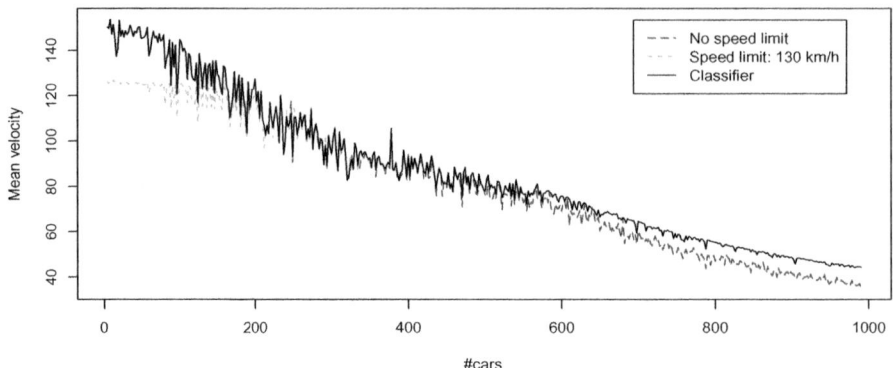

Fig. 3. Comparison: Classifier vs. fixed actions

is not beneficial. As a first scenario, we thus want to learn the point from which a homogenization in form of a speed limit of 130km/h leads to a higher mean velocity of all cars in comparison to not setting a speed limit. The probability for rear-end collision accidents decreases with an increasing homogenization of traffic. In our simulation, whenever two cars are involved in an accident, they will be set to stay on the right lane for 600 iterations.

The simulation server is set up to let the simulation clients run experiments with 4, 6, ... , 998, 1000 cars, each setting five times. The fraction of trucks is not fixed, but its maximum is set to 10% of the number of cars. Each client places the given number of cars on the road randomly and initiates the simulation according to the scheme of Figure 2. After a settlement phase of 1000 iterations, recording of the traffic flow in cars per time at a defined point and the mean velocity of all simulated cars in each iteration is started. After further 1000 iterations, the state of the simulation is stored. A situation description is generated, using the following features: Traffic flow, traffic density (sum of the vehicle lengths divided by overall road length), mean velocity, standard deviation of velocity, and truck percentage. The first action, in this case "no speed limit" is done and another settlement phase of 1000 iterations follows. After this phase, the mean velocity of all cars during further 1000 iterations is taken as fitness for the action.

Now, the saved simulation state gets restored and the next action gets investigated: "speed limit 130km/h" for the whole road. The fitness for this action is computed analogously. The client then sends the state description and the action with the highest mean velocity and the according fitness back to the server. The server records all received results and lets the clients simulate until the multitude of traffic densities is run through.

The server uses an interface to *WEKA* [9] to build a classifier, when to use which action. For learning, we use *WEKA's* J4.8 implementation of the *C4.5* algorithm [15]. The classifier is then tested on 494 new runs (with 4, 6, ... , 1000 cars) of the same scenario and compared to the fixed usage of any of both

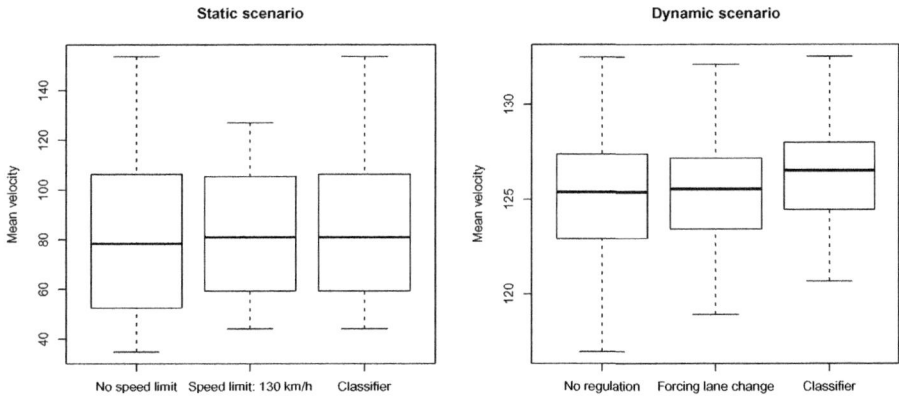

Fig. 4. Comparison: Classifier vs. fixed actions

actions. The results are shown in figure 3. The classifier chooses "no speed limit" at low traffic densities and switches to "speed limit 130km/h" for high traffic densities. Analyses have shown that the classifier chooses the best action for 85% of the simulated situations. This leads to the mean overall velocities for taking action "no speed limit": 82.71, "speed limit 130km/h": 82.83, and classifier: 85.85km/h. The corresponding boxplot is shown in Figure 4 on the left. A one-sided paired t-test with error level $\alpha = 0.05$ indicates a greater mean velocity for the classifier ($p < 2.2e - 16$ in both cases). Even if multiple testing (two tests) is taken into account using the "familywise error rate" (Bonferronis FWER), the statistical tests indicate a greater mean velocity of the classifier compared to the fixed settings.

5.2   Dynamic Scenario: Forcing Lane Changes

In the second scenario, there is a part of a motorway divided into 20 segments $EI_0 \cdots EI_{19}$, each with a length of 500m. Each EI has two lanes. The NI between EI_{14} and EI_{15} is connected to the one lane link road EI_{20}. Figure 5 shows an excerpt of the road map. One kilometer ahead the junction point on the motorway, a variable-message sign (VMS) is used to dynamically advise drivers to use the left lane in order to let the ones coming from the right enter the motorway. In our simulation, if this signal is given, drivers will change from the right to the left lane in the corresponding region if it is possible in the current situation. Therefore, a classifier is trained using the features $density\,(EI_{15,16})$, $density\,(EI_{17,18})$ and $density\,(EI_{20})$ as situation description. The two actions "turn off VMS" and "turn on VMS" (show message to use left lane till junction point) are compared and the better one is used as the target attribute value for the training input. During simulation, varying traffic densities on the two entry points into the road network are simulated. Each training example is generated from the analysis of 60s simulated time, according to the method

Fig. 5. Screenshot showing part of the motorway (blue), containing the VMS and the junction (green). The arrows indicate the direction of travel.

```
meanV <= 101.907816                    dEI(20) <= 0.019705
|    flow <= 214: a0 (62.0/18.0)       |   dEI(20) <- 0.01273: a0 (13773.0/4413.0)
|    flow > 214: a1 (1724.0/391.0)     .
meanV > 101.907816                     :
|    flow <= 14
|    |    flow <- 2: a1 (5.0)           |   |   |   dEI(17,18) > 0.004072: a1 (1311.0/526.0)
|    |    flow > 2: a0 (30.0/2.0)       |   |   dEI(17,18) > 0.011574: a1 (3771.0/1061.0)
|    flow > 14: a0 (660.0/66.0)         |   dEI(20) > 0.02811: a1 (3818.0/433.0)

with     a0 = no speedlimit            with     a0 = turn off VMS
         a1 = speed limit 130km/h               a1 = turn on VMS
                                        dEI(x) = density(EI_x)
```

Fig. 6. Classifier of static and dynamic scenario

described in the last subsection. After this time slice, the result is transmitted to the server and situation after having applied the better action is used for the subsequent simulation. The server lets the clients simulate until 10,000 data sets are generated.

The classifier is tested on the same scenario and with a duration of 48h simulation time (172,800 iterations). The classifier determines the action to take for a period of 60s. The traffic volumes on the two starting points vary over time. The simulation is performed 100 times and the mean overall velocities for the different strategies are computed: "turn off VMS": 125.12, "turn on VMS": 125.44, and classifier: 126.41km/h. The corresponding boxplot is shown in Figure 4 on the right. Statistical tests with the same setting as before lead to the same result ($p < 2.2e - 16$ in both cases comparing the classifier to the fixed settings) and thus, indicate a greater mean velocity of the classifier. The trained classifiers and the confusion matrices of both scenarios can be seen in Figures 6 and 7.

The average travel times per car in the different settings are: a_0 : 289.53, a_1 : 282.15, and $classifier$: 279.89 seconds. Scaling these numbers to the simulated time of 48 hours and the average number of cars in each scenario (43148.09), using the classifier approx. 120h are saved in comparison to the fixed a_0 and 27h in comparison to the fixed a_1 setting.

	Classified as:	
Class	**No limit**	**Max 130km/h**
No limit	705	352
Max 130km/h	158	1266

	Classified as:	
Class	**turn off VMS**	**turn on VMS**
turn off VMS	12185	3049
turn on VMS	6709	8057

Fig. 7. Confusion matrices of classifiers in static and dynamic scenario (cross-validation on training data)

6 Conclusion

In this paper, we have presented an approach to learning dynamic adaptation strategies using the example of traffic simulation experiments. Simulation provides the clear advantage to perform "what if" studies and thus, allows for investigating alternative behaviors in identical settings. In the evaluation we have tested two different behaviors in two scenarios (speed limit vs. no speed limit and forcing cars to change the lane at a feeder road vs. letting them drive as usual) in order to check if a strategy based on traffic features can be used to gain an advantage in traffic flow. The results have shown that the trained classifiers lead to a greater mean velocity in both scenarios in comparison to fixed strategies where the current situation is not taken into account. Although the increase of the average velocities per road user is not very high (especially in the second setting), it is worthwhile taking into account the potential for reduction of CO_2 emission as well as for gas consumption for the total amount of road users by such dynamic adaptations. The results of the evaluation might not be too surprising – e.g., having learned a classifier what speed limit to use in dependence on the traffic flow or traffic densities (Fig. 6) – but they show the principal feasibility of the approach generating comprehensible decision rules or trees. In future work, it would be interesting to investigate more complex settings.

One of the disadvantages of the approach as presented here is that with an increasing number of options to be taken into account, the number of simulation runs will increase constantly. Even more problematic is a situation where multiple criteria are to be evaluated, e.g., forcing lane change behavior, different speed limits, and overtaking prohibition for trucks. In this case the Cartesian product of options could be used for investigation. However, due to the huge number of combinations, such an approach would not be feasible any more. We are currently working on a new approach where successful settings are identified from a set of independent simulation runs with different behaviors of different aspects (potentially selected probabilistically). The basic idea is to estimate the quality of behaviors by taking into account results of similar situations and thus, identifying behavior rules which are expected to be advantageous in similar settings. This approach has the advantage that even an unstructured set of experiments could be taken into account.

Acknowledgments. This work was partly supported by the *MainCampus* scholarship of the *Stiftung Polytechnische Gesellschaft Frankfurt am Main*.

References

1. Baqueiro, O., Wang, Y.J., McBurney, P., Coenen, F.: Integrating data mining and agent based modeling and simulation. In: Perner, P. (ed.) ICDM 2009. LNCS, vol. 5633, pp. 220–231. Springer, Heidelberg (2009)
2. Bazzan, A.L.C.: Opportunities for multiagent systems and multiagent reinforcement learning in traffic control. Autonomous Agents and Multi-Agent Systems 18, 342–375 (2009)
3. Bazzan, A.L.C., de Oliveira, D., Klügl, F., Nagel, K.: To adapt or not to adapt – consequences of adapting driver and traffic light agents. In: Tuyls, K., Nowe, A., Guessoum, Z., Kudenko, D. (eds.) ALAMAS 2005, ALAMAS 2006, and ALAMAS 2007. LNCS (LNAI), vol. 4865, pp. 1–14. Springer, Heidelberg (2008)
4. Bull, L., Sha'Aban, J., Tomlinson, A., Addison, J., Heydecker, B.: Towards distributed adaptive control for road traffic junction signals using learning classifier systems, pp. 279–299. Springer, New York (2004)
5. Dallmeyer, J., Lattner, A.D., Timm, I.J.: From GIS to Mixed Traffic Simulation in Urban Scenarios. In: Proceedings of the 4th International ICST Conference on Simulation Tools and Techniques (SIMUTools 2011) (2011)
6. Fiosins, M., Fiosina, J., Müller, J.P.: Change point analysis for intelligent agents in city traffic. In: The Seventh International Workshop on Agents and Data Mining Interaction (ADMI 2011) at the 10th International Conference on Autonomous Agents and Multiagent Systems (AAMAS 2011), Springer, Heidelberg (2011)
7. Gehrke, J.D., Wojtusiak, J.: Traffic prediction for agent route planning. In: Proceedings of the 8th International Conference on ComputationalScience, Part III, ICCS 2008, pp. 692–701. Springer, Heidelberg (2008)
8. Hafstein, S.F., Pottmeier, A., Wahle, J., Schreckenberg, M.: Cellular automaton modeling of the autobahn traffic in north rhine-westphalia. In: Troch, I., Breitenecker, F. (eds.) Proc. of the 4th MATHMOD, pp. 1322–1331 (2003)
9. Hall, M., Frank, E., Holmes, G., Pfahringer, B., Reutemann, P., Witten, I.H.: The WEKA data mining software: An update. SIGKDD Explorations 11(1), 10–18 (2009)
10. Helbing, D.: Empirical traffic data and their implications for traffic modeling. Phys. Rev. E 55(1), R25–R28 (1997)
11. Kerner, B.S.: Introduction to Modern Traffic Flow Theory and Control: The Long Road to Three-Phase Traffic Theory. Springer, Heidelberg (2009)
12. Moussa, N.: Car accidents in cellular automata models for one-lane traffic flow. Phys. Rev. E 68(3), 36127 (2003)
13. Nagel, K., Schreckenberg, M.: A cellular automaton model for freeway traffic. Journal de Physique I 2(12), 2221–2229 (1992)
14. Nagel, K., Wolf, D.E., Wagner, P., Simon, P.: Two-lane traffic rules for cellular automata: A systematic approach. Physical Review E 58(2), 1425–1437 (1998)
15. Quinlan, J.R.: C4.5 - Programs for Machine Learning. Morgan Kaufmann Publishers, Inc., San Francisco (1993)
16. Stevanovic, A.: Adaptive Traffic Control Systems: Domestic and Foreign State of Practice (NCHRP Synthesis 403, Transportation Research Board). National Academy of Sciences, Washington D.C (2010)

Value of Incomplete Information in Mobile Target Allocation

Marin Lujak[1], Stefano Giordani[2], and Sascha Ossowski[1]

[1] University Rey Juan Carlos, Madrid, Spain
[2] Dip. Ingegneria dell'Impresa - University of Rome "Tor Vergata", Italy

Abstract. In this paper, we consider a decentralized approach to the multi-agent target allocation problem where agents are partitioned in two groups and every member of each group is a possible target for the members of the opposite group. Each agent has a limited communication range (radius) and individual preferences for the target allocation based on its individual local utility function. Furthermore, all agents are mobile and the allocation is achieved through a proposed dynamic iterative auction algorithm. Every agent in each step finds its best target based on the auction algorithm and the exchange of information with connected agents and moves towards it without any insight in the decision-making processes of other agents in the system. In the case of connected communication graph among all agents, the algorithm results in an optimal allocation solution. We explore the deterioration of the allocation solution in respect to the decrease of the quantity of the information exchanged among agents and agents' varying communication range when the latter is not sufficient to maintain connected communication graph.

1 Introduction

In dynamic multi-robot target assignment, multirobot planning and execution requires cooperative and coordinated control of each robot's actions. Resources must be used as efficiently as possible to minimize the cost and time of execution and to maximize the benefit and efficiency of a multi-robot team. Completing the mission in an arbitrary feasible way does not necessarily make a multi-robot mission performance satisfactory. For these reasons, algorithms that can adequately correspond to the changing communication network topologies are an important topic of the collaborative robotics research. Typically these algorithms rely on modeling the systems as graphs, where every robot is a node and edges correspond to communication links between pairs of robots defined according to a pre-specified communication model [13].

A multi-agent system in which agents have limited communication capabilities may achieve an optimal target assignment solution if the global information is up- to-date and at the disposal of all decision makers (agents) at least in a multi-hop fashion; sufficient condition for optimal solution is that the communication graph among agents is connected [20,19]. Recall that a graph is said to be connected, if for every pair of nodes there exists a path between them; otherwise it is disconnected and formed of more than one connected component. The ability to form a single connected communication graph as well as the frequency of its disconnections depends on the choice

F. Klügl and S. Ossowski (Eds.): MATES 2011, LNAI 6973, pp. 89–100, 2011.

of the agents' transmitting range (radius): the larger the range, the less likely it is that the network becomes disconnected. From a communication-theoretic perspective, the critical transmitting range (CTR) for connectivity is a minimum common value of the agents' transmitting range that produces a connected communication graph in order to achieve and maintain network connectivity. At CTR, all global data is available to each agent. Under this value, starts the creation of detached connected components and when the value of communication range is zero, the agents communicate only over the target states (free or occupied). If communication range is under CTR and, therefore, the information at the disposal of agents (decision makers) is not up-to-date and complete, then we naturally expect to achieve a poor group decision making and lower levels of cooperation and hence assignment performance.

In this paper, we consider the problem of dynamic assignment of two groups of mobile agents with the objective of minimization of the total distance of movement of both. Each agent of one group has to be assigned to at most one mobile target agent of the opposite group. We propose a dynamic auction algorithm with mobility for multi-agent coordination since the classical Bertsekas' auction algorithm [2] will not guarantee an optimal or even feasible assignment with insufficient communication range for complete communication graph, and certain modifications are necessary. To respond to this open issue, in [12], was presented a distributed and dynamic version of Bertsekas' auction algorithm [2] for the case when one group of mobile agents moves toward the targets placed on static positions in the environment. The algorithm finds minimum total length routes from agents' initial to distinct final positions (targets) in the multi-agent target assignment problem with a disconnected communication graph. In the present work, we go a step forward and present a modified auction algorithm for the case when both the robots and their targets are mobile agents that if assigned to one another, move closer until they don't intercept. Through this algorithm, we explore the connection between the assignment solution of two mobile agent groups and the sparsity of communication graph varying from a connected communication graph to the case with only isolated vertices. Furthermore, we investigate how the lack of communication network connectedness among agents and the varying quantity of the information exchanged among communicating agents in the negotiation process influences the assignment solution. We prove through simulations that in the context of dynamic unpredicted environments and the communication range insufficient to maintain connected communication network, the policy of no exchange of assignment information, resulting in a selfish behavior, is the most adequate policy.

The paper is organized as follows. In Section 2 we treat a related work. In Section 3, problem formulation and definitions are presented. In Section 4, the modified distributed auction algorithm for the case of mobile agents and their targets and disconnected communication graph is presented. Section 5 contains simulation results demonstrating the performance of the presented auction algorithm. The conclusions are found in Section 6.

2 Related Work

Market-based coordination approaches have been implemented in many multirobot systems (e.g., [5,14,1,3,8,11,12,20]). Robot-agents in a market-based multi-agent system

are designed as self-interested participants in a virtual economy in which they negotiate on the target cost [3], maximizing their individual rewards and minimizing their
individual costs.

In a general case of the multi-robot task assignment (MRTA) problem, any robot
agent can be assigned to a task which consists of a target location that needs to be
visited by a robot. A formal analysis and review of the MRTA problem and algorithms
can be found in e.g., [6,7]. Approaching the MRTA problem through a market-based
mechanism can be found in, e.g., [3,10,8].

Dynamic task reallocation allows robots to change their behavior in response to
environmental changes or actions of other robots in order to improve overall system
performance. There are a number of task allocation algorithms and most of them require a complete communication graph among agents (e.g., [20,2,1,1,8,9,10,13,14,19]).
Coordination algorithm for task allocation that uses only local sensing and no direct
communication between robots was presented in [11]. In a real-world distributed multi-
robot operation, updated shared information is necessary in all the applications requiring cooperative and coordinated multiple robot task assignment. A multi-agent system
in which agents have limited communication capabilities achieves an optimal target
assignment solution if the global information is up- to-date and at the disposal of all
decision makers (agents) at least in a multi-hop fashion; sufficient condition for optimal
solution is that the communication graph among agents is connected [20,19]. Dynamic
breaking and (re)-establishment of communication links among robots can be due to
e.g., unpredicted environmental obstacles, wireless transceiver imperfections, fading or
robots drifting beyond the range of the wireless radios link bandwidth, delays, need for
encryption, message mis-ordering, as well as range constraints due to physical setup of
the network or to the power limitations on communications [9].

The critical transmitting range (CTR) for connectivity is a minimum common value
of the agents' transmitting range that produces a connected communication graph. At
CTR, all global data is available to each agent and if the communication range is lower
than CTR, agents' decisions are sub-optimal due to the lack of updated information.
Critical transmitting range was a topic of diverse works, e.g., [15,16,17,18]. In [16],
CTR in an obstacle free area of limited size was proven to be $\rho_M = c\sqrt{\ln n/(\pi n)}$ for
some constant $c \geq 1$, where n is the number of network nodes (agents) and M is some
kind of node mobility.

Within the context of two mobile groups of agents, the correlation between the dynamics of the solution of the distributed multi-agent target assignment problem in respect to the variation of the agents' communication range under the critical transmitting
range, has not been explored so far to the best of our knowledge.

3   Problem Formulation and Definitions

Considering a time horizon made of T time periods, given are two distinct groups, each
one made of n collaborative mobile robot agents: group $A = \{a_1, \ldots, a_n\}$ and group
$\Theta = \{\theta_1, \ldots, \theta_n\}$, both represented by points in the plane. The agents are positioned,
w.l.o.g., in a square environment $E = [0, l]^2 \subset \mathbf{R}^2$ of side length $l > 0$, with $p_a(t) \in E$
being the position of agent $a \in A$ at the beginning of time period $t = 1, \ldots, T$, and
$q_\theta(t) \in E$ being the position of agent $\theta \in \Theta$ at time $t = 1, \ldots, T$.

Each agent, $a \in A$, is autonomous and independent decision maker which is described by the touple

$$a = \{p_a(t), \ \rho_a, \ d_{max}^{[a]}\} \ , \qquad (1)$$

and, similarly, agent $\theta \in \Theta$ by the touple

$$\theta = \{q_\theta(t), \ \rho_\theta, \ d_{max}^{[\theta]}\} \ , \qquad (2)$$

where $\rho_a \in \mathrm{R}_{>0}$ and $\rho_\theta \in \mathrm{R}_{>0}$ are a fixed transmitting (communication) range (radius) of agent a's and agent θ's wireless transceiver for limited range communication respectively. $d_{max}^{[a]}$ and $d_{max}^{[\theta]}$ are the maximum movement distance (maximum step size) of agent $a \in A$ and agent $\theta \in \Theta$ respectively, at the beginning of time period t. At any time period t, each agent a knows its position $p_a(t)$ and the position $q_\theta(t)$ of each opposite group's agent $\theta \in \Theta$. Let $c_{a\theta}(t)$ be the (Euclidean) distance between the positions of agents a and θ.

Examples of such a two-group agent setup can be found in mobile sensor networks and in unmanned aerial vehicles (UAVs) where mobile agents can move to follow and track mobile targets, the position of which is globally known to all the agents (through, e.g., global positioning system).

As the agents of both groups move in the environment toward their preferred target agents, the conditions of the relative proximity of the agents of two groups in the environment change so that the closest agent $a(\theta)$ in one period can become more distant than some other agent which was further away in the period before. In each period t, each agent a is able to communicate to a set of agents $C_a(t) \subseteq A$ (belonging to the same connected component of its own group) reachable in a multi-hop fashion within the communication graph; at any time period t, the latter is a random geometric graph (RGG) [4], that is the undirected graph $G_a(t) = (A, E_a(t))$ with vertex set A randomly distributed in some subset of R^2, and edge set $E_a(t)$ with edge $(i, j) \in E_a(t)$ if and only if

$$\|p_i(t) - p_j(t)\|_2 \leq \rho_a \ . \qquad (3)$$

The exact same logic applies to the agents of the opposite group Θ which are able to communicate to a set of agents $C_\theta(t) \subseteq \Theta$ reachable in a multi-hop fashion within the communication graph $G_\theta(t) = (A, E_\theta(t))$. In this way, two agents of a same group which are not within the communication range of each other can communicate over a third agent within the same group (communication relay point) in a multi-hop fashion as long as the latter is placed within the communication range of the both. Therefore, agent a together with the set of agents communicating with the same induce a connected subgraph (connected component) of $G_a(t)$. The same principle stands for agent $\theta \in \Theta$ and its communicating agents resulting in a connected component of $G_\theta(t)$.

We consider the problem of dynamic assignment of two groups of mobile agents: A to Θ, and Θ to A where each agent of one group has to be assigned to at most one mobile target agent of the opposite group. The total traveled distance of all agents which move towards their assigned targets has to be dynamically minimized. We assume that no a priori global assignment information is available and that agents are collaborative and only receive information through their local interaction with the environment and with the connected agents in the communication graph of the same group. Agents communicate the assignment data and negotiate with the agents of the same group while there is no direct communication of the agents of opposite groups. T is the upper bound on the number of time periods in which all the agents reach their distinct assigned targets.

4   Dynamic Online Auction with Mobility

Each robot agent has its own copy of the modified auction algorithm which serves as a controller of its actions as it moves toward its assigned target in each period. Since the auction algorithm's structure is equal for all agents, in the following we will present the version for the agents belonging to the group A but the same reasoning stands for the agents of the group Θ which negotiate on their targets: agents of the group A.

Each agent a keeps in its memory the value $v_{\theta a}$, that is, its most recent knowledge about the actual value of target θ, for each $\theta \in \Theta$, and the set S_a of its most recent knowledge about all the agents' assignments. Both $v_{\theta a}$ and S_a do not have to coincide with the actual target value and agents' assignments, respectively; they may also differ from one agent to another due to the dynamics of their previous communication and local interaction with the other agents and targets in the environment. Each agent can be occupied or free depending if there is or there is not present an agent of the opposite group on the same position.

- Initially, i.e., at time $t = 1$ and auction iteration $h = 0$, for each robot agent $a \in A$, set $S_a(t = 1, h = 0)$ of assignments is assumed empty and all target values $v_{\theta,a}(1, 0)$ are set to zero.

At the beginning of each time period $t \in [1, \ldots, T]$, a new round of iterative auction is performed, starting from the assignments and target values locally available to the agents from the end of the round before. In more detail, during iteration h of round t:

- each agent broadcasts within its connected component its identity, the assigned target (if any) and its status on that target (whether it has arrived or not to the target).
- depending on one of the four applied information exchange policies which are motivated by different communication costs when different amounts of information are exchanged, each agent sends and receives:
  1. all target values $v_{\theta,a}(t, h - 1)$ and assignments $S_a(t, h - 1)$ for all $\theta \in \Theta$ from/to the agents within the connected component $C_a(t)$ agent a belongs to;
  2. target values $v_{\theta_{C_a(t)},a}(t, h - 1)$ and assignments within $S_a(t, h - 1)$ for targets θ assigned only within connected component $C_a(t)$ agent a belongs to on the beginning of time period t;
  3. target value $v_{\theta_a,a}(t, h - 1)$ and assignment in $S_a(t, h - 1)$ related only to agent a's momentary assignment θ_a and exchanged only with the agents which share the same assignment (if any) within the same connected component $C_a(t)$;
  4. no information to/from other agents. Each agent keeps its information for itself.
- Each agent updates its local list of the assignments $S_a(t, h)$ and target values $v_{\theta,a}(t, h)$ by adopting the largest value $v_\theta(t, h - 1)$ among the set of agents $C_a(t)$ within the connected component for each target of interest $\theta \in \Theta$ and the assignment resulting from this value. However, if the target θ_a is assigned to more than

one agent, its assignment is canceled making it unassigned and eligible for bidding in the ongoing round unless if it has already come to its target position q_{θ_a}; in that case, the agent on the target position remains assigned to the target while other agents within the connected component update the value of the target θ_a and cancel the assignment to the same.

- All the agents scan the environment for closer targets than their assigned ones; if one is found, they break the assignment with their assigned target and become eligible for biding in the ongoing round.
- If agent a is unassigned, it finds its best target, calculates the bid value and bids for that target using the following bidding and assignment procedure.

4.1   Bidding

To submit a bid, each agent a unassigned in its partial assignment $S_a(t, h)$:

- finds target θ_a which offers the best possible value $\theta_a = \arg\min_{\theta \in \Theta}\{c_{a\theta}(t) - v_{\theta a}(t, h)\}$, and calculates bid for target θ_a as follows: $b_{a\theta_a}(t, h) = v_{\theta_a u}(t, h) + u_a(t, h) - w_a(t, h) + \epsilon = c_{a\theta_a}(t) - w_a(t, h) + \epsilon$, where $u_a(t, h) = \min_{\theta \in \Theta}\{c_{a\theta}(t) - v_{\theta a}(t, h)\}$ and $w_a(t, h) = \min_{k \neq \theta_a \in \Theta}\{c_{ak}(t) - v_{ka}(t, h)\}$ is the second best utility that is, the best value over targets other than θ_a.
- raises the value of its preferred target by the bidding increment γ_a so that it is indifferent between θ_a and the second best target, that is, it sets $v_{\theta a}(t, h)$ to $v_{\theta a}(t, h) + \gamma_a(t, h)$, where $\gamma_a(t, h) = u_{\theta a}(t, h) - w_a(t, h) + \epsilon$.

The bidding phase is over when all the unassigned agents calculate their bid.

4.2   Assignment

Let $P(\theta_a)(t, h) \subseteq C_a(t)$ be the set of agents with bids pending for target θ_a. Only one agent $a_{coord} \in P(\theta_a)(t, h)$ is responsible for the assignment of target θ_a and if there is more than one agent in $P(\theta_a)(t, h)$, the first one in the lexicographic ordering coordinates the auction for that target.

Each agent $a \neq a_{coord} \in P(\theta_a)(t, h)$, broadcasts its bid $b_{a\theta_a}(t, h)$. Agent a_{coord} receives the bids $b_{k\theta_a}(t, h)$ of all other agents $k \in P(\theta_a)(t, h)$, $k \neq a_{coord}$, regarding θ_a. Following steps are performed to resolve the assignment:

- Agent a_{coord} selects agent $a_{\theta_a} = \arg\max_{a \in P(\theta_a)(t,h)} b_{a\theta_a}$ with the highest bid $b_{a\theta_a \max} = \max_{a \in P(\theta)(t,h)} b_{a\theta_a}$.
- If $b_{a\theta_a \max} \geq v_{\theta_a a}(t, h) + \epsilon$ then $v_{\theta_a a}(t, h) := b_{a\theta_a \max}$, the updated assignment information is broadcasted to all the agents $k \neq a_{coord} \in C_a(t)$ which update their sets of assignments $S_a(t)$ by replacing the current agent assigned to it (if any), with agent a_{θ_a}.
- If $b_{a\theta_a \max} < v_{\theta_a a}(t, h) + \epsilon$ then all bids for target θ_a are cleared, no reassignment or target value change is made.

If there are any unassigned agents left within $C_a(t)$, the assignment algorithm starts again from the bidding phase within iteration $h + 1$. This process terminates when each agent $a \in A$ has a target assignment.

4.3 Agent Movement

When all agents are assigned to their respective targets in the final auction iteration, say $h_{fin}(t)$, at round t of the iterative auction, the agent movement phase takes place:

- if agent $a \in A$ is not at its target position p_{θ_a}, it moves one step toward θ_a, covering at most a maximum distance $d_{max}^{[a]}$.
- Once when agent a comes to the position of its assigned and available target, it sets its target value $v_{\theta_a a}(t, h_{fin}(t))$ to $-\inf$, and broadcasts the latter to the interested agents in $C_a(t)$ based on its information exchange policy; this will disable (discourage) assigning the rest of interested agents to the same target.

If the initial targets' values $v_\theta(1, 0)$ are identically zero, the ϵ-CS condition (see, e.g., [2]) will be satisfied because the value of any assigned target is strictly increasing during the auction process and must be at least ϵ. To assure the convergence of the algorithm and to exclude the possibility of multiple exchanges of agents on the target positions, and therefore of infinite loops, the target value is modeled in the way that it decreases infinitely when an agent arrives on its assigned available target position so that once arrived, an agent remains on the same. Since there is a limited number of bids for any target while there still exist targets that have not yet received any bids, the dynamic auction algorithm will finish when all targets have been given at least one bid and the last agent comes to its target.

The presented algorithm works also when the number of agents differs from the number of targets. In fact, if the number of targets is not less than the number of agents, the assignment process terminates when each agent reaches its assigned target; otherwise, the assignment process terminates when all the unassigned agents realize that all the targets are occupied.

5 Simulation Setup and Results

We simulate a Multi-Agent (robot) System with the forward auction algorithm implemented in MatLab. The dynamic modified auction algorithm is experimented with 4 different kinds of information exchange among agents within each $C_a(t)$, $\forall a \in A$, and, similarly for all $\theta \in \Theta$ within their $C_\theta(t)$, for $t \in \{1, \ldots, T\}$, and $h \in \{0, \ldots, h_{fin}(t)\}$. In each experiment, both groups of agents A and Θ apply within their group one of the following information exchange policies:

- exchange of all assignment data in S_a and target values $v_{\theta,a}(t, h)$ for targets $\theta \in \Theta$ among all agents $a \in C_a(t)$;
- partial exchange of target values $v_{\theta_a,a}(t, h)$ and assignments in S_a regarding only the targets assigned to connected agents $a \in C_a(t)$;
- exchange only of the target value $v_{\theta_a,a}(t, h)$ among the agents assigned to the same target θ_a;
- no information exchange at all. The result is a greedy algorithm where each agent behaves in a selfish and greedy way.

W.l.o.g., and for simplicity, we model the agents as points in plane which move on a straight line towards their assigned targets. Experiments were performed for up to 60 agents (30 agents in each group) in $[0, 50]^2 \subset \mathbf{R}^2$ where the initial robot agent positions were generated uniformly randomly. The value of communication range ρ is set from 0 to 25; furthermore, maximum step size d_{max} varies from 1 to 40 since above the latter values, the number of exchanged messages, crossed distance, and the number of algorithm runs remain unchanged due to high probability of communication graph connectedness. For each group's number of robots n varying from 1 to 30,

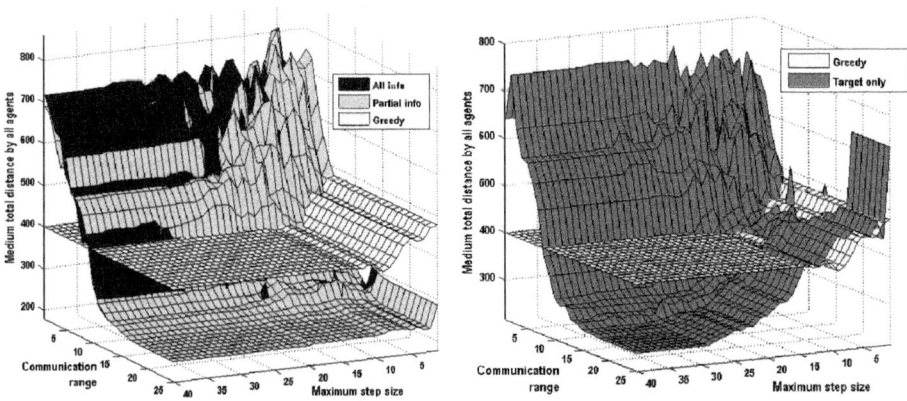

Fig. 1. Medium total distance crossed by 60 agents in $[0, 50]^2$ environment in respect to communication range ρ and maximum step size d_{max} equal for both groups: left, for all, partial, and no information exchange (greedy), right: for target only vs. greedy no information exchange

we considered 10 different instances. We assume maximum distances crossed in each time period to be equal for the two groups, that is, $d_{max}^{[a]} = d_{max}^{[\theta]} = d_{max}$; the same assumption applies to the communication range of the two groups, i.e., $\rho_a = \rho_\theta = \rho$, $\forall a \in A$ and $\forall \theta \in \Theta$. The average assignment solution (over 10 instances) for the problem with 60, $(30 + 30)$ agents is presented in Figure 1. The latter represents the dynamics of the total distance crossed by all the agents in respect to varying maximum step size d_{max} and the communication range ρ when the multi-agent system used one of the four information exchange policies.

Figures 2 and 3 present the medium total number of runs of the algorithms with the applied policies of the information exchange and a medium number of messages exchanged during the total running time of the algorithm.

As can be visible from the Figures, the presented auction algorithm with included mobility is stable, i.e., it always produces a feasible allocation solution. The experiments show that the average total crossed distance for all the 3 cases with information exchange give the same optimal solution as Bertsekas' algorithm in the case of connected communication graph among all the agents. All and partial information exchange result in very similar average total distance, the former having slightly superior

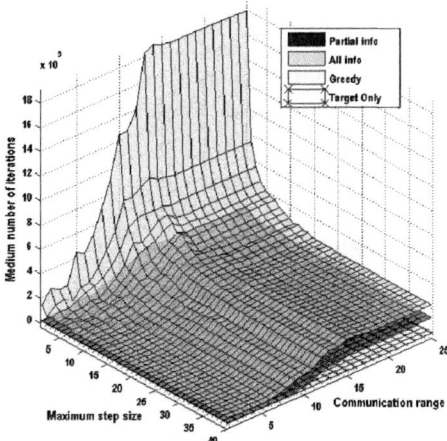

Fig. 2. Medium total number of iterations of the algorithms with exchange of all of the information vs. partial exchange of information , target only, and greedy for 60 agents

performance than the latter one. Moreover, it is visible from Figure 1 that the dynamics of the assignment solution when the communication graph is connected with high probability is better within the all and partial information exchange than the greedy approach with no communication.

On the other hand, surprisingly, as the communication graph gets more and more disconnected and the communication range decreases, the assignment solution of the greedy policy approach becomes superior than the other information exchange policies and the target-only policy has the worst assignment dynamics in respect to decreasing communication range. This is explained through the fact that outdated past information regarding the global assignment solution in dynamic and unpredictable environments is not sufficient to compose locally a satisfactory assignment as is the case in the assignment problem in [12] where agents move towards static targets and their assignment information converges faster to feasible sub-optimal solutions with limited bounds in respect to optimal solutions. However, in all of these cases, the solution in average degrades gracefully with the decrease of the communication range ρ and the maximum step size d_{max}.

For the case of initial zero prices, the total number of iterations of one auction run (one step) in which each target agent receives a bid from the agents of the opposite group is no more than $\max_{(a,\theta)} |c_{a\theta}|/\epsilon$. Once all objects receive at least one bid, one auction step terminates and agents move one step towards their targets. In the worst case, if all the agents of one group form a single connected component and if each iteration of a single run involves one bid by a single person, the total number of iterations is no more than $n \cdot \max_{(a,\theta)} |c_{a\theta}|/\epsilon$ and since each bid requires $O(n)$ operations, the running time of each algorithm step (moving one step towards assigned targets) is $O(n^2 \max_{i,j} |a_{ij}|/\epsilon)$. The total running time of the allocation is $s \cdot n \cdot \max_{(a,\theta)} |c_{a\theta}|/\epsilon$, where s is a number of steps from agents' initial to final target positions. For further information regarding the general auction algorithm complexity, see, e.g., [2].

The total number of messages exchanged within each group in one step in a multi-agent system made of two groups of 30 agents (in total 60 agents) is seen in Figure 3, left, while the target-value only information exchange is shown in Figure 3, right. The highest number of exchanged messages is achieved by the model with target only

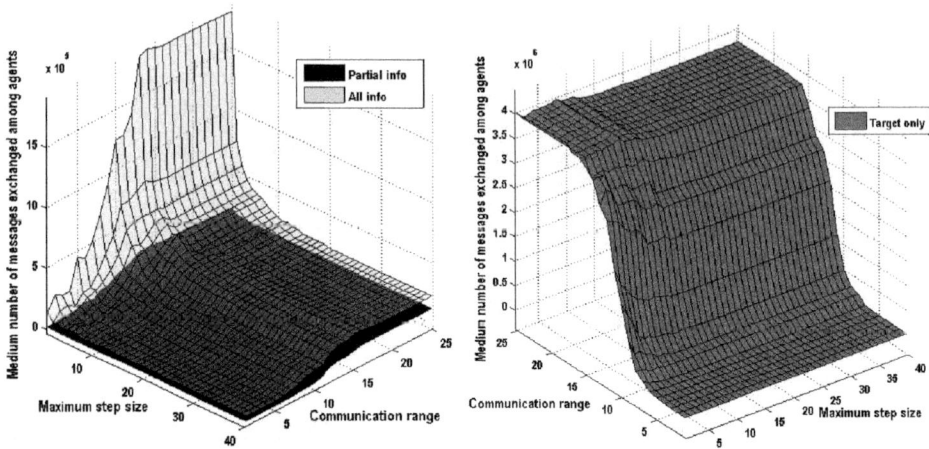

Fig. 3. Left: Medium total number of messages exchanged among agents for the algorithm with all vs. partial information exchange; right: Medium total number of messages of the algorithm with target only information exchange for 60 agents

information exchange, Figure 3. This is due to the fact that unpredicted assignment events caused by moving targets put increased uncertainty into the system so that the past information exchanged in each group can be misleading and might degrade the assignment solution. The quantity of each assignment information exchanged among the agents in each step is at least n times less than the available information and, therefore in each step an agent has to contact at least n times other agents repeating the whole bidding process in sequence for each auctioned target. This large amount of information that must be passed over the agents' communication network is a potential problem if the latter is subject to imperfections such as delays, noise, and changing topology.

The models with all and partial information exchange show very close crossed distance results, while in the terms of the medium number of exchanged messages, the model with target-only information exchange is more demanding than the all information exchange model.

The most surprising result of the simulation with two groups of mobile agents, compared to the results of the simulation with only one mobile agent group while the other is static [12], is that in the former, the greedy approach gives a better global solution than any other approach as the communication range decreases under the CTR. There emerges a conclusion that when the environment is influenced by unknown factors and its behavior is therefore unpredictable, it is more convenient to follow the greedy policy where agents don't exchange the assignment information with other agents than to rely on the information which in the dynamic environment with high probability is obsolete and old. When the communication graph is connected or connected with high probability, it is, however, more convenient to share the data. Furthermore, from the experiments it is visible that the assignment algorithms of two groups of agents where both groups are mobile and moving towards one another, converges more rapidly than the algorithm [12] with only one moving group.

6   Conclusions

In this paper, we explored how social behaviors, such as compromise, selflessness or selfishness, and negotiation influence the total group's assignment solution when the agents' communication range is insufficient for connected communication graph. A decentralized implementation of the Bertsekas' auction algorithm was presented to solve a Multi-Agent (robot) Target Assignment problem with two groups of mobile agents. We examined the dynamics of the assignment solution in respect to the maximum distance stepped by the agents between two consecutive time periods and the quantity of the information exchanged within the communicating agents. When uncertainty in the environment is elevated due to possible unpredicted events, past information dependent on time of observation, exchanged among agents, may be inaccurate and prove a distraction for agents. We proved through the simulations that in a dynamic environment with mobile targets, with the communication range under the CTR, the selfish approaches in information exchange result in better system's performance. In the future work we plan to implement the presented algorithm on a collaborative scenario in the coordination of ambulances in the medical emergency management and an antagonistic scenario for the case of reunion of two military groups on an unknown enemy area.

Acknowledgements. This work was supported in part by the Spanish Ministry of Science and Innovation through the projects "AT" (Grant CONSOLIDER CSD2007-0022, INGENIO 2010) and "OVAMAH" (Grant TIN2009-13839-C03-02).

References

1. Beard, R.W., McLain, T.W.: Multiple UAV cooperative search under collision avoidance and limited range communication constraints. In: Proc. of Conf. on Decision and Control, vol. 1, pp. 25–30. IEEE, Los Alamitos (2003)
2. Bertsekas, D.P.: Auction algorithms for network flow problems: A tutorial introduction. Comput. Opt. and Applications 1(1), 7–66 (1992)
3. Dias, M.B., Zlot, R., Kalra, N., Stentz, A.: Market-based multirobot coordination: A survey and analysis. Proc. of IEEE, Spec. iss. on multirob. coord. 94(7), 1257–1270 (2006)
4. Díaz, J., Mitsche, D., et al.: On the connectivity of dynamic random geometric graphs. In: Proc. of 19th ACM-SIAM Symposium on Discrete Algorithms, pp. 601–610 (2008)
5. Elango, M., Nachiappan, S., Tiwari, M.K.: Balancing task allocation in multi-robot systems using k means clustering and auction based mechanisms. Expert Systems With Applications 38(6), 6486–6491 (2010)
6. Gerkey, B.P., Matarić, M.J.: A formal analysis and taxonomy of task allocation in multi-robot systems. The Intern. Journ. of Rob. Research 23(9), 939–954 (2004)

7. Gerkey, B.P., Matarić, M.J.: Multi-robot task allocation: Analyzing the complexity and opti-mality of key architectures. In: Proc. of ICRA 2003, vol. 3, pp. 3862–3868 (2003)
8. Gerkey, B.P., Matarić, M.J.: Sold!: Auction methods for multi-robot control. Proc. IEEE Trans. on Robotics and Automat. 18(5), 758–768 (2002)
9. Gil, A.E., Passino, K.M., Ganapathy, S., Sparks, A.: Cooperative scheduling of tasks for networked uninhabited autonomous vehicles. In: Proc. of 42nd IEEE Conf. on Decision and Control, pp. 522–527 (2003)
10. Hoeing, M., Dasgupta, P., Petrov, P., O'Hara, S.: Auction-based multi-robot task allocation in comstar. In: Proc. of the 6th Inter. Joint Conf. on Auton. Agents and Multiagent Systems, pp. 1–8 (2007)
11. Lerman, K., Jones, C., Galstyan, A., Matarić, M.J.: Analysis of dynamic task allocation in multi-robot systems. The Intern. Journal of Robotics Research 25(3), 225–253 (2006)
12. Lujak, M., Giordani, S.: On the communication range in auction-based multi-agent target assignment In: Bettstetter, C., Gershenson, C. (eds.) IWSOS 2011. LNCS, vol. 6557, pp. 32–43. Springer, Heidelberg (2011)
13. Michael, N., Zavlanos, M., Kumar, V., Pappas, G.: Maintaining connectivity in mobile robot networks. Experim. Robotics, 117–126 (2009)
14. Nanjanath, M., Gini, M.: Repeated auctions for robust task execution by a robot team. Robotics and Autonomous Sys. 58(7), 900–909 (2010)
15. Penrose, M.: Random geometric graphs. Oxford Univ. Press, USA (2003)
16. Santi, P.: The critical transmitting range for connectivity in mobile ad hoc networks. IEEE Trans. on Mob. Comp. 4(3), 310–317 (2005)
17. Santi, P., Blough, D.M.: An evaluation of connectivity in mobile wireless ad hoc networks. In: Proc. of Int. Conf. on Depend. Sys. and Netw., pp. 89–98 (2002)
18. Santi, P., Blough, D.M., Vainstein, F.: A probabilistic analysis for the range assignment prob-lem in ad-hoc networks. In: Proc. of ACM Mobihoc, pp. 212–220 (2001)
19. Savkin, A.V.: The problem of coordination and consensus achievement in groups of au-tonomous mobile robots with limited communication. Nonlinear Analysis 65(5), 1094–1102 (2006)
20. Zavlanos, M.M., Spesivtsev, L., Pappas, G.J.: A distributed auction algorithm for the assign-ment problem. In: Proc. of 47th IEEE Conf. on Dec. and Contr., pp. 1212–1217 (2008)

Dynamic Coalition Adaptation for Efficient Agent-Based Virtual Power Plants*

Radu-Casian Mihailescu, Matteo Vasirani, and Sascha Ossowski

Rey Juan Carlos University, Madrid, Spain
{raducasian.mihailescu,matteo.vasirani,sascha.ossowski}@urjc.es

Abstract. An agent-based organizational model for a smart energy system is introduced relying on a dynamic coalition formation mechanism for virtual power plants. Central to this mechanism we propose a solution concept that stems from the existent stability notions in coalitional games. The process is intended as an open-ended organizational adaptation, concerned with achieving stable configurations that meet the desired functionalities within stochastic scenarios. We deploy the mechanism in distributed environments populated by negotiating agents and give empirical results that prove a significant improvement of organizational efficiency.

1 Introduction

In recent years, there is an increasing interest in the integration of distributed, small-scale, renewable generation into the power system. An efficient use of distributed energy resources (DER) may increase the flexibility and the resilience of the power system at distribution level. Furthermore, it is possible to reduce the dependence from large-scale, non-renewable, power plants and therefore to contribute to a sensible reduction of CO_2 emissions. According to the US department of Energy, a 5% increase in grid efficiency is equivalent to the fuel and CO_2 emission of 53 million cars.

The potential allure of the multiagent system paradigm (MAS) to the power industry has been extensively documented so far [8]. To this respect, several management systems have been proposed for the organization of the grid. On the one hand micro-grids [6] have been advocated as a subsystem of the distribution network, formed by generation, storage and load devices, interconnected at the electrical and the informational level. Micro-grids can be intended as a systemic approach to realize the emerging potential of distributed generation.

Setting aside from this approach that aims at imposing an architectural control, whether centralized or not, on already predefined micro-grids, our vision is intended at proposing a method for congregating the smart-grid actors (DERs and consumers alike) to dynamically approximate optimal micro-grid configurations. To this end, the procedure is designed such that it develops on the concept of integrating DERs in the form of virtual power plants [10]. A virtual power plant (VPP) is conceived as a bundle

* This work was supported by the projects AT (CONSOLIDER CSD2007-0022, INGENIO 2010) and OVAMAH (TIN2009-13839-C03-02).

F. Klügl and S. Ossowski (Eds.): MATES 2011, LNAI 6973, pp. 101–112, 2011.

of DERs that are connected through an informational infrastructure and act in a coordinated way as a single entity. The challenging problem related to the implementation of the VPP concept is the distributed control of the DERs, mainly due to the stochastic behaviour of the system and the heterogeneity of the devices involved.

The aim of this work is modelling the coordination of virtual power plants in the sense of coalitional games. Instead of considering centralized architectures [10], we claim that a dynamic, bottom-up, approximation of optimal VPP configurations is more effective to ensure flexibility and robustness to the system.

The remaining of this paper is organized as follows. We begin in Section 2 by generally discussing existing techniques for team formation in MAS. In Section 3 we discuss the formalization of the problem. Our agent-based organizational model is introduced in the fourth section with emphasis on the coalition self-adaptation scheme proposed. In Section 5 we present experimental results and point towards future work, while Section 6 concludes the paper.

2   Related Work

In the following we give a brief review, addressing teamwork in agent organizations and more precisely, the problem of structuring a set of individuals as a team of cooperative agents that pursue an institutional goal, then asses their applicability to MAS scenarios.

Coalitional games are denoted by a *set of players* $\mathcal{A} = \{1, 2, \ldots n\}$ that seek to coalesce into cooperative groups, which represent in fact an agreement of the respective players for acting within the game as a single entity. The outcome that each of these coalitions can achieve for itself is defined in terms of a *characteristic function* v, which weights the worth (utility) of a coalition S in a game, $v(S)$. Thus, a coalitional game can be uniquely defined as a pair $(\mathcal{A}, v)$.

An important body of work has been devoted to the question of how to best partition a group of agents (the problem domain is non-superadditive), which is essentially a combinatorial problem with an exponential search space [14]. The proposed solutions can be analysed according to different attributes of the solution method, such as optimality, centralisation, dynamism and stability.

A first class of algorithms are those that are run centrally by an omniscient agent that tries to find an optimal solution, or at least a solution that is bounded from optimal. As a subclass, a common practice is that of employing dynamic programming solutions [12]. The complexity of such algorithms, although significantly better than an exhaustive enumeration of all coalition structures, is prohibitive in the number of agents, being usually suitable for situations of at most 20 agents. The second subclass of this category of algorithms is built upon interpreting the problem in the sense of a coalition structure graph, introduced by Sandholm in [13]. Extensions of this approach consider different pruning techniques in order to establish solutions bounded from optimal, such as the one proposed in [4]. For instance, using this algorithm one may compute a faster solution when smaller bounds are desirable. Still, this type of algorithms remain severely prohibitive in terms of scalability. Same is the case for the state-of-the-art algorithm [11], which divides the search space into partitions based on integer partition and performs branch and bound search.

The second class of algorithms are oriented towards providing solutions rapidly, however not guaranteeing optimality, nor worst-case bounds for the solution. This type of algorithms is known to be scalable and more applicable to real scenarios. Amongst them we mention several notable efforts employing, genetic algorithms [14], swarm optimization [17] or constraint satisfaction techniques [3]. However, the limitation of these algorithms lies in that they represent a centralized, one-shot optimization procedure.

Thirdly, we identify the class of decentralized and dynamic methods. Here, quite the opposite, considering a multi-agent environment, it is desirable that computing the solution could be achieved in a decentralized manner, based on the agents' local utility computations, that seek to find feasible coalition structures through series of negotiations. The suitability of decentralized scenarios, apart for advocating for the autonomy of the agents in such setings, applies to manifold scenarios where coalitions have to adapt their structure due to the dynamic nature of the environment. Along these lines, Klush et al. introduced in [7] a distributed and completely decentralized process for coalition formation, able of operating in open systems. Another relevant instances of such an algorithm is the one proposed by Apt et al in [2], though limiting, in the sense of allowing transformations only to make use of simple split and merge rules. A satisfying coalition formation algorithms is proposed in [15]. Here, agents have an incomplete view of the world, time and computational constraints, the coalition formation goal being one of meeting minimum requirements rather than achieving maximum performance. This allows for a more malleable framework of negotiation in contrast to the typical techniques based on optimization of utility functions. Moreover, the dynamism of the system does not allow the agents to rationalize optimally, but rather to engage in opportunistic negotiations and of high-risk, as the success of the formation of a coalition cannot be guaranteed.

In this paper, we propose a mechanism that addresses the domain-dependent constraints posed by the electricity domain, which classifies our approach to the decentralized and dynamic solutions.

3   Problem Representation

The coalition games we aim to address in our approach are the ones where the coalition formation problem is projected on an underlying network topology, given that the cost for cooperation also plays a major role. This class of games is primarily characterized by non-superadditivity, in the sense that gains resultant from forming coalitions are limited by the actual cost of coalition formation[1] and coordination, thus the grand coalition is seldom the optimal structure. Furthermore, the coalitional game is subject to the dynamism of the environment. The challenge is to develop mechanisms that permit large number of autonomous agents to collectively achieve a desired functionality by permanent adaptive dynamics. In contrast to static coalition formation, dynamic coalitional games represent a more complex issue since the focus is not merely in analyzing the coalitional structure, but the main aspect under investigation is how the formation of the coalitional structure takes place through the players' interactions and its adaptability to

---

[1] The cost of forming a coalition can be perceived through the negotiation process and information exchange which incur costs.

environmental variations or externalities, which denote the evolution of the system. The two major approaches of addressing this are either to search for the coalitional structure that maximizes the total utility of the system (social welfare), or to find the structure with Pareto optimal payoff distribution for the agents involved. Generally, computing this through a centralized approach is NP-complete. The complexity of the problem addressed is due to the fact that the utility of adding or removing actors from a coalition has a dynamic valuation, as it depends on the other actors already comprising the coalition at each moment in time. Therefore, it is desirable that the coalition formation process takes place in a distributed manner, leveraging on the autonomy of the agents, which spontaneously organize into topologies and functionalities to meet the desired objectives. We believe that in order to solve these issues, the problem must be understood in the context of self-organization by providing a minimum set of interaction rules that would lead to an efficient achievement of the underlined desiderata.

Returning to our initial application, the algorithm we propose is illustrated as a case study in the context of smart energy systems. We set to investigate the integration of renewable energy resources to the grid in the form of virtual power plants by means of aggregating the power generating potential of various devices in a novel way in the context of MAS. As system designers, we choose to enable the autonomous agents with the basic coordination primitives, and leave to the agents to self-organize and coordinate as the situation may demand, in a fully distributed manner.

We model the problem as a dynamic coalition formation game with the following formalization:

Let $M = \langle \mathcal{A}, \mathcal{G}, \beta_i, \mathcal{S}, \Phi, v \rangle$ be a multi-agent system where:

- $\mathcal{A} = \{a_1, a_2, ..., a_n\}$ represents the set of agents of a given portion of the distribution grid. We assume that each stakeholder that is connected to the grid is represented by a software agent that manages the corresponding device (e.g., generators, storage devices, intelligent loads).
- $\mathcal{G} = (\mathcal{A}, E)$ is the underlying communication network denoted as an undirected graph where the set of vertices is the set of agents and edges are communication links. $\mathcal{N}_i$ represents a_i's set of neighbours s.t. $\forall a_i, a_j \in \mathcal{A}$, if $(a_i, a_j) \in E$ then $a_i \in \mathcal{N}_j$ and $a_j \in \mathcal{N}_i$
- β_i is the forecast amount of electricity for the following day associated with agent a_i. If $\beta_i > 0$, then agent a_i is a *provider*, whilst if $\beta_i < 0$ then agent a_i is a *consumer* (or load). Let $\mathcal{P} \subseteq \mathcal{A}$ denote the set of providers, and $\mathcal{L} \subseteq \mathcal{A}$ the set of consumers. In this work we assume that an agent is either a provider or a load, and therefore $\mathcal{P} \cup \mathcal{L} = \mathcal{A}, \mathcal{P} \cap \mathcal{L} = \emptyset$. We will refer onwards generically, to an agent belonging to set $\mathcal{P}$ as PA, and to an agent belonging to set $\mathcal{L}$ as LA.
- $CS = \{S_1, S_2, ..., S_m\}$ is the set of coalitions that partition the set $\mathcal{A}$. We assume that all coalitions are disjoint, and therefore:

$$\bigcup_{j=1}^{m} S_j = \mathcal{A}, \ S_j \cap S_k = \emptyset, \forall j \neq k$$

- $\Phi = \{\phi_1, \phi_2, \phi_3\}$ is a set of constraints that must hold for every coalition. In this work, we enforce that the number of members of each coalition does not exceed a predefined value N, which corresponds to the safety limit imposed by technological constraints (ϕ_1). We also want that each coalition is able to supply electricity to all the loads, so as the energetic balance between generation and consumption must be positive (ϕ_2). Finally, each coalition must realise a desired generation profile of electricity that would qualify them as VPP (ϕ_3). Formally:

$$\phi_1 : |S_j| \leq N \ \forall j \in \{1, ..., m\}$$

$$\phi_2 : \sum_{a_i \in S_j} \beta_i > 0$$

$$\phi_3 : \sum_{a_i \in \mathcal{P}_j} \beta_i = \psi$$

where $\mathcal{P}_j = \mathcal{P} \cap S_j$, and ψ represents the desired energetic profile that each coalition wants to achieve.

- $v : \mathcal{S} \rightarrow [-1, 1]$ is a function that for every coalition of the set $\mathcal{S}$ returns its utility value. Each provider agent a_i is characterized by an *association coefficient* $\gamma_{i,j}$ that represents the percentage contribution of a_i to coalition S_j's desired energetic profile ψ, accounting as well for the encountered power loss in the course of transmission. Thus, the utility function of the coalition, v, is defined as the sum of the association coefficients of the PA members:

$$v(S_j) = \sum_{a_i \in \mathcal{P}_j} \gamma_{i,j}$$

A resulting value of 1 signifies the ideal situation of an energetically equlibrated coalition able of supplying demand.

The goal of the coordination problem is obtaining a partitioning of $\mathcal{A}$ into a coalition structure $\mathcal{S}$ that complies with the set of constraints Φ and at the same time maximises the social welfare[2] of the system, without jeopardizing the functionality of any of the coalitions. We leave aside for now what this trade-off implies and further develop on this issue in Sections 4 and 5.

4 Coalition Self-adaptation Mechanism

The mechanism presented hereafter proposes an organizational design for managing the smart grid actors, that operates at the level of the electricity distribution network. Namely, the foremost issue we address in this paper regards the notion of stability that a system of a given random coalition structure is capable to achieve, given the dynamism of the environment. This represents an adaptive process, providing much needed flexibility and functional scalability.

The mechanism proceeds as follows. Each coalition designates a coordinator agent (CA) which shall be performing the inter-coalition negotiations. There are numerous

---

[2] For computing the social welfare of the system we mean the typical interpretation of averaging over the utilities of all coalitions.

possible procedures for leader election [16], though in order of placing into focus our mechanism we have chosen a straightforward approach of assigning this role for each coalition to the PA with the highest association coefficient.

We note in advance that the process executes asynchronously and in parallel for all agents. Communication amongst agents assumes the use of time-outs by means of which agents place upper bounds, specifying the amount of time allocated for receiving a reply. In case no reply is received in due time, the particular agent is simply disregarded from being considered as a candidate for coalition reorganization. Given the classification of Section 2, our proposed approach belongs to the class of decentralized and dynamic methods. Here coalition adaptation is achieved in a self-organizing fashion by opportunistic aggregation of agents, while maximizing coalitional benefits by means of taking advantage of local network resources.

As it had been described in Section 3, all actors a_i submit on a daily basis their forecasted profile β_i, which typically does not differ exceedingly from their previous one. Nevertheless these cumulative variations might entail a reorganization of the coalition structure CS for the following forcasted period in order to assure enhanced coordination at the coalition level. Therefore, consequent to calculating the energetic balance ϕ_2 of the coalition given the existing LAs and PAs comprising it, it is to be determined the PA actors that would qualify to be signed-off, or the profile of the actors that would be eligible to be signed-in to the coalition. The association coefficients $\gamma_{i,j}$, revealing the existing interdependencies within the coalition, play a key role at this stage. The weakest links signify the actors the coalition is least dependent on, based on which agents are to be proposed for being signed out of a coalition. Interconnected coalitions should incorporate a control mechanism for achieving a basic energy optimization for the entire system via a close coordination with neighboring coalitions. Otherwise, the security and stability of the main grid could be threatend severely. The mechanism is in such a way designed that it proves to be consistent with our proposed solution concept introduced hereafter.

Thus, the problem we are facing in open organizations requires a modification of the coalition structure due to the variations occurring within the system. With these considerations in mind we seek a notion of equilibrium that intrinsically provides an argumentation scheme, which allows for a reorganization of the coalition structure. Furthermore, the solution concept should reflect the decentralization outlook of our scenario, while minimizing the structural adaptations by providing a minimum set of interaction rules in order of attaining the desired stability properties amongst negotiating agents.

The solution we propose can be directly referenced to game-theoretic approaches on issues of stability and negotiation. For further considerations on notions of stability, their strength, limitations and interrelations we refer the reader to [9]. In our scenario, of utmost importance is the agents' capability to coordinate and reorganize into groups or coalitions by transforming traditional game-theory criterions of stability towards operating in dynamic environments. Moreover, we advocate for reorienting game-theory to accomodate situations where coordination is a more likely descriptor of the game rather than simply self-interested settings. As it is emphasized in [9], an equivalent formulation for solution concepts can be in interpreted in terms of objections and counter-objections. More formally, let x be an imputation in a coalition game with transferable payoff $(\mathcal{A}, v)$, we define our argumentation scheme as follows:

- (S, y) is an objection of coalition S to x against T if Sexcludes i and $e\left(S \cup \{i\}, x\right) > e\left(S, y\right)$
- coalition T counteracts to the objection of coalition S against accepting player i if $e\left(T \cup \{i\}, y\right) / e\left(T, x\right) > 1 + \mu$ or $e\left(T \cup \{i\}, y\right) + e\left(S, y\right) > e\left(T, x\right) + e\left(S \cup \{i\}, x\right) - \tau$.

To correlate the game-theoretic terms introduced above to our setting, we give the interpretation of these terms for our scenario. Specifically, by imputation we mean the distribution of utilities over the coalitions' set, whereas the excess e of each coalition represents the difference between its potential maximum in utility (which corresponds to meeting the desired energetic profile, see Section 3) and its current utility v.

We reason that the excess criteria applied for solution concepts such as the kernel and the nucleolus appears to be an appropriate measure of the coalition's efficiency, especially in games where the primary concern lies rather in the performance of the coalition itself. This basis further advocates for argumentation settings where objections are raised by coalitions and not by single players, such as the case of the bargaining set or the kernel. The objection (S, y) may be interpreted as an argument of coalition S for excluding i resulting in imputation y where its excess is being decreased. Our solution models situations where such objections cause unstable outcomes only if coalition T to which the objection has been addressed fails to counterobject by asserting that S's demand is not justified since T's excess under y by accepting i would be larger than it was under x. Such a response would have hold if we simply presumed players to be self-interested and not mind the social welfare of the system. If on the contrary, players are concerned with the overall efficiency of the system, they would consider accepting the greater sacrifice of y in comparison to x only if this would account for an improvement of S that exceeds the deterioration of T's performance by at least the margin τ. Thus, τ is the threshhold gain required in order for justifying the deviation, whereas μ represents S's tolerance to suboptimal gains.

Recalling our collaborative VPP scenario, it becomes imperative, as system designers, endowing the system with the possibility for relaxing standards of their individual performance in the interest of the social welfare. Our proposed mechanisms, thus aims at assessing how and to what extent this may be achieved in order to satisfy the desired system functionalities. We further elaborate on this matter in Section 5 based on the experiments performed.

For applying this solution concept to our setting, we additionally need to take into account the underlying topology and thus restrain the inter-coalition argumentation to the given network structure, representing a particularization of the more generic outline presented herein. Thus, each coalition perceives a local solution with respect to its neighborhood. Accordingly, from coalition S_i's local view point at iteration l the local solution is:

$$CS_i(l) = \{S_{i1}, S_{i2}, ..., S_{ik}\}, S_{ik} \in \mathcal{N}_{S_i}$$

A potential argument of one coalition would trigger reactions in its vicinity and so, coalitions need to make local adaptive decisions. Therefore, the system is able to determine the most appropriate organizational structure at run-time in the absence of a central controller and in a scalable manner.

When multiple objections are being adressed to one coalition, its decision of considering one would be based on the criteria of maximizing parameter τ, while minimizing parameter μ. The distribution of PA agents amongst VPPs is repeated until there are no neighbor VPPs that would gain a higher utility value in terms of the interaction scheme described above. Also worth remembering is that the procedure is ought to occur with the domain dependent constraints, that impose maintaining the profile of the coalition within certain limits (see Section 3). Finally, we stress that the aim for our proposed scheme is intended towards an open-ended organizational adaptation concerned with achieving stable configurations in dynamic environments where one-shot optimization procedure are unapplicable.

5   Experimental Results

In this section we focus on emphasizing the results attained during the inter-coalition interaction phase, based upon the solution concept introduced and projected on arbitrary grid configurations. We use hereafter the notion of a coalition interchangingly with the term VPP[3]. We simulate a system comprising of up to 1000 coalitions deployed in arbitrary topological configurations. The generated configurations correspond to generic meshed suburban network models, being identified as the most suitable setting for the deployment of small-scale VPPs. This entails that each resulting VPP is considered to be directly connected to at most 6 neighboring ones. Thus, we are referring to coalitional graphs limited to a 6-node connectivity, as depicted by a plausible VPP scenario for this particular type of topologies. For generating the random graph structure we have used the model proposed in [5]. The energetic capacity for the virtual power plants is assumed at an average of 6MW (small-scale VPP, consisting of at most 500 DERs per VPP). The simulations assume daily variations for the generated energy of each coalition, bounded to an extent of at most 20%. For these experiments we have considered commercially available residential DERs of 3 capacity classes of at most 25kw. We presume the distribution of DERs in the grid capable of matching the overall consumers' demand. The results presented have been obtained by averaging over 20 realisations (statistically significant for reducing to very low levels the results' variance).

To begin with, we first evaluate the performance of our algorithm attained through the argumentation scheme introduced. Given the cooperative scenario reflected by our chosen solution concept we have set aside from the Pareto optimal instance[4] where self-interested agents agree to participate in a trade if and only if the contract increases the agent's immediate payoff. This basic type of negotiations alone (unrestricted by topological configurations), where DERs would have individually been transferred between coalitions, has proved to reach a local optima, with higher social welfare than others [1].

Alternatively, our chosen scheme for negotiation is primarily aimed at increasing the social welfare of the system and thus, avoiding some of the imbalances that could

---

[3] By VPP we divert from the common understanding per se and rather denote an ensemble of both LAs and PAs, instead of merely PAs.

[4] Represented in the graphs as the individualistic approach.

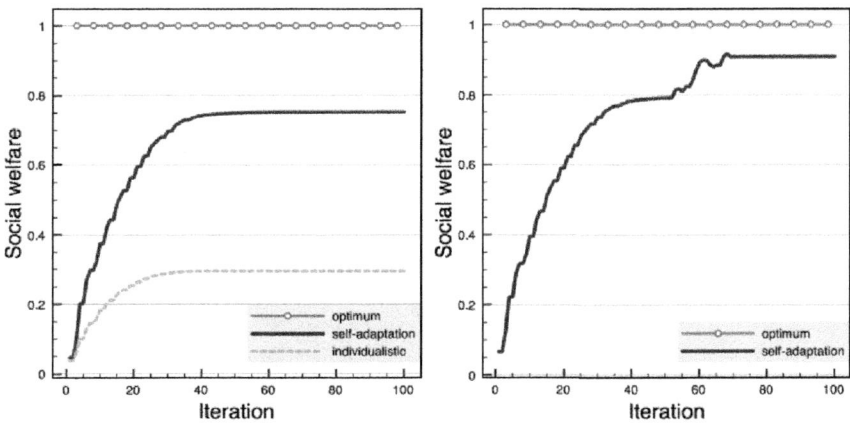

Fig. 1. Social welfare of the system in number of steps. a) normal behavior ; b)induced variations

occur otherwise at the coalition level and which would severely affect the VPP in our scenario. Such a situation would have corresponded to the undesired case of a VPP unable to assure an acceptable match of supply with demand. In by doing so, the mechanism proposed herein is able of improving on the quality of the local optima reached, while still employing a straightforward self-organizing scheme that avoids an otherwise exponential lookahead. The negotiation is based on the actor's local perspective, not assuming the configuration of the other coalitions to be known. The experiments performed reveal that the procedure leads to a local optimum rapidly, to a higher average social welfare and even more importantly, decreases the occurrence of coalitions far from equilibrium.

Figure 1 points out the average percent increase in social welfare, that the system manages to attain from an initial state to a stable one, achieved during the course of the adaptation phase. The system proves to reach a stable organization in approximately 50 steps by agreeing on reassigning DERs between coalitions according to the argumentation scheme proposed. The optimal allocation of DERs, given the sufficient availability of energy in the grid would yield a social welfare of 1. However, achieving this is not always necessarily the case, as the coalitions are highly dependent on the actual distribution of DERs in the network, while being ought to obey as well the constraints referring to their energetic potential.

As the graph in Figure 1(a) illustrates, a stable configuration of the system is abruptly reached, meaning that the agreements realized earlier improve the social welfare more than the ones performed later. Furthermore, the solution applied is an anytime algorithm that achieves a monotonic improvement of the global (social) welfare of the system, which can thus only improve at each time step. This is obviously an important aspect when the best solution needs to be reached in a bounded amount of time. Hence we comply with our objective of converging abruptly to an efficient and stable configuration of the system.

Transferring actors individually between coalitions as opposed to bundles of actors, although more time consuming, avoids a known outcome, that of concentrating the

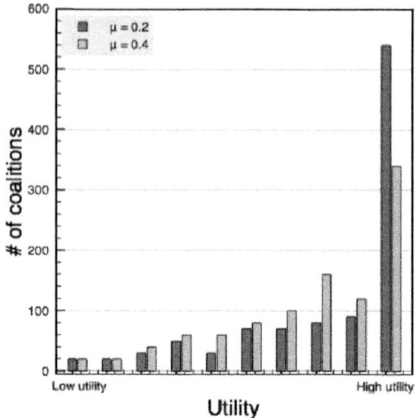

Fig. 2. Histogram representation for the utilities of the coalitions

actors among only a few coalitions [1]. Single transfers have been shown to have the tendency of diffusing the spread of actors into more evenly configurations. This is clearly a desired state for our organization structure. Another important aspect achieved as a result of this is as well, performing a minimization of the structural adaptation required.

Moreover, the organizational model proposed proves to be able to operate in open environments and dynamically stabilize behavior while actors are being added or removed to the system. In fact its adaptable features leverage on the inherent variations in the system permitting it to escape local optima. In Figure 1(b) we plot a less usual instance, where the system undergoes considerable variations during the adaptation phase, as some of the actors of the coalitions are removed (possibly due to failures) and some have joined the system. We consider a rather extreme situation where the proportion of coalitions that experience such modifications is considered at 30%, while within each coalition up to 10% of the actors have been disconnected or alternatively, have been appended to the system. The system demonstrates a capability to reorganize and reach a stationary configuration as the spikes injected into the system are flattened in a small number of steps.

Subsequently we perform a series of experiments to draw more insight to the solution concept introduced. On one hand, our negotiation scheme implies that deviations would only occur if a certain minimum gain τ has been achieved. On the other hand, the extent to which a coalition is willing to decrease its efficiency in detriment of the gain in social welfare is represented by a satisfactory parameter μ. This represents in effect a percentage, which defines what an acceptable performance would be and how tolerant is one coalition towards suboptimal performance. For our simulations we chose an initial value of 0.4 and considered a homogenous population of actors in the system. Although this does not make the objective of our scenario, heterogeneity amongst the actors involved may as well be introduced.

Following, we analyzed the implications of the dependency on this parameter for a better understanding of its functionality. Thus, we have analyzed the stationary states the system falls into as a function of μ. For large values of μ, meaning that coalitions are willing to significantly decrease their utility with respect to the improvement of the global welfare of the system, we encountered an expected global increase in utility, but a considerable variation in the allocation of utilities in the system. Instead, when only lower decrease in performance is accepted by each coalition the results obtained are plotted in Figure 2. The diagrams of Figure 2 illustrate a histogram representation of the coalitions' utilities discretised in increasing order of their worth. It can be seen that a 20% increase of μ reduced significantly the number of coalitions operating at high efficiency denoted by the first column of the histogram, while the number of coalitions operating at lower levels of efficiency has been increased. The results emphasized that the best performance[5] of the system was obtained for values of μ in the vicinity of 0.2 . Somewhat surprisingly, what the experiments show is that being willing to accept lower efficiencies in the benefit of the global performance is only advantageous to a certain extent. In actuality, there is a trade-off to be taken into account. Although the overall system utility increases, the ratio between the number of coalitions with low utility and those with high utility is increasing as well. So, for assesing the efficiency of the system not only should we be interested in the global utility, but also in having a uniform distribution of high utilities for the majority of the coalitions.

Future work will further look to a greater extent at the electrical features of the power system and incorporate in a more factual form load-flow computation analyses, that verifies for contingencies and maintain the system within its operational limits. Also, taking into account that at present the proliferation of DERs in the grid is still yet to achieve an adequate level, we intent to address in our future work, at a more granular level, the most suitable techniques for efficiently deploying such devices throughout the topology of the grid.

6 Conclusions

As a proof of concept, our work has introduced a dynamic coalition-based model deployed in distributed environments of negotiating agents. The adaptation mechanism introduced performs an open-ended adaptation of groups of organizational agents, converging towards stable configurations. In particular, we have highlighted the applicability of this approach through the design of a distributed adaptive scheme for the smart electricity grid. This process resulted in virtual partitions of the grid that would be able to commit to a steady and robust generation profile requiring less energy from real power plants especially during high-demand periods and providing a mechanism able of reducing the complexity of the management process.

---

[5] In our acceptation of best performance we restrict the results to a number of threshhold values. In terms of utility distribution, namely we would like the number of coalitions pertained by the highest utility class(last column of Figure 2) to represent a minimum of 50% of all coalitions, while the remaining classes to be below the limit of 10%. Moreover what we have achieved is to maintain the inferior fraction of lower utility classes, each below 5% of the total number of coalitions. In terms of average percent increase in social welfare we impose an 80% improvement.

References

1. Andersson, M., Sandholm, T.: Contract types for satisficing task allocation: II experimental results. In: AAAI Spring Symposium Series: Satisficing Models, Stanford University, CA (1998)
2. Apt, K., Witzel, A.: A Generic Approach to Coalition Formation. In: Proceeding of the International Workshop on Computational Social Choice, COMSOC (2006)
3. Brams, S.J., Jones, M.A., Marc, D.: Dynamic models of coalition formation: fallback vs. build-up. In: Proceedings of the 9th Conference of Theoretical Aspects of Rationality and Knowledge archive (2003)
4. Dang, V.D., Jennings, N.R.: Generating coalition structures with finite bound from the optimal guarantees. In: Proceedings of the Third International Joint Conference on Autonomous Agents and Multiagent Systems (AAMAS), pp. 564–571 (2004)
5. Erdos, P., Renyi, A.: On the evolution of random graphs. Publ. Math. Inst. Hung. Acad. Sci. 5, 17–61 (1960)
6. Hatziargyriou, N.D., Dimeas, A.L.: Operation of a Multiagent System for Microgrid Control. IEEE Transactions on Power Systems (August 2005)
7. Klusch, M., Gerber, A.: Dynamic coalition formation among racional agents. IEEE Intelligent Systems 17(3), 42–47 (2002)
8. Mcarthur, S.D.J., Davidson, E.M., Catterson, V.M., Dimeas, A.L., Hatziargyriou, N.D., Ponci, F., Funabashi, T.: Multi-Agent Systems for Power Engineering Applications - Part I: Concepts, Approaches, and Technical Challenges. IEEE Transactions on Power Systems 22(4), 1743–1752 (2007)
9. Osborne, M., Rubinstein, A.: A Course in Game Theory. MIT Press, Cambridge (1994)
10. Pudjianto, D., Ramsay, C., Strbac, G.: Virtual power plant and system integration of distributed energy resources. Renewable Power Generation IET(1), 10–16 (2007)
11. Rahwan, T., Ramchurn, S.D., Dang, V.D., Giovannucci, A., Jennings, N.R.: Anytime optimal coalition structure generation. In: Proceedings of the 22nd National Conference on Artificial Intelligence (2007)
12. Rothkopf, M.H., Pekec, A., Harstad, R.M.: Computationally manageable combinatorial auctions. Management Science 44(8), 1131–1147 (1995)
13. Sandholm, T.W., Larson, K., Andersson, M., Shehory, O., Tohme, F.: Coalition structure generation with worst case guarantees. Artificial Intelligence 111(1-1), 209–238 (1999)
14. Sen, S., Dutta, P.: Searching for optimal coalition structures. In: Proceedings of the Fourth International Conference on Multiagent Systems, pp. 286–292 (2000)
15. Soh, L.-K., Tsatsoulis, C.: A Real-Time Negotiation Model and A Multi-Agent Sensor Network Implementation. Autonomous Agents and Multi-Agent Systems 11(3), 215–271 (2005)
16. Tel, G.: Introduction To Distributed Algorithms, 2nd edn. Cambridge Univ. Press, Cambridge (2000)
17. Zhang, G., Jiang, J., Xia, N., Su, Z.: Particle swarms cooperative optimization for coalition generation problem. In: Wang, T.-D., Li, X., Chen, S.-H., Wang, X., Abbass, H.A., Iba, H., Chen, G.-L., Yao, X. (eds.) SEAL 2006. LNCS, vol. 4247, pp. 166–173. Springer, Heidelberg (2006)

Monotonic Mixing of Decision Strategies for Agent-Based Bargaining

Jan Richter, Matthias Klusch, and Ryszard Kowalczyk

Swinburne University of Technology, Melbourne, Australia
German Research Center for Artificial Intelligence, Saarbrücken, Germany
{jrichter,rkowalczyk}@swin.edu.au, klusch@dfki.de

Abstract. In automated bargaining a common method to obtain complex concession behaviour is to mix individual tactics, or decision functions, by a linear weighted combination. In such systems, the negotiation process between agents using mixed strategies with imitative and non-imitative tactics is highly dynamic, and non-monotonicity in the sequence of utilities of proposed offers can emerge at any time even in cases of individual cooperative behaviour and static strategy settings of both agents. This can result in a number of undesirable effects, such as delayed agreements, significant variation of outcomes with lower utilities, or a partial loss of control over the strategy settings. We propose two alternatives of mixing to avoid these problems, one based on individual imitative negotiation threads and one based on single concessions of each tactic involved. We prove that both produce monotonic sequences of utilities over time for mixed multi-tactic strategies with static and dynamically changing weights thereby avoiding such dynamic effects, and show with a comparative evaluation that they can provide utility gains for each agent in many multi-issue negotiation scenarios.

1 Introduction

Automated negotiation between rational software agents is considered key to facilitate intelligent decision-making between two or more parties which are in conflict about their goals. In such environments, the agents acting on behalf of their users (buyers, sellers) have no or only uncertain knowledge about opponent's behaviours and can use a range of different strategies to conduct negotiation. In automated bargaining or bilateral negotiation, two rational agents negotiate by alternatively exchanging offers over issues of a service or product where each agent has the preference to achieve the highest possible utility from an outcome while the common interest is to find an agreement before the deadline. A common approach for the agents to propose offers is to use individual decision functions, also called tactics, and mix them based on linear weighted combinations to create complex concession behaviour in the form of negotiation strategies. For instance, the prominent service-oriented negotiation model by Faratin et al [4] proposes different types of tactics such as behaviour-, time- or resource-dependent that can be mixed together. In this paper, we demonstrate

F. Klügl and S. Ossowski (Eds.): MATES 2011, LNAI 6973, pp. 113–124, 2011.

that non-monotonic behaviour in the form of non-monotonic offer curves and utility sequences can easily emerge at any time as a result of the *dynamic effects of an agent system in which the agents use mixed strategies* involving behaviour-dependent and -independent tactics[1]. In other words, such a system created by negotiating agents using mixed strategies may generate non-monotonic behaviour even when strategy settings and mixing weights of both agents are *static* and all involved tactics are cooperative in that their individual concession behaviour is monotonic. As a result, the agent's own aggregated utilities over all negotiated issues can be non-monotonic as well, implying that it proposes offers increasing its own overall utility. These effects are often considered undesirable for automated single- and multi-issue negotiations [9] [4] as they may delay final agreements, have significantly varying outcomes with lower utilities, or result in a partial loss of the agents' control over their strategy due to the high sensitivity of parameters. In this paper, we therefore provide examples as well as an analysis and evaluation of the traditional mixing method with respect to the self-emergence of non-monotonic behaviour in the implied negotiation process. In particular, we propose two alternative mixing mechanisms based on linear weighted combination of tactics that solve this problem: the first using individual imitative negotiation threads, and the second combining individually proposed concessions of each tactic involved. We prove that both methods avoid these dynamic effects and ensure monotonic behaviour, the first for static and the second for dynamic weights. We further demonstrate by means of a comparative experimental evaluation that the proposed mechanisms provide utility gains for both parties in many negotiation settings.

In the next section, we briefly introduce the basic model as well as pure and mixed tactics for agent-based bargaining and discuss the emergence of non-monotonic behaviour in multi-tactic strategies. The two alternative mixing mechanisms are proposed in Section 3, while the results of an experimental evaluation are given in Section 4. Related work is presented in Section 5, and, finally we conclude in Section 6.

2   Mixing Negotiation Tactics

The negotiation model we consider in this paper has been introduced in [4] where two agents a and b exchange offers and counteroffers on a number of real-valued issues such as price or delivery time. The sequence of all offers exchanged between agents a and b until time t_n is termed a negotiation thread:

$$X_{a\leftrightarrow b}^{t_n} = (x_{a\leftrightarrow b}^{t_i})_{i=1,\ldots,n} = (x_{a\rightarrow b}^{t_1}, x_{b\rightarrow a}^{t_2}, x_{a\rightarrow b}^{t_3}, \ldots, x_{b\rightarrow a}^{t_n}). \qquad (1)$$

The offer $x_{b\rightarrow a}^{t_n}$ at time t_n indicates the last element of the negotiation thread where t_i represent discrete time points where $t_{i+1} > t_i$ with $i = 1, 2, \ldots, n$ and $n \in \mathbb{N}$. The next counteroffer of agent a given the thread is then $x_{a\rightarrow b}^{t_{n+1}}$. We assume that each agent has a negotiation interval $D_j^a = [min_j^a, max_j^a]$ for each issue j

---

[1] This paper is a major extension of [10].

where min_j^a and max_j^a are the initial and reservation values, respectively, if a is a buyer agent whereas the opposite holds for a seller, and D_j is the issue domain with $D_j^a, D_j^b \subseteq D_j$. Each agent has a utility function $U_j^a : D_j^a \to [0,1]$ associated to each issue which assigns a score to the current value within its acceptable interval. We assume that utility functions are monotonically increasing or decreasing depending on the issue and the role of the agent. For example, for issue *price* the utility function is decreasing for a buyer and increasing for a seller. For each offer x of an agent a, the aggregated utility function $U^a(x) = \sum_j w_j^a U_j^a(x_j)$ determines the score for all issues j, where the weight w_{aj} represents the relative importance of issue j to agent a with $\sum_{1 \leq j \leq p} w_j^a = 1$. Agents may include discounts or negotiation costs, however, for simplicity we do not consider such a case here. The agents exchange offers alternately until one agent accepts or withdraws from the negotiation. An offer is accepted by agent a if the overall utility of agent b's last offer is equal or higher than a's next offer, such that $U^a(x_{b \to a}^{t_n}) \geq U^a(x_a^{t_{n+1}})$. An agent withdraws if it reaches its deadline t_{max}^a. Even though the utility structure may be more complex and of a different shape the functioning of the negotiation strategies described in this paper are best measured when using above linear utility function. Accordingly, it has been shown [7] that strategies well-suited for monotonic utility models do not cope well with non-monotonic utility spaces, so that we restrict to the former.

2.1   Negotiation Tactics and Strategies

A common method to generate offers is to use tactics or decision functions which utilize changes in the negotiation environment such as proposals from negotiation partners, or available resources such as time or the number of negotiating agents. In particular, a tactic τ_j^a is as a function mapping the mental state (about its environment) of an agent a to the issue domain D_j with $\tau_j^a : MS_a \to D_j$. Typical examples of such tactics are the time-, resource- or behaviour-dependent tactics proposed in [4]. A wide range of different negotiation strategies can be created by an agent through mixing of pure tactics. Faratin et al [4] introduces the concept of strategies where tactics are mixed based on a weight matrix

$$\Gamma_{a \to b}^{t_{n+1}} = \begin{pmatrix} \gamma_{11} & \gamma_{12} & \cdots & \gamma_{1m} \\ \gamma_{21} & \gamma_{22} & \cdots & \gamma_{2m} \\ \vdots & \vdots & \ddots & \vdots \\ \gamma_{p1} & \gamma_{p2} & \cdots & \gamma_{pm} \end{pmatrix} \tag{2}$$

where $\gamma_{ji} \in [0,1]$ is the weight of tactic i for issue j. The weighted linear combination of tactics is then defined by the weighted sum of proposed offers of each tactic $x_{a \to b}^{t_{n+1}}[j] = \sum_{i=1}^{m} \gamma_{ji} \cdot \tau_{ji}$ where weights are normalized with $\sum_{i=1}^{m} \gamma_{ji} = 1$. The weighted counterproposal extends the negotiation thread by appending $x_{a \to b}^{t_{n+1}}$ whereby each row in the matrix represents a weighted linear combination of m tactics for one issue. Different types of negotiation behaviour can be obtained by weighting a given set of tactics in different ways. For example, the agent's mental state can change and generate a new weight matrix [3] depending on the current environment and belief of the agent. The above method of using pure or mixed tactics represent decision functions which an agent uses to make *concessions* such that $U^a(x_{a \to b}^{t_{n+1}}) < U^a(x_{a \to b}^{t_{n-1}})$. In multi-issue negotiations, an agent can also make trade-offs where the next offer has the same utility as its previous offer (both are on the same indifference curve) with $U^a(x_{a \to b}^{t_{n+1}}) = U^a(x_{a \to b}^{t_{n-1}})$. In this paper, we focus on the concession-making mechanisms as detailed above and refer to [11,5] for well-discussed trade-off mechanisms.

2.2   Definition of Monotonic Tactics

To determine if a mixed strategy generates a monotonic offer sequence we distinguish between monotonic behaviour-dependent and -independent pure tactics:

Definition 1. *Given a negotiation between agents a and b, a monotonic behaviour-independent tactic $\tau_j^a(t_k)$ of agent a for issue j is a function generating offers at any times $t_k, t_i \in T_n$ such that $\tau_j^a(t_k) \geq \tau_j^a(t_i)$ if U^a is decreasing or $\tau_j^a(t_k) \leq \tau_j^a(t_i)$ if U^a is increasing under the condition that $k, i \in \{1, 2, \ldots, n\}$ and $k > i$.*

Definition 2. *Given a negotiation between agents a and b at time t_n, a monotonic behaviour-dependent tactic $\tau_j^a(\widetilde{X}_{a \leftrightarrow b}^{t_n})$ generates an offer using any sequence $\widetilde{X}_{a \leftrightarrow b}^{t_n} = (x_{a \leftrightarrow b}^t)_{t \in \widetilde{T}_n}$ where $\widetilde{T}_n \neq \emptyset$ and $\widetilde{T}_n \subseteq T_n = \{t_1, \ldots, t_n\}$ under the conditions that there exists at least one offer $x_{b \to a}^{t_i} \in D_j^b$ of agent b in the sequence such that*

- *$\tau_j^a(\widetilde{X}_{a \leftrightarrow b}^{t_n}) \geq \tau_j^a(\widetilde{X}_{a \leftrightarrow b}^{t_{n-2}})$ if the sequence of opponent's offers $(x_{b \to a}^t)_{t \in \widetilde{T}_n}$ and U^a is monotonic decreasing or*
- *$\tau_j^a(\widetilde{X}_{a \leftrightarrow b}^{t_n}) \leq \tau_j^a(\widetilde{X}_{b \leftrightarrow a}^{t_{n-2}})$ if the sequence of opponent's offers $(x_{b \to a}^t)_{t \in \widetilde{T}_n}$ and U^a is monotonic increasing.*

Definition 1 typically represents tactics depending on a particular resource which state may change over time. Throughout the paper we denote this class of tactics with $\tau_{j,\text{time}}$ for issue j. In the simplest case the tactic may depend on time or the number of negotiation rounds. For instance, the polynomial and exponential time-dependent decision functions proposed by Faratin et al [4] represent such tactics as they generate offers in a monotonically decreasing or increasing manner. In the case of a resource-dependent tactic, however, the resource may diminish and increase over time such that a monotonic sequence of offers is not guaranteed. An imitative tactic according to Definition 2 uses historical offers from the opponent to propose counteroffers by preserving a monotonic offer sequence as long as the opponent's sequence is monotonic as well. We refer to such imitative tactics as $\tau_{j,\text{beh}}$. For instance, the imitative tit-for-tat tactics in [4] fulfil this definition. Once non-monotonicity is introduced by one partner it can in turn cause a non-monotonic offer sequence of the opponent depending on the degree of how much the concessions are copied. As a result, if monotonic tactics are mixed together, non-monotonic behaviour can emerge even when both agents apply monotonic tactics as we demonstrate in the next section.

2.3   Monotonicity of Mixed Strategies

It is often argued [9,3] that the process of negotiation should be designed in a way that agents make concessions, or seek for joint improvements, i.e. in the form of trade-off proposals, in a negotiation. This implies monotonic behaviour: an agent makes proposals such that the aggregated utility of its next offer is equal (trade-off) or lower (concession) than the aggregated utility of its previous offer, such that $U^a(x_{a \to b}^{t_{n+1}}) \leq U^a(x_{a \to b}^{t_{n+1}})$. In the following, we say that agents have monotonic concession behaviour if they propose offers according to this principle. In single-issue negotiations agents typically have opposing utility structures such that a non-monotonic sequence of offers increases the risk of a withdrawal of the opponent. In that sense an agent a is acting rational in single-issue negotiations if it concedes towards the last offer of its opponent, thereby trying to increase the opponent's utility such that the sequence of its own utilities is monotonically decreasing. In multi-issue negotiations, however, an offer of an agent a with a higher aggregated utility for a as compared to its previous offer can not easily be detected by the opponent as the utility structures are unknown to each other. If, in turn, the opponent's utility for a's last offer is lower as a's previous offers, the opponent may assume that a made a trade-off proposal and can therefore not detect the cause of such non-monotonic behaviour. It is also argued that agents behaving non-monotonic under time-constraints can be advantageous and the question whether automated negotiation should be designed in a way that non-monotonic behaviour is ensured is widely discussed in the research literature [12]. However, non-monotonicity in the sequence of proposed offers and their respective aggregated utilities of an agent can easily emerge at any time as a result of the *dynamic effects of an agent system in which the agents use mixed strategies*. Intuitively, non-monotonic behaviour can occur when an agent changes its strategy, e.g. the mixing weights, during the encounter. However, automatic non-monotonic behaviour can also be observed when imitative and non-imitative tactics are mixed by a linear weighted combination without the agent changing its strategy, i.e. even in the case of *static strategy settings and mixing weights*. A simple example shall demonstrate this:

Example 1: Assume a negotiation between two agents a and b at time t_n where agent a applies a mixed strategy with static weight γ using one time-dependent tactic $\tau_{\text{time}}^a(t_{n+1})$ and one imitative tactic simply copying the concession of the partner (basic absolute tit-for-tat): $\tau_{\text{beh}}^a(x_{b \to a}^{t_{n-2}}, x_{a \to b}^{t_{n-1}}, x_{b \to a}^{t_n}) = x_{b \to a}^{t_{n-2}} - x_{a \to b}^{t_n} + x_{a \to b}^{t_{n-1}}$ such that agent a's next offer is $x_{a \to b}^{t_{n+1}} = \gamma \cdot \tau_{\text{time}}^a(t_{n+1}) + (1 - \gamma) \cdot \tau_{\text{beh}}^a(x_{b \to a}^{t_{n-2}}, x_{a \to b}^{t_{n-1}}, x_{b \to a}^{t_n})$. Given the thread $(\ldots, x_{b \to a}^{t_{n-2}}, x_{a \to b}^{t_{n-1}}, x_{b \to a}^{t_n}) = (\ldots, 30, 10, 20)$, agent a's next time-dependent proposal $\tau_{\text{time}}(t_{n+1}) = 11$ and the mixing weight $\gamma = 0.5$, the next counteroffer is $x_{a \to b}^{t_{n+1}} = 0.5 \cdot 11 + 0.5 \cdot 20 = 15.5$. Now assume, agent b replies with a comparatively small concession $x_{b \to a}^{t_{n+2}} = 19$ and agent a's next time-dependent proposal is $\tau_{\text{time}}(t_{n+3}) = 12$, then agent a's response is lower than its previous offer and thus non-monotonic with $x_{a \to b}^{t_{n+3}} = 0.5 \cdot 12 + 0.5 \cdot 16.5 = 14.25$. In this example the non-monotonic behaviour emerges in static mixed strategies with imitative and non-imitative tactics even though

	Buyer Agent	Seller Agent
Issue 1	$min_1 = 10, max_1 = 25, w_1 = 0.7$	$min_1 = 15, max_1 = 30, w_1 = 0.5$
	Mixed Strategy ($\gamma_1 = 0.3$):	Mixed Strategy ($\gamma_1 \in \{0.1, 0.12\}$):
	$\tau_{1,time}$: polynomial, $\beta = 5$	$\tau_{1,time}$: polynomial, $\beta = 1$
	$\tau_{1,beh}$: absolute tft, $\delta = 1$	$\tau_{1,beh}$: absolute tft, $\delta = 1$
Issue 2	$min_2 = 20, max_2 = 40, w_2 = 0.3$	$min_2 = 30, max_2 = 50, w_2 = 0.5$
	Mixed Strategy ($\gamma_1 = 0.4$):	Mixed Strategy ($\gamma_1 = 0.2$):
	$\tau_{2,time}$: polynomial, $\beta = 2$	$\tau_{2,time}$: polynomial, $\beta = 0.3$
	$\tau_{2,beh}$: absolute tft, $\delta = 1$, $R = 0$	$\tau_{2,beh}$: relative tft, $\delta = 1$

(a) Example 2: Negotiation settings

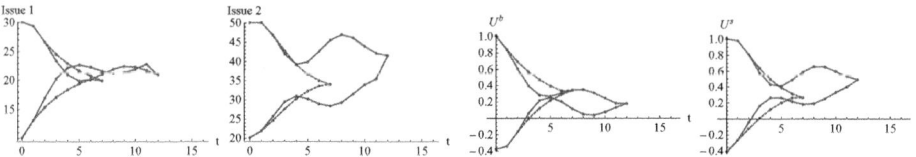

(b) Buyer's and seller's offer curves for issue 1 and 2 ($\gamma = 0.12$)

(c) Buyer's (left) and seller's (right) aggregated offer utilities ($\gamma = 0.12$)

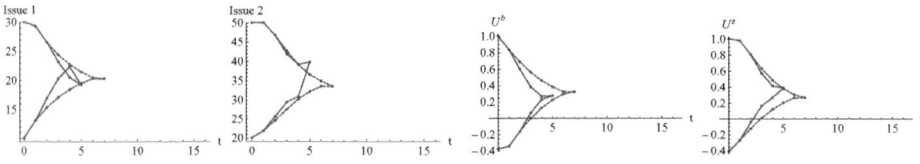

(d) Buyer's and seller's offer curves for issue 1 and 2 ($\gamma = 0.1$)

(e) Buyer's (left) and seller's (right) aggregated offer utilities ($\gamma = 0.1$)

Fig. 1. Example 2 settings and offer and utility curves using the traditional (straight) or the negotiation thread-based mixing (dotted)

the sequence of opponents' offers is monotonic and all involved tactics are monotonic as well. This is because the imitative tactic is *not independent* from the other tactics in the mix since it uses the last offer of the current negotiation thread which is different from the individually proposed one. In addition, if both agents have imitative tactics in their mix a non-monotonic sequence of offers is copied to some degree and may thus reproduce the non-monotonicity in the sequence of opponent's offers and vice versa. If agents have opposing utility functions, such that a non-monotonic utility sequence of one agent then also causes a non-monotonic utility sequence of the partner's offers. This can result in a delay of agreements, varying outcomes as compared to mixing methods with monotonic offer sequences, and a high sensitivity in terms of the strategy parameters making it difficult for an agent to apply such strategies in real world scenarios. In such cases, the described dynamics of the system result in a partial loss of the agent's control over its strategy since small changes of parameters may change the offer curves to a large degree.

Example 2: The settings of the second example with multiple issues are shown in the table in figure 1(a), and figure 1(b-e) shows the non-monotonic offer and utility curves of both agents (straight) and how it is reproduced if the traditional mixing method is used (as a comparison the dotted curves show the thread-based mixing from next section). As a result, the utility curves of both agents are non-monotonic with a delayed agreement. In the case of the agents having different deadlines this behaviour might also result in no agreement. The example further demonstrates that in such scenarios it is difficult to find suitable strategy parameters since the outcome utility may change significantly for slightly different settings as shown in figure 1 for different γ settings (the difference in utility is 0.1 for both agents when the seller changes γ_1 from 0.1 to 0.12). The agent can avoid non-monotonic behaviour by applying a simple min- or max-*constraint* (if it is a buyer or seller, respectively) to the next offer proposal to ensure that the agent's own utility does not increase with the new offer. However, the offer curve then rapidly changes to linear and the agent may propose the same offer over a long time period which may also increase the risk of the opponent's withdrawal. In the next section, we therefore present two alternative mixing mechanisms producing monotonic offer and utility sequences.

3   Monotonic Mixing Mechanisms

3.1   Mixing Based on Negotiation Threads

To calculate the imitative tactics in mixed strategies using the traditional mixing method the last offer in the current thread is used. The imitative part of the strategy does therefore not represent an individually applied behaviour-dependent tactic. Another intuitive method is to use the last offers of each imitative tactic involved in the mix. This can be interpreted as using individual negotiation threads $X_{a \leftrightarrow b}^{t_n}[j, k]$ where k denotes the k'th behaviour-dependent tactic $\tau_{jk}(\tilde{X}_{a \leftrightarrow b}^{t_n}[j, k])$ for issue j. As a result, offers from all imitative functions have to be stored in order to be used in the calculation of next proposals. Formally, the linear weighted combination of tactics can now be written as:

$$x_{a \to b}^{t_{n+1}}[j] = \sum_{i=1}^{l} \gamma_{ji} \cdot \tau_{ji}(t_{n+1}) + \sum_{k=l+1}^{m} \gamma_{jk} \cdot \tau_{jk}(\tilde{X}_{a \leftrightarrow b}^{t_n}[j, k]) \qquad (3)$$

where m and l denote the total number and the number of behaviour-independent tactics, respectively. Unlike the traditional mixing method in Section 2.1 this method can be regarded as a true linear weighted combination of tactics in which all involved tactics are independent from each other.

Theorem 1. *The mixing mechanism using individual negotiation threads for each behaviour-dependent tactic results in a monotonic offer curve if monotonic tactics from definitions 1 and 2 are used with static weights for all tactics.*

Proof. Let $X_{a \leftrightarrow b}^{t_n}$ be the negotiation thread at time t_n with $x_{b \to a}^{t_n}$ being the last offer and $x_{a \to b}^{t_{n+1}}$ being the next counteroffer of agent a then according to Definition

1 and 2 $\gamma_k \cdot \tau_k(\tilde{X}^{t_n}_{a \leftrightarrow b}[k]) \geq \gamma_k \cdot \tau_k(\tilde{X}^{t_{n-2}}_{a \leftrightarrow b}[k])$ and $\gamma_i \cdot \tau_i(t_{n+1}) \geq \gamma_i \cdot \tau_i(t_{n-1})$ if U^a is decreasing and all $\gamma_i, \gamma_k \geq 0$. Since each term of the sum in (3) at t_n is larger than the corresponding term of the sum at t_{n-2} it follows that $x^{t_n+1}_{a \to b} \geq x^{t_{n-1}}_{a \to b}$. The same line of reasoning can be followed for increasing utility functions U^a. □

Figure 1 shows the monotonic offers curves and the resulting monotonic utility sequence when both agents use this mixing mechanism for Example 2 (dotted). The outcome is changed in favour of the seller and agreement is reached earlier. Agents using this mechanism do not expose the dynamic effects as described in section 2.3. However, the mechanism does not force the agent to propose offers in a monotonic manner. For instance, if the opponent still proposes offers in a non-monotonic sequence, an imitative tactic in the mix may still copy it to some degree. The agent can choose to strictly ensure monotonicity by applying a constraint C to the imitative tactic: $C(\tau_{jk}(\tilde{X}^{t_n}_{a \leftrightarrow b}[j, k]), x^{t_n}_{a \to b}[j, k])$ where $C \equiv \min$ if U^a decreasing and $C \equiv \max$ if U^a increasing. The individual imitative thread used by this method does not represent the actual negotiation thread. This seems counter-intuitive as the offer curve and the outcome of the individually applied imitative tactics might indeed be different from the mixed strategy.

3.2　Mixing Based on Single Concessions

This mixing type calculates individual next concessions for each tactic to mix behaviour-dependent and -independent tactics as defined in Section 2.2:

$$x^{t_{n+1}}_{a \to b}[j] = x^{t_{n-1}}_{a \to b}[j] + \sum_{i=1}^{l} \gamma_{ji} \cdot (\tau_{ji}(t_{n+1}) - \tau_{ji}(t_{n-1})) + \ldots$$
$$+ \sum_{k=l+1}^{m} \gamma_{jk} \cdot (\tau_{jk}(\tilde{X}^{t_n}_{a \leftrightarrow b}[j]) - x^{t_{n-1}}_{a \to b}[j]) \tag{4}$$

with m and l denoting the total number and the number of behaviour-independent tactics respectively. In order to use concessions at least two offers of the opponent are necessary. Any of the former mechanisms can be used for initial offers as they propose the same offers in the first round. Concessions for behaviour-independent tactics are, since they do not depend on opponent' offers, the difference $\tau_{ji}(t_{n+1}) - \tau_{ji}(t_{n-1})$ between the calculated offer at t_{n+1} and the previous individual offer at t_{n-1}. For the imitative tactic we can not follow the same line of reasoning because, as described in the previous section, the last offer of the individually applied imitative tactic is unknown. However, suppose that the agent changed its strategy to the pure imitative tactic at time t_{n+1} the last offer is still be $x^{t_{n-1}}_{a \to b}$ and hence the next offer is given by $\tau_{jk}(\tilde{X}^{t_n}_{a \leftrightarrow b}[j])$. We can hence calculate the behaviour-dependent concession by the difference between the proposed imitative offer and the last offer of the agent. This approach provides monotonic offer curves similar to the negotiation thread-based mixing and also avoids non-monotonic aggregated utilities over time. The major advantage, however, is that a monotonic sequence of utilities is also never introduced if the agent changes weights for tactics dynamically.

Theorem 2. *The mixing mechanism based on single concessions of pure tactics results in a monotonic offer curve (and therefore preserves a monotonic sequence of utilities) if monotonic tactics from Definitions 1 and 2 are used.*

Proof. Let $X_{a \leftrightarrow b}^{t_n}$ be the negotiation thread at time t_n with $x_{b \rightarrow a}^{t_n}$ being the last offer and $x_{a \rightarrow b}^{t_{n+1}}$ being the next counteroffer of agent a then according to Definition 1 the behaviour-independent concession $\tau_{ji}^a(t_{n+1}) - \tau_{ji}^a(t_{n-1})$ is always greater zero if U_a is increasing. The offer proposed by the pure behaviour-dependent tactics $\tau_{jk}^a(\tilde{X}_{a \leftrightarrow b}^{t_n}[j])$ for issue j is greater than the previous offer $x_{a \rightarrow b}^{t_{n-1}}[j]$ if monotonic tactics from Definition 2 are used and the opponent never introduces non-monotonicity. The behaviour-dependent concession $\tau_{jk}^a(\tilde{X}_{a \leftrightarrow b}^{t_n}[j]) - x_{a \rightarrow b}^{t_{n-1}}[j]$ is therefore always greater zero. For all weights $\gamma_i, \gamma_k \geq 0$ follows that each term of the sum in Eq. (4) is greater zero and hence $x_{a \rightarrow b}^{t_{n+1}} \geq x_{a \rightarrow b}^{t_{n-1}}$. The same line of reasoning can be followed for an increasing scoring function U_a.   □

Similar to the previous method the agent can strictly avoid imitating a non-monotonic sequence of opponent's offers by applying a constraint C to each imitative concession in (4) written as $C(\tau_{jk}(\tilde{X}_{a \leftrightarrow b}^{t_n}[j]) - x_{a \rightarrow b}^{t_{n-1}}[j], 0)$ where $C \equiv \min$ if U^a decreasing or $C \equiv \max$ if U^a increasing. In contrast to the thread-based mixing this mechanism needs no separate negotiation threads and produces monotonic offer curves even for dynamically changing weights.

4   Evaluation

We present the results of a comparative evaluation of the mixing mechanisms with respect to their non-monotonic behaviour and its respective effects in different bilateral single- and multi-issue negotiation settings. As the number of possible mixes of tactics is infinite, we focus on a mix of two tactics from [3], one behaviour- and one time-dependent, for each agent with static weights throughout the encounter and settings as follows:

- *Time-dependent (polynomial)*: (C)onceder: $\beta \in \{3, 5, 7\}$; (B)oulware: $\beta \in \{0.1, 0.2, 0.3\}$
- *Behaviour-dependent*: (a)bsolute tft: $\delta = 1, R(M) = 0$; (r)elative tft: $\delta = 1$
- *Weights*: (S)mall: $\gamma \in \{0.1, 0.2, 0.3\}$; (L)arge: $\gamma \in \{0.7, 0.8, 0.9\}$

Initial letters indicate strategies, for example, 'CaS' denotes the strategy group containing conceder time-dependent and absolute tit-for-tat tactics mixed by small weights. Before considering a multi-issue scenario we are interested in when and to what degree non-monotonic behaviour occurs in static mixed strategies. For that reason, we consider first a single-issue scenario with two agents, a buyer b and a seller s, who negotiate about issue 1 from example 1. To enable a more realistic setting deadlines of both agents can be different with $t_{max}^b = 20$ and $t_{max}^s \in \{10, 20, 30\}$. The tables in figure 2 illustrates the rate (%) of negotiations with non-monotonic offer curves in the case of both agents applying the traditional linear weighted combination for a particular strategy group. Numbers below the rate are the maximum variation in terms of non-monotonicity occurred in utility for either the seller or buyer agent. As shown, the dynamic occurrence of non-monotonic behaviour in static strategy settings is not a negligible side-effect. In such scenarios the variation is higher in the case of oppositional applied time-dependent tactics in the mix, such as conceder against boulware. In the second, multi-issue scenario we use issue 1 and 2 from example 2 with

s / b	CaS	CaL	BaS	BaL
CaS	0/0	7/0.03	30/0.45	100/0.19
CaL	9/0.06	23/0.03	88/0.45	100/0.18
BaS	89/0.36	89/0.43	0/0	0/0
BaL	88/0.06	100/0.16	0/0	0/0

s / b	CrS	CrL	BrS	BrL
CrS	4/0.09	4/0.09	70/0.47	100/0.14
CrL	16/0.01	22/0.04	99/0.24	100/0.09
BrS	74/0.46	48/0.55	0/0	0/0
BrL	99/0.13	100/0.26	0/0	0/0

(a) Non-monotonicity in single-issue negotiation (rate in %/max. variation in utility)

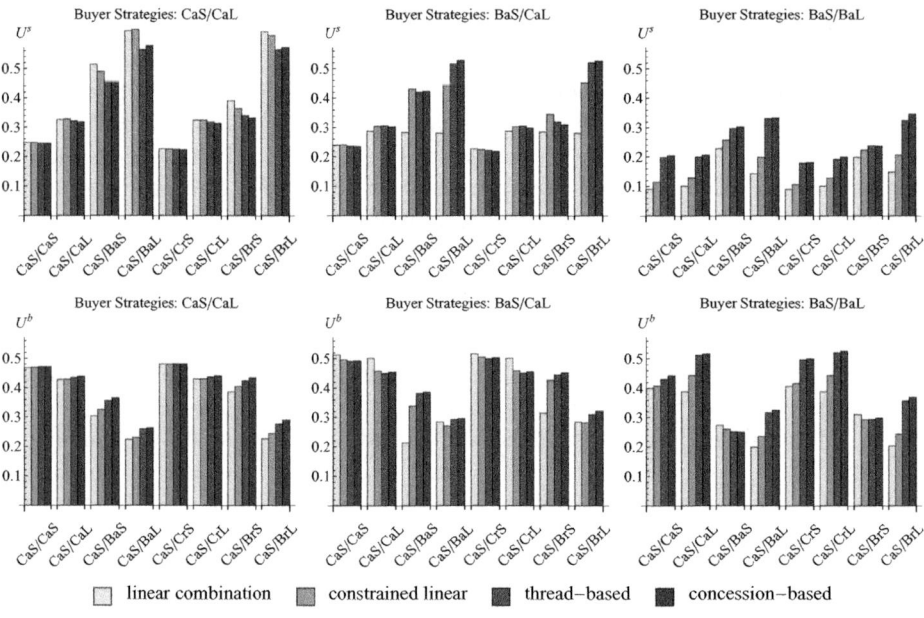

Fig. 2. Buyer's (bottom) and seller's (top) aggregated utilities

the above deadline settings to compare the different mixing mechanisms (cf. 2.1 to 3.2) applying the same strategy groups. Due to the large number of possible strategy assignments we choose three scenarios where the buyer applies more cooperative (CaS/CaL), more competitive strategies (BaS/Bal) for both issues, or a mixture of both (BaS/CaL), whereas the seller is cooperative for issue 1 (CaS) and applies different combinations for issue 2. The results in Figures 2(b) and 2(c) show that choosing a different mechanism for mixing the same set of tactics has a strong effect on the negotiation outcomes in many scenarios. In each diagram a group of bars represent the aggregated linear utility (cf. Section 2.1) for the different mixing mechanisms applied for one strategy group, from left (light) to right (dark) as follows: (1) Linear weighted combination, (2) Constrained linear weighted combination, (3) thread-based) and (4) concession-based mechanism. The monotonic mixing mechanisms tend to shift utility from an agent that gained advantage through its non-monotonic utility sequence to the other agent with monotonic concession behaviour (e.g. for buyer strategy CaS/Cal), whereas both agents may also gain significantly higher utilities in some scenarios when using the proposed mechanisms (e.g. buyer applying the competitive BaS/Bal mixed strategy). The results also demonstrate that both monotonic mechanisms perform similar because of the independent treatment of pure tactics in both methods. In general, we further observed the effect that the difference between traditional and the monotonic mixing mechanisms increases when the time-dependent tactics and the mixing weights are oppositional, i.e. one agent uses conceder with small mixing weights while the other agent employs boulware tactics with large mixing weights and vice versa. For instance, if both agents use similar strategies (both cooperative or both competitive) utilities are similar for all mixing mechanisms. These observations correspond to the results from the first experiment (cf. figure 2(a)) where oppositional concession behaviours exposed the highest rate of non-monotonicity.

5   Related Work

A large number of negotiation scenarios have been studied to provide effective negotiation mechanisms and strategies, while, however, many focus on single families of tactics [4], trade-off mechanisms [3] or meta-strategies [11], but do not consider the dynamic effects in the negotiation process. For example, Fatima et al [6] investigate scenarios of single- and multi-issue negotiation where agents have only partial information about each other trying to find optimal strategies that most exploit the opponent. The work focus on the effect of time, information states and discounting factors on the outcome while comparisons are made to equilibrium solutions but are limited to time-dependent tactics. Evaluation results for pure, static and dynamic mixed strategies are presented in [3] with focus on the influence of long and short term deadlines, and initial offers. Matos et al [8] propose the application of genetic algorithms to determine most successful mixed strategies that evolve depending on the environment and strategy of the opponent. Both approaches demonstrate that mixed strategies perform better than pure tactics in terms of gained utility and negotiation cycles, but do not investigate the mechanism of their mixing with respect to the emergence of non-monotonic behaviour. Cardoso et al [2], and Brzostowski et al [1] consider the mixing of different tactic families to evaluate adaptive strategies based on reinforcement learning, respectively, heuristic predictive methods or regression analysis with respect to their negotiation outcomes only. Sierra and Ros [11] propose to let an agent make concessions through single or mixed tactics whenever a deadlock occurs, i.e. the opponent's last offer does not improve the utility of the offer two steps before, otherwise a trade-off tactic is used. However, utilities of offers may also decrease when pure tactics are combined as shown in this paper. Our work is different in that it focuses on the analysis of the mixing mechanism itself, and proposes new mechanisms that, in contrast to the commonly used mixing, avoid the dynamic emergence of non-monotonic utility sequences during the negotiation process, thereby also avoiding the drawbacks described above.

6   Conclusions

We provided an investigation of (non-)monotonic behaviour of multi-tactic strategies created by different mechanisms for mixing pure tactics in single- and multi-issue bargaining. The traditional mixing based on linear weighted combination can undesirably expose non-monotonic utilities over time, even in cases of individual cooperative behaviour and static strategy settings of both agents, if behaviour-dependent and -independent tactics are used. As alternative, we proposed two mixing mechanisms that solve this problem by provably producing monotonic concession behaviour for static and dynamic weights: the first using imitative negotiation threads and the second single concessions for each involved tactic. A comparative evaluation showed that both mechanisms yield higher utilities for the agents in many multi-issue negotiation scenarios as compared to traditional mixing when both agents use the same mixing mechanism.

References

1. Brzostowski, J., Kowalczyk, R.: Predicting Partner's Behaviour in Agent Negotiation. In: AAMAS 2006, pp. 355–361. ACM, New York (2006)
2. Cardoso, H.L., Oliveira, E.: Using and Evaluating Adaptive Agents for Electronic Commerce Negotiation. In: Monard, M.C., Sichman, J.S. (eds.) SBIA 2000 and IBERAMIA 2000. LNCS (LNAI), vol. 1952, pp. 96–105. Springer, Heidelberg (2000)
3. Faratin, P.: Automated Service Negotiation Between Autonomous Computational Agents. PhD Thesis, University of London (2000)
4. Faratin, P., Sierra, C., Jennings, N.R.: Negotiation Decision Functions for Autonomous Agents. Robotics and Autonomous Systems 24(3-4), 159–182 (1998)
5. Faratin, P., Sierra, C., Jennings, N.R.: Using Similarity Criteria to make Issue Trade-offs in Automated Negotiations. Artificial Intelligence 142, 205–237 (2002)
6. Fatima, S.S., Wooldridge, M., Jennings, N.R.: Bargaining with Incomplete Information. Annals of Mathematics and Artificial Intelligence 44(3), 207–232 (2005)
7. Ito, T., Hattori, H., Klein, M.: Multi-Issue Negotiation Protocol for Agents: Exploring Nonlinear Utility Spaces. In: 20th Int. Joint Conference on Artificial Intelligence, pp. 1347–1352. Morgan Kaufmann Publishers Inc., San Francisco (2007)
8. Matos, N., Sierra, C., Jennings, N.R.: Determining Successful Negotiation Strategies: An Evolutionary Approach. In: 3rd Int. Conf. on Multi-Agent Systems. IEEE Computer Society, Washington (1998)
9. Raiffa, H.: The art and science of negotiation. Harvard University Press, Cambridge (1982)
10. Richter, J., Klusch, M., Kowalczyk, R.: On Monotonic Mixed Tactics and Strategies for Multi-Issue Negotiation. In: AAMAS 2010, pp. 1609–1610 (2010)
11. Ros, R., Sierra, C.: A Negotiation Meta Strategy Combining Trade-off and Concession Moves. Autonomous Agents and Multiagent Systems 12, 163–181 (2006)
12. Winoto, P., McCalla, G.I., Vassileva, J.: Non-Monotonic-Offers Bargaining Protocol. Autonomous Agents and Multi-Agent Systems 11(1), 45–67 (2005)

Agent Factory: A Framework for Prototyping Logic-Based AOP Languages

Sean Russell[1], Howell Jordan[2], Gregory M.P. O'Hare[1], and Rem W. Collier[1]

[1] CLARITY: Centre for Sensor Web Technologies, University College Dublin, Ireland
[2] Lero - The Irish Software Engineering Research Centre, University of Limerick, Ireland

Abstract. Recent years have seen the emergence of a number of AOP languages. While these can mostly be characterized as logic-oriented languages that map situations to courses of action, they are based on a variety of concepts, resulting in obvious differences in syntax and semantics. Less obviously, the development tools and infrastructure - such as environment integration, reuse mechanisms, debugging, and IDE integration - surrounding these languages also vary widely. Two drawbacks of this diversity are: a perceived lack of transferability of knowledge and expertise between languages; and a potential obscuring of the fundamental conceptual differences between languages. These drawbacks can impact on both the languages' uptake and comparability.

In this paper, we present a Common Language Framework that has emerged out of ongoing work on AOP languages that have been deployed through Agent Factory. This framework consists of a set of pre-written components for building agent interpreters, together with a set of tools that can be easily adapted to different AOP languages. Through this framework we have been able to rapidly prototype a range of different AOP languages, one of which is presented as a case study in this paper.

1   Introduction

The last 10 years has seen the emergence of a number of logic-based Agent-Oriented Programming (AOP) languages, such as 3APL [5], Jason/AgentSpeak [2,10], GOAL [8], and AFAPL2 [3]. A common criticism of these languages is the associated learning curve, which is often compounded by the lack of supporting tools that facilitate development, deployment and debugging. While some languages do offer reasonable levels of tool support, a secondary criticism is often that there is such cross-language diversity in this tool support that it can be difficult to transfer experience between languages. For example, a developer who learns to program Jason agents may not be able to easily apply their experience to learn how to program in AFAPL2. This issue was demonstrated at a recent Agent-Oriented Software Engineering course held in University College Dublin, in which around 40 students (all professional software engineers with 5+ years industry experience) enrolled in the Advanced Software Engineering Masters programme were asked to develop agent systems using both Jason and AFAPL2. The main criticism raised by the students arose not in understanding the different language concepts, but in the diversity of the supporting machinery. For example, in AFAPL2, students were required to develop perceptors, actuators, modules, and platform services to link the

F. Klügl and S. Ossowski (Eds.): MATES 2011, LNAI 6973, pp. 125–136, 2011.

language to their environment, whilst in Jason, the students were required to develop an Environment class that played a similar role. While such diversity reflects differing approaches to building multi-agent systems, it also acts as a barrier to entry for the wider software engineering community as it makes direct comparison and evaluation of AOP languages more difficult. As an aside, informal feedback from the students indicated no clear consensus as to which language was preferred, as some students preferred AFAPL2 whilst others preferred Jason.

With these criticisms in mind, recent work on the Agent Factory framework [4] has focused on supporting heterogeneous logic-based agent architectures with the goal of providing a common toolset that can be adapted to different agent models, ranging from custom Java agents, through to reactive agent architectures and finally to high-level agent programming languages. Whilst primarily these components have been designed to support languages based on first-order logic, Non logic based languages can also be developed using the framework, as long as the language is compatible with the FIPA based Agent Factory Runtime Environment.

Specifically we have redeveloped the AFAPL2 logic framework in order to make it modular and extensible, this was required as it was previously limited to only first order structures. Additionally we have decoupled language syntax and underlying logic structure to allow the component be used in different languages easily. A new planing mechanism has been developed based on the intention stack concept within AgentSpeak(L). Furthermore we have reimagined the environment interface to allow aggregation of relates sensors and actions in the form of modules.

Agent Factory is by no means the only framework or platform that supports heterogeneous multi-agent architectures. Platforms such as JADE [1] provide essential runtime infrastructure such as agent discovery, inter-agent communication, and fault tolerance; through Java APIs, these services are made available to both native Java agents and high-level AOP language interpreters. Though such platforms often provide low-level development tools for deployment and debugging, they typically offer no direct support for high-level AOP languages.

Language-independent frameworks for high-level AOP languages have been the subject of relatively little research. Dennis et al developed an extensible model checker for Beliefs-Desires-Intentions (BDI) agent programs, by distilling the common features of several AOP languages to create an intermediate language called Agent Infrastructure Layer (AIL) [7], and an AIL verifier called Agent Java PathFinder [6]. In this approach, the developer of a new AOP language X can obtain a model-checking tool for X by simply implementing an X-to-AIL compiler; AIL makes no assumptions regarding the source language's interpreter cycle, and has clear semantics, making this task relatively easy. We regard this work as complimentary to our own. Rather than modelling the commonalities of existing languages, Agent Factory aims to provide greater flexibility, in the form of tool and platform components that can be reused to quickly implement and explore novel agent programming language features.

Section 2 presents the various sub-frameworks that make up the CLF. Following this, section 3 describes the process of creating a language using the CLF, and section 4 describes the evaluation of the framework. Finally, section 5 presents some concluding remarks.

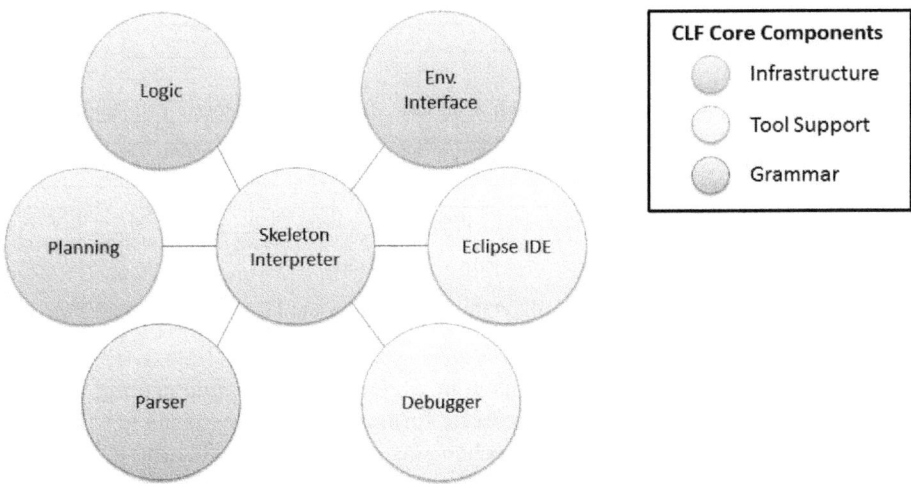

Fig. 1. Schematic of the Common Language Framework

2   Multi-language Support in Agent Factory

Agent Factory (AF) is an open-source framework for the development of agent-based systems [4]. Since 2001, AF has been structured over a number of layers, with the lower run-time environment layer providing FIPA-standards based support for agent interoperability much in the same way as is done in other agent platforms, such as JADE [1]. The upper levels of the AF framework then deliver support for the fabrication of agents using the AFAPL2 agent programming language [3].

In order to facilitate ongoing work on Agent Factory and AFAPL2, we have attempted to develop a range of sub-components that can be easily adapted and reused as necessary. We believe that these components have reached a level of maturity that will allow AOP language developers to utilise them to rapidly prototype new agent programming languages. As is depicted in figure 1, these components are known collectively as the Common Language Framework (CLF), and they are outlined below.

2.1   Infrastructure Support

The infrastructure components provided by the CLF are concerned with the internals of the agent. They provide support for: representing and manipulating first-order logic; plan representation and execution; and a standardised interface between the agent and its environment.

Logic Framework: Agent Factory utilises a standard predicate logic language, similar to those used in other systems such as GOAL[8] and Jason[2], which is based on the one originally developed for AFAPL2 [3]. Two key interfaces are used to represent well formed formulae within the language; IFormula and ITerm. Figure 2 shows the

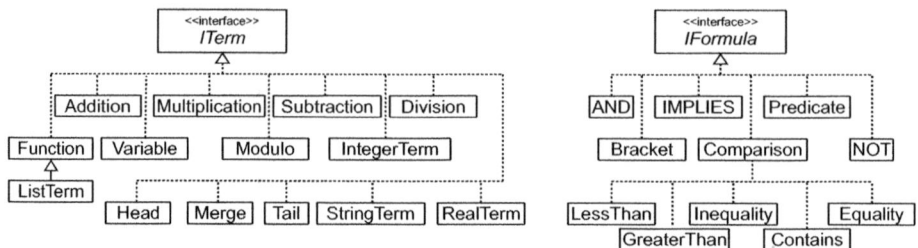

Fig. 2. UML diagrams of IFormula and ITerm

constructs supported within the language in which operators implementing ITerm are used to represent the arguments of predicate formulae and comparisons.

Agent Factory provides support mechanisms designed to enable the easy creation and conversion of these constructs through two interfaces: *ILogicFactory* and *ILogicPresenter* respectively. Default implementations are provided for both interfaces which can process any of the logical operators shown in Fig. 2, assuming the input consists of well formed formulae only.

Finally, support for reasoning with logic is provided via multiple logic reasoning engines allowing queries over sets of well formed formulae or the generation of beliefs based on these formulae and a set of inference rules. Both of these systems implement the the *IQueryEngine* interface and where neither is appropriate, additional reasoning engines can be built. The IQueryEngine interface is designed to support multiple sources, such as the belief and goal bases of an agent; when a query is run the IQueryEngine determines the applicable sources to check based on the underlying type of logic object. Sources are specified by implementing the *IQueryable* interface.

In summary, the logic framework of Agent Factory implements the standard functionality one would expect to see in a basic logic system and provides clearly defined extension points that allow the logic to be modified for a specific language. However, in many cases, we expect that such modifications will focus on specific formulae that are based on the standard AFAPL2 logic syntax and will not require modification of the reasoning engines or the re-implementation of the default logic engine and logic presenter. In cases where languages do not employ our syntax, we have preferred to adapt the language syntax rather that undertake more time-consuming modifications to the framework.

Environment Interface: The interface between an agent and its environment is based around two core components: *sensors* and *actions*. Generally speaking, sensors are the components that are responsible for generating the agents model of its environment, while actions are the components that cause some change to occur in the environment. As such, the core focus of a sensor is belief generation and the core focus of an action is to facilitate manipulation of the environment. The term action differs from other systems where it is usually referred as actuator, this difference is due to the desire to differentiate actions from perceptors, which are the equivalent concepts in the AFAPL2 logic system.

Experience in developing agent-based systems has shown that actions and sensors alone are insufficient - there are many cases where actions and sensors must interact through some shared data structure or API, for example: a graphical interface, a connection to a remote system (e.g. controlling a robot via bluetooth), or something simpler, such as a queue. While it is possible to model all of this through the FIPA notion of a platform service, the approach is not appealing because platform services are typically shared resources, whereas these resources are more often private (to the agent). As a result, we introduce a third component, known as a *module*. This component is an aggregation of related sensors and actions that share a common data structure (the module). Typically, the sensors and actions associated with the module are implemented as inline classes, making the component self-contained, but this is not required, and the implementation can just as easily be spread over multiple classes. Modules are named so as to maintain a clear distinction between them and services, which are a runtime environment concept.

By introducing the notions of actions, sensors and modules, we offer a simple model for integrating with the environment that engenders reuse of components both across applications and across languages. In particular, modules can be viewed as a form of API that can be used by any CLF-based agent. Currently, module's exist for: creating and manipulating Stack and Queue data structures; and interacting with various pre-existing platform services, including the FIPA Agent Management Service, and our EIS and CARTAGO services. As hinted above, they can also be used to implement clients to connect to remote systems or graphical interfaces for agent-user interaction.

Planning. Support for planning comes in the form of an extensible set of plan operators and a plan executor that is based on the intention stack approach adopted in Jason [2]. The default implementation includes: brackets, if-else statements, while loops, state querying, plan expansion (foreach), assignment (assigning a value to a variable), failure handling (try-recover), and durative actions. Each of these operators has an associated class that implements the *IPlanStep* interface. The key method of this class is the *handle(...)* method, which implements the operational semantics of that plan operator. This method is called by the plan executor. Additional operators can be added, for example, in Af-AgentSpeak, goal invocation is implemented as a custom plan step.

2.2 Skeleton Interpreter

The recommended hierarchy of the agent classes is shown in Fig. 3. Whilst it is not required that agents extend the AbstractLanguageAgent class, it is the easiest and quickest way to incorporate Agent Factory's Environment Interface, FIPA standard platform services, and runtime environment features such as scheduling algorithms. The AbstractLanguageAgent class provides basic agent action and sensor functionality, such as printing, ACL communication, migration, state monitoring, and platform service availability.

When prototyping languages we recommend the following naming scheme. The primary functionality of the agent is encapsulated within the *AbstractXXXXAgent* class, where XXXX is replaced with the name of the language. This scheme is also applied

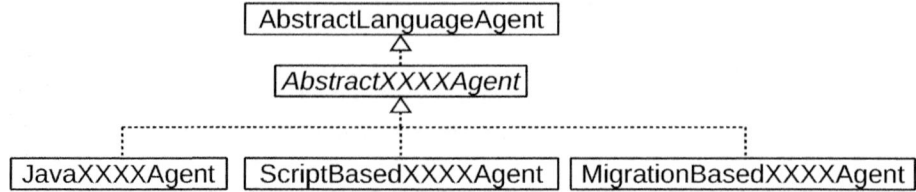

Fig. 3. Recommended agent class hierarchy

to the three recommended subclasses, *JavaXXXXAgent, ScriptBasedXXXXAgent* and *MigrationBasedXXXXAgent*, which will be further explained in section 3.

As is shown in figure 4, the interpreter of the language is represented by the method *execute()* in the AbstractXXXXAgent class. This method performs a single step of the interpreter, during which the agent perceives its environment, deliberates, and performs an action. The 3-step process shown below is not enforced, but is indicative of a typical execution step.

```
public class AbstractXXXXAgent extends AbstractLanguageAgent {
    protected BeliefSet beliefs;
    protected IQueryEngine queryEngine;

    <constructor>(String name) {
        super(name);
        queryEngine = new ResolutionBasedQueryEngine()
        beliefs = new BeliefSet();
        queryEngine.addSource(beliefs);
    }

    public void execute() {
        // 1. Sense environment
        senseEnvironment();

        // 2. Deliberate...

        // 3. Act: Select one or more activities:
        for (Predicate activity : activities)
            performActivity(activity);

        endOfIteration();
    }

    protected void noSuchAction(Predicate activity) {
        ...
    }
}
```

Fig. 4. Recommended structure of an AbstractXXXXAgent

2.3   Parser Support

Parser support is provided using JavaCC and JJTree. While a separate parser must be developed for each language, CLF includes sample JavaCC production rules demonstrating the use of each infrastructure component, which can easily be customised. The CLF provides standard visitor implementations to generate compiler code from these production rules; only the CodeGeneratorVisitor must be modified to handle the new language constructs. At runtime, the ScriptBasedXXXXAgent outlined in section 2.2 invokes this compiler, and uses the resulting object files to initialise the interpreter.

2.4   Tool Support

Debugger Framework. The Agent Factory Debugger is a highly extensible tool designed to be easily customisable for different agent architectures. The debugger allows agents to be collectively suspended or resumed as well as individually resumed, suspended and stepped.

The debugger provides a default inspector for all agent factory agents which details the platform services subscribed to and a log of incoming and outgoing messages. This default inspector also manages the state history of the agent and can be easily extended to include much more information, requiring only the extension of two components: the state manager and the inspector.

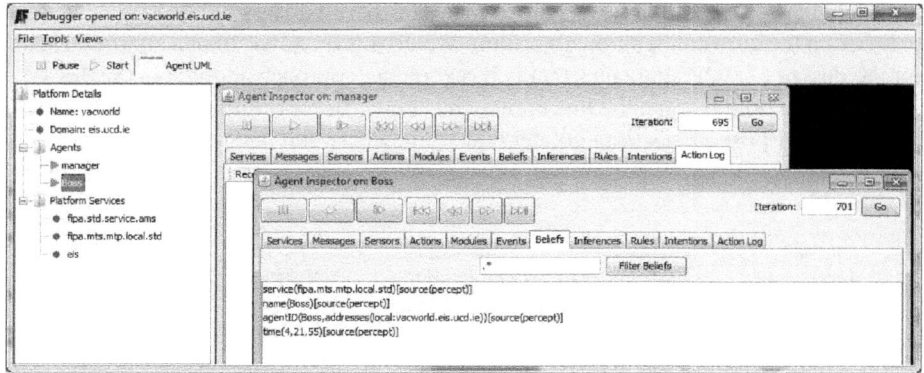

Fig. 5. Screeenshot of the debugger

A screen shot of the Agent Factory debugger is shown in Figure 5, this shows the the Agent Inspectors and controls for two agents of the same type. In this situation there is only one instance of the *StateManagerFactory* and *InspectorFactory*, these factories create a seperate *StateManager* and *Inspector* (Visible in the right pane of the figure) for each agent .

Each agent's StateManager is responsible for updating its Inspector at the end of every execution cycle. To this end the StateManager creates a *Snapshot* of the current internal state of the agent and passes it to the Inspector. Extending the functionality of the inspector requires the addition of new InspectorPanels formatted to display the required information and the extension of the Snapshot class to include the data required to update the Inspector.

Eclipse Integration. Eclipse integration with Agent Factory is provided through the use of a number of plugins, one which provides the Agent Factory libraries as well as a number of support classes and an individual plugin for each of the languages developed using the common language framework.

The core functionality provided by each of the individual plugins consists of;

1. An *Editor* to provide syntax highlighting on the various elements of the language.
2. A *Builder* to provide a mechanism for the automatic compilation of the agent code and reporting of errors through eclipse.
3. A new file Wizard to automatically create an agent file from a template.

3   Prototyping an AOP Language

AOP language developers typically employ a wide range of techniques in the design and implementation of an AOP language that includes the design of the underlying reasoning mechanisms, the definition of an interface to the environment, and the integration of the interpreter with an associated run-time framework, and potentially the creation of an associated development toolkit. In this section, we outline an approach to prototyping AOP languages that attempts to remove many of these barriers to allow the developer to focus on the core deliberation algorithm. We do this by advocating a simple structure for the design of AOP languages that is based on the approach adopted in the design of AFAPL2. We do not argue the this approach is better or more suitable, but advocate its use for the purpose of ensuring greater consistency between languages.

Fig. 6. CLF Language Development Process

The specific approach advocated combines the default logic implementation outlined in section 2.1 together with the environmental interface described in Section 2.1.

In order to develop a new AOP language using AF, there are a number of key steps to be followed. In this section, we outline these steps through a set of high level instructions, should the reader require more detailed information this is available through the Agent Factory website[1].

3.1   Language Design

First the specifications of the language must be defined, this includes both the syntax of the language as well as the operation semantics of the interpreter. The former can be achieved through the construction of a Backus-Naur Form (BNF) grammar describing the unique constructs of the language, this can be done by creation of a grammar in the case of a new language or the modification of an existing grammar when the language

---

[1] http://www.agentfactory.com

already exists. The latter requires the definition of the operation semantics of the interpreter which will be used to structure the actions of the interpreter in the next section. Finally it is recommended that a suitable example agent program is written, as this will make later testing much easier.

3.2 Skeleton Interpreter

Based on the recommended structure provided in Section 2.2, implementation of the skeleton interpreter requires the creation of an abstract class *AbstractXXXXAgent*. This class requires the creation of custom data structure to represent the constructs of the language and the agents belief, goals, etc.. The operational semantics defined in Section 3.1 are then used to structure the implementation of the *execute()* method within the class thus providing the functionality of a single step of the interpreter.

It is also recommended that the class *JavaXXXXAgent* should be created which extends AbstractXXXXAgent, this allows the direct injection of the example agent program into the data structures of the agent without the need for a parser. Through this class the operation of the interpreter and the functionality of the data structures can be tested.

3.3 Debugger Implementation

The next logical step in the development process is the implementation of the debugger as it allows the mental state of the agent be viewed during the operation of the agent. This is instrumental in ensuring the correct operation of the developed interpreter. In short this process requires the creation of a number of classes used for the representation of the agents state and it display within the debugger, namely;

 – *XXXXSnapShot*, which holds all the required state information.
 – *XXXXStateManager*, which creates the snapshots at the end of an interpreter cycle.
 – *XXXXInspector*, which displays the recorded information
 – *XXXXStateManagerFactory* and *XXXXInspectorFactory* which manage the automatic creation of the StateManagers and Inspectors respectively.

3.4 Parser Implementation

Having successfully tested the interpreter using the debugger and the JavaXXXXAgent, the next step is the implementation of the parser for the language and its integration with the system. This process involves a number of complex steps;

 – Based on the grammar developed in Section 3.1 and the template provided within Agent Factory, complete the JavaCC grammar defining the language. As production rules are supplied for parsing the logic and environmental interface components this is not an overly difficult task.
 – Using JJTree, which constructs a parse tree during processing, modify the *CodeGeneratorVisitor* template provided to harvest and store the required data structures from the parse tree.

- Finally the creation of the *ScriptBasedXXXXAgent*, which utilises the parser and CodeGeneratorVisitor to populate all the agent code into the class, thus allowing the creation of agents within the language.
- To fully connect the agent type with Agent Factory we must create the *XXXXArchitectureFactory* which is responsible for automatic creation of agents using the ScriptBasedXXXXAgent class, automatic creation is achieved through the association of the file extension to the agent type.
- A supplementary step in the process is the creation of the *MigrationBasedXXXXAgent* which is similar to the ScriptBasedXXXXAgent in that it allows the creation of an agent of the language on the system. Rather that through the use of the parser it uses the state information from another platform to instantiate the agent.

3.5   Eclipse Integration

At this point the language is fully developed and functional, however the final step of Eclipse integration is recommended as it makes designing agents within the language easier. As discussed in Section 2.4 there are three components to the eclipse integration, the builder, editor and new file wizard. An Eclipse plugin is provided which provides the structure and an example implementation of all the features described.

- The builder is implemented by integrating the parser developed in Section 3.4 and display the errors through eclipse's built in marker system.
- The editor requires only the modification of the example implementation such that the correct keywords, labels and operators are highlighted.
- Finally the new file wizard is created through the modification of the example and the provision of a sample agent file.

4   Evaluation

Scientific evaluation of this system is not an easy task, initial evaluation has been completed and further evaluation is planned.Informally it is the opinion of the authors that the provided components simplify the process of developing AOP languages. The initial evaluation comprised of the use and comparison of two languages created using the framework during participation in the 2010 Multi Agent Contest[2][11].

The contest scenario consisted of developing a multi-agent system to solve a cooperative task in a dynamic environment. The environment was a grid-like world in which virtual cows move around collectively in one or more herds exhibiting a swarm-like behavior. There were two corrals, each belongs to one of the two agent teams. The teams of agents competed to control the behavior of animals and lead them to their own corral. The winning agent team being the one which scored highest.

The two languages used were AF-TeleoReactive (AF-TR), which is based on Nils Nilsson's Teleo-Reactive formalism [9], and AF-AgentSpeak (AF-AS), an implementation of AgentSpeak(L). The scenario is very much suited to having two types of agents, a leader agent and a herder agent. The CLF allowed us do develop modules which could

---

[2] http://www.multiagentcontest.org/2010

be used with both languages and made it possible to rapidly develop a number of prototype agents with those languages. Through these prototypes, we were able to identify that AF-AgentSpeak was suited to the Leader role, this is due to the comprehensive planning support available, and AF-TeleoReactive was suited to the Herder role, as it is designed to react quickly to a changing environment.

This pilot evaluation serves to justify the comparability of the created languages. As this project was completed by members of the team responsible for the creation of the framework, evaluation of the CLFs ease of use is currently future work. This thorough evaluation will be performed when the Agent-Oriented Software Engineering course runs again (Jan 2012). The planned evaluation similarly allows the assessment of the CLF in terms only of the usability and comparability of the produced languages, whilst this evaluation is useful it is not sufficient to validate the goal of providing a common toolset that can be adapted to different agent models.

To properly validate the usefulness of the components for the development of AOP languages would require a large number of people creating languages both with and without the support of the framework. Whilst ideally we would like the feedback this would bring, for logistical reasons alone we will not be attempting it.

5 Conclusions

Our main objective making these changes to Agent Factory is to develop versions of existing AOP languages for Agent Factory, that are adapted to employ a consistent underlying infrastructure which we hope will allow developers to focus on understanding the strengths and weaknesses of the languages rather than the supporting machinery. By providing this common infrastructure and implementing various AOP languages, we also hope to gain additional insight into the weaknesses of the current state-of-the-art in AOP with the goal of identifying and exploring potential features that will underpin the next generation agent programming languages. Finally, we hope that Agent Factory will help to foster the development of new AOP languages by reducing the complexity of AOP language development.

Acknowledgements. This work was supported, in part, by Science Foundation Ireland grant 07/CE/I1147 to CLARITY: Centre for Sensor Web Technologies and by Environmental Protection Agency Ireland project number 2008-WRM-MS-1-S1, WAIST - Waste Augmentation and Integrated Shipment Tracking, funded under STRIVE- Waste, Resource Management and Chemicals Call 2007.

References

1. Bellifemine, F.L., Caire, G., Greenwood, D.: Developing multi-agent systems with JADE. Wiley, Chichester (2007)
2. Bordini, R.H., Hübner, J.F., Wooldridge, M.J.: Programming multi-agent systems in AgentSpeak using Jason. Wiley Interscience, Hoboken (2007)
3. Collier, R.W., O'Hare, G.M.P.: Modeling and programming with commitment rules in agent factory. In: Giurca, Gasevic, Tavater (eds.) Handbook of Research on Emerging Rule-Based Languages and Technologies: Open Solutions and Approaches. IGI Publishing (2009)

4. Collier, R.W.: The realisation of agent factory: An environment for the rapid prototyping of intelligent agents. Master's thesis, University of Manchester Institute of Science and Technology (UMIST), England (1996)

5. Dastani, M.M., van Riemsdijk, M.B., Dignum, F.P.M., Meyer, J.-J.C.: A programming language for cognitive agents goal directed 3APL. In: Dastani, M.M., Dix, J., El Fallah-Seghrouchni, A. (eds.) PROMAS 2003. LNCS (LNAI), vol. 3067, pp. 111–130. Springer, Heidelberg (2004)

6. Dennis, L.A., Farwer, B., Bordini, R.H., Fisher, M.: A flexible framework for verifying agent programs. In: Proceedings of the 7th International Joint Conference on Autonomous Agents and Multiagent Systems. International Foundation for Autonomous Agents and Multiagent Systems, pp. 1303–1306 (2008)

7. Dennis, L.A., Farwer, B., Bordini, R.H., Fisher, M., Wooldridge, M.J.: A common semantic basis for BDI languages. In: Dastani, M.M., El Fallah Seghrouchni, A., Ricci, A., Winikoff, M (eds.) ProMAS 2007. LNCS (LNAI), vol. 4908, pp. 124–139. Springer, Heidelberg (2008)

8. Hindriks, K.V.: Programmingrationalagents in goal. Multi-Agent Programming, 119–157 (2009)

9. Nilsson, N.J.: Toward agent programs with circuit semantics, Stanford University. Computer Science Dept. Citeseer (1992)

10. Rao, A.: Agentspeak (l): Bdi agents speak out in a logical computable language. Agents Breaking Away, 42–55 (1996)

11. Russell, S., Carr, D., Dragone, M., OHare, G., Collier, R.: From bogtrotting to herding: a ucd perspective. Annals of Mathematics and Artificial Intelligence, 1–20 (2011), doi:10.1007/s10472-011-9236-z

Agent-Based Container Terminal Optimisation

Michael Winikoff[1], Hanno-Felix Wagner[2], Thomas Young[3], Stephen Cranefield[1],
Roger Jarquin[4], Guannan Li[1], Brent Martin[3], and Rainer Unland[2]

[1] University of Otago, Dunedin, New Zealand
[2] Universität Duisburg-Essen, Essen, Germany
[3] University of Canterbury, Christchurch, New Zealand
[4] Jade Software Corporation, Christchurch, New Zealand

Abstract. Container terminals play a critical role in international shipping and
are under pressure to cope with increasing container traffic. The problem of managing container terminals effectively has a number of characteristics which make
agents a suitable technology to consider applying. Container terminals involve
the operation of distributed entities (e.g. quay cranes, straddle carriers) which
coordinate to achieve competing goals in a dynamic environment. This paper describes a joint industry-university project which has explored the applicability of
agent technology to the domain of container terminal management. We describe
a simulation platform of a container terminal based on the JADE agent framework, along with two optimisations that have been developed and integrated with
the simulator: allocating container moves to machines through negotiation, and
allocating containers to yard locations through an evolutionary algorithm.

1 Introduction

Container terminals play a crucial role in the process of shipping containerised goods.
Due to their critical role, and the growth in the amount of container traffic, container
terminals are under pressure to increase their operating capacity and efficiency.

The goal of the work described in this paper was to investigate how agent-based
solutions could be used to improve the efficiency of container terminals. A number of
characteristics of container terminals make them a natural candidate for agent-based
solutions. Firstly, they can be naturally described as a system of interacting entities
(e.g. cranes) which are distributed and autonomous, and which interact to solve a problem (e.g. loading and unloading ships) in an efficient way. Secondly, the environment is
dynamic: the situation is subject to change, and things can (and do) go wrong. Taken together, these three characteristics make it natural to investigate agent-based techniques
for container terminal management and optimisation.

This paper reports on a joint industry-university project. The industry partner was
Jade Software Corporation, whose portfolio of products includes Jade Master Terminal
(JMT), a comprehensive container terminal management solution. The project included
visits to a local container terminal port in order to obtain a detailed understanding of the
problem and its associated complexities. Additionally, real (but anonymised) data from
the port was used for evaluation purposes. This data included machine movements and
container arrival and departure information.

F. Klügl and S. Ossowski (Eds.): MATES 2011, LNAI 6973, pp. 137–148, 2011.
© Springer-Verlag Berlin Heidelberg 2011

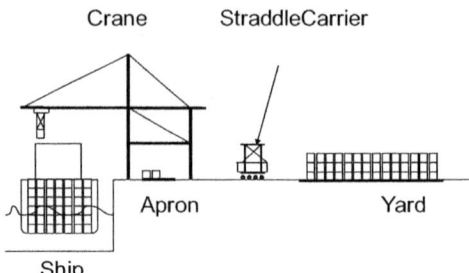

Fig. 1. Port Scenario

Note that the aim of this project is not to automate container handling: the domain is sufficiently complex that we cannot hope to capture all relevant situations and constraints. Instead, our ultimate aim is to develop an intelligent decision support tool that can assist human decision makers who are running a container terminal.

The key contributions of this paper are: (1) An agent-based container terminal simulation platform, which can be used to assess (static) policies, or to guide decision makers during day-to-day operation (Section 4), (2) A negotiation-based algorithm for optimising allocation of container moves to straddle carriers (Section 5), and (3) A genetic algorithm approach for optimising the allocation of containers to yard locations (Section 6).

This paper is structured as follows. In Section 2 we introduce the domain of container terminals, along with associated problems; followed by a discussion of related work (Section 3). Section 4 presents the agent-based simulator which we have developed. We then discuss specific optimisations that address allocating container moves to straddle carriers (Section 5) and allocating container locations in the yard (Section 6). Finally, Section 7 concludes with discussions and future plans.

2   Container Terminal Operation

In this section we briefly introduce the domain of container terminal operations, and the associated problems that confront a container terminal manager. Note that the discussion here is necessarily brief and omits various details and complexities. We aim to capture the essence of the problem, and give some sense of the various constraints and factors that make the problem challenging, without describing all such constraints and factors.

A container terminal consists of a number of different areas, depicted in Figure 1. The *apron* is the area directly beside the ship, into which containers are unloaded from the ship, and from which containers are loaded onto the ship. Note that the apron is of limited size. The bulk of the container terminal is taken up by the *yard* where containers are stored. Figure 1 does not show the structure of the yard, some specific areas (such as empty container storage, or container cleaning), or the rail and truck areas, where trucks and trains arrive to collect and/or drop off containers.

Whilst the basic areas (e.g. apron, yard) are somewhat consistent between different container terminals, the machines used vary. The local port that we have worked with has a particular setup that involves two types of machines: Quay Cranes (QCs) and Straddle Carriers (SCs). Quay Cranes ("Crane" in Figure 1) are able to move along the shore and can load containers from the apron to the ship, or unload them from the ship to the apron. Straddle Carriers are mobile cranes, able to move freely within the container terminal. They are able to lift containers and stack them up to a certain height.

Given these areas and machines, the basic process of unloading a ship is as follows. Containers are unloaded from the ship to the apron by the QC. While this is being done, Straddle Carriers are clearing the apron by transporting containers from the apron to the yard, and stacking them. The process for loading a ship is the reverse. This process sounds fairly simple, but is made complicated by a range of factors and constraints. For instance:

- There may be more than one QC operating on a given ship, so SCs need to be shared between the QCs. Additionally, two QCs operating on the one ship need to maintain a safe separation distance.
- When retrieving containers from the yard, the container needed may be beneath other containers, which requires these containers to be moved in order to access the desired container. It is worth noting that yard space is limited, and that container terminals sometimes operate at a high level of yard capacity utilisation, so that one cannot avoid stacking containers in a sub-optimal way.
- Some containers are refrigerated ("reefers"), and these cannot be without power for an extended period. Additionally, for safety reasons, humans and machines cannot be in the same area at the same time. Since (dis)connecting reefers to power is done by humans, but moving reefers is done by machines, meeting the safety and power constraints requires coordination.
- Issues may arise during operations such as machines breaking down, or finding that certain containers cannot be stacked on top of certain other containers. Finally, Straddle Carrier operators are human and may make mistakes in data entry. This may lead to situations such as a later driver attempting to pick up container C1 from the yard, only to find that C1 is not where it is meant to be.

Note that the ship arrival times follow a known schedule, but that for various reasons they sometimes do not follow this schedule. Planning of unloading can be partially done before a ship arrives, but may need to be redone because the ship docks with reversed orientation due to tides, or to accommodate dealing with trains and trucks.

The key metric for container terminal efficiency is ship turnaround time: any delays to a ship's schedule are bad (and may involve a financial penalty to the port, if it fails to meet the contracted service level agreement with shipping companies). Two key decisions that the terminal operators need to make as part of day-to-day operations, and which we have focussed on, are:

- How should SCs be allocated between QCs, yard rearrangement operations, and trucks and trains? The management of straddle carriers has a big impact on the terminal's efficiency. If QCs are not adequately served, then they may need to wait for containers to be moved, which delays ship loading/unloading.
- Where should a given (incoming) container be placed in the yard? The placement of containers in the yard can make a big difference to the cost of moving the container later to where it is needed.

3   Related Work

There are a few papers that propose to apply multi-agent systems in the domain of container terminal management and optimisation. Thurston and Hu [1] proposes to use a multi-agent system to automate container terminal operations. They focus on the loading process only. Like us, they have agents for each of the machines (quay cranes, straddle carriers). While their work is promising, the paper is early work: it outlines the approach and reports on an early Java prototype. No experimental evaluation is reported, and (from personal contact with the author) it appears that no subsequent work has been done. Rebollo *et al.* [2] also propose to automate container terminal operations using a multi-agent system. Again, the paper is abstract: it provides a system architecture, but does not provide details about how the individual agents would operate. Implementation appears to have been in progress, but we have not found any subsequent papers describing the resulting implementation, or results from evaluation. Note that such work, which attempts to address all of the problems of a container terminal, is quite ambitious, and is in danger of needing to make simplifying assumptions that render it inapplicable to real ports. Our approach is firstly to not attempt to automate a terminal, but to provide decision support; and secondly, to deal with parts of the problem separately, while trying to avoid oversimplifying the problem.

Other work that seeks to apply agents to container terminals has been more modest in scope, seeking either to tackle part of the problem only, or to simulate but not to control. An example of the latter is Henesey *et al.* [3], which describes a simulation tool ("SimPort"). Unlike the earlier described work, they do not aim to automate the operation of a container terminal, but instead to provide a tool that can be used to analyse the performance of (static) policies. This analysis can then be used to select static policies to implement.

In addition to agent-based approaches, there have been other (non-agent-based) approaches that aim to tackle various aspects of the management and optimisation of container terminals (see [4,5] for recent surveys). A common limitation of such work, which is often based on operations research techniques, is that it computes solutions up-front, but does not address well the dynamic nature of the problem.

The work of Chen *et al.* [6] is in some ways quite close to our work on optimising container moves (Section 5), and, indeed, their formalisation was the starting point for our work. However, they make a number of assumptions that are unreasonable in practice, and which we have relaxed. In particular, they assume that the processing of loading and unloading is handled separately. Additionally, they assume a three-stage process and do not provide for "buffering" where, for example, a Quay Crane can unload a second or third container even though the first container has not yet been taken to the yard.

Considering now the yard allocation problem (which we cover in Section 6), there is a range of work that tackles this problem. Zhang *et al.* [7] consider the problem of allocating inbound and outbound containers to blocks in the yard, within the context of an overall planning hierarchy for a container terminal. A two-stage process first determines the number of containers that are to be assigned to each block to evenly balance the overall workload. This is followed by the allocation of individual containers to specific blocks, without considering the specific placement of containers within each block.

Preston and Kozan [8] propose a Container Location Model (the plan for container storage in the yard) based on an Evolutionary Algorithm (EA) to optimise outbound transfers for a single ship assuming one of three deterministic types of loading schedule.

4   An Agent-Based Simulator

As basis for the optimization approaches, we present the open source port simulation model *ContMAS*[1]. It consists of several types of agents, which cooperate through (asynchronous) message communication to achieve a common goal, namely the (intelligent) unloading of containers from a ship to the yard. Although it is configured to do so using QCs and SCs to fit the situation in the given local port, the model is flexible and can easily be configured to match any different port setup. *ContMAS* is designed as a tool for general port simulations. It can be used for planning a new or re-planning a present port, to test and compare optimization and operation strategies, to simulate utilization scenarios or to run a just-in-time troubleshooting support tool in an actual port.

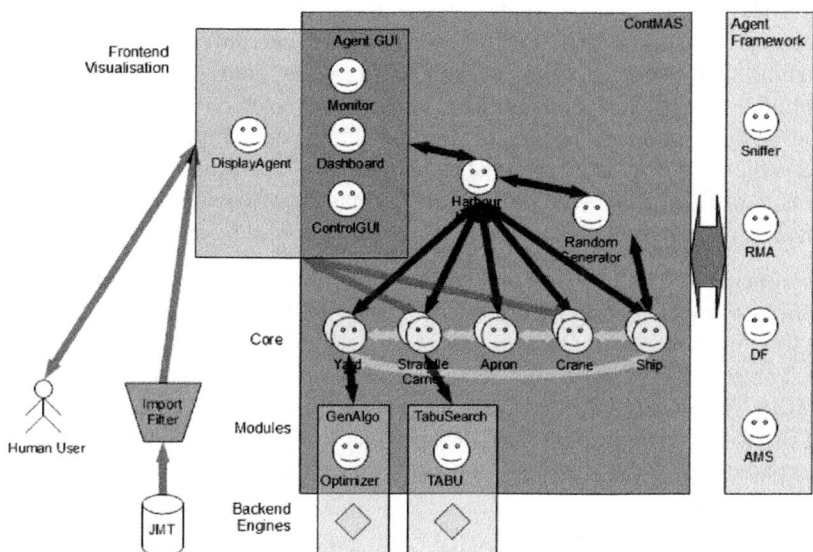

Fig. 2. Simulation Architecture

4.1   Model Description

Architecture: *ContMAS* utilizes the *Java Agent DEvelopment Framework* (*JADE*[2]) maintained by Telecom Italia. It is plain Java and uses *Jena* to access .owl files for certain features. It can be run as a project in the agent platform management tool

---

[1] LGPL,   available   at   `http://www-stud.uni-due.de/~sehawagn/contmas/`
`page/index_en.html`

[2] Not to be confused with the Jade product from Jade Software Corporation.

AgentGUI[3], which then provides a bird's eye view of the physical layout. The *Protégé* ontology editor serves as a tool for the development of the communication ontology and configuration interface. The system is structured into core agents, user interface agents, administrative agents and module agents (see Figure 2). Core agents represent the different handling devices in a port, but are generally modeled as one generic type with multiple options of configuration. This provides a flexible approximation of the reality while reducing the complexity by abstraction. *ContMAS* realizes a decentralised planning process since agents maintain and are solely responsible for individual plans for the execution order of container moves. In its basic version *ContMAS* allows the simple simulation of the activities within a harbor. However, in order to test different optimization strategies agents can be equipped with "intelligence", which means that a specific strategy can be added to each agent. Alternatively, agents can use advisors in order to come to a better decision. In this paper we will present two already developed optimization strategies, one which deals with the optimization of the allocation of container moves to straddle carriers (Section 5), and one to optimize the allocation of container positions in the yard (Section 6).

Agents: The core agents are called *ContainerHolderAgents*. Those are the agents which can pick up, transport ("hold") and drop containers, one for each individual device or other actor, such as cranes, ships, straddle carriers, yard areas or apron areas. There are several other agents in the model. The *HarbourMaster* controls the setup and events such as creation of a new agent e.g. for a newly arriving ship. The *ControlGUIAgent* provides the graphical interface for the human user. The *RandomGenerator* provides random numbers or events for simulations. Agents are also used for visualisations such as a bird's eye map or 3D rendering of the containers held by an agent.

Environment: The logical structure of the port is modelled as a tree of *Domains*. Each *Domain* lies in exactly one parent *Domain* and can contain several sub-*Domains*. An agent lives in exactly one *Domain* and can be capable of accessing several other *Domains*. For example, a *Crane* lives in the *Domain CraneRails* and can access the *Domain TrainRails, ShipBerth* and *StraddleCarrierStreet* to exchange containers with agents living in those *Domains*. This structure permits to dynamically calculate the shortest logical path through the port for a container, along with possible alternatives for comparison and weighing.

Data Structures: Agent communication uses a data structure called *TransportOrderChain (TOC)* which represents the path of a container through the port as a list of *TransportOrders*, each representing a single step (e.g. ship→crane). Each TOC is marked with a *TransportOrderChainState* indicating the state of the negotiation, e.g. whether a call for proposals has been issued, a drop planned, etc.

4.2   Simulator Operation

Operation: All negotiations between the agents are carried out by means of an extended contract net protocol. We selected the contract net since it is a standard generic

---

[3] Currently under development by Dipl.-Ing. Christian Derksen and Nils Loose at University Duisburg-Essen   http://www.dawis.wiwi.uni-due.de/team/christian-derksen/

protocol for task distribution. Any agent currently holding a container, e.g. a ship, initiates a call for proposals (CFP) to other suitable agents, e.g. cranes. They respond with a REFUSE or PROPOSE message, in the latter case containing the possible time of pick-up. The initiating agent then decides on one of the proposals and sends an ACCEPT message to that agent; all other agents get a REJECT message. Through this message exchange, the issuing agent and the determined contractor established a time and place to meet physically to hand over the container in question. Both agents move independently and can also negotiate with other agents about more containers in the meantime, thus building up a local plan. When the agreed upon time is reached, both agents should have moved to their negotiated position and the initiating agent issues a REQUEST to execute the appointment, i.e. to hand over the container. The contractor will acknowledge with an INFORM message. At this point, the administration over the container changes from the initiating agent to the contractor, which can itself become an initiator and issue a CFP for the next step of transportation, e.g. from crane to apron, adding a new *TransportOrder* to the *TransportOrderChain*. The communication between very different types of handling devices and other agents therefore is homogeneous and the *TransportOrderChain* builds up during negotiation. The set of all TOCs reaching the yard in one run contains a complete record of all container transfers and the corresponding time represents a trace or resulting global plan for a given setup.

Additional Features: In *ContMAS*, it is also possible to import *TOC*s with varying amounts of detail to determine the level of freedom the agents have. This allows the simulation to be used for several purposes, such as testing pre-planned runs against plans that have been produced just-in-time through negotiation or "replay" data from a real port, as was done in our project.

5   Optimisation of Allocation of Moves to Straddle Carriers

As mentioned in Section 2, Straddle Carrier management is an important sub-problem. We have therefore developed a negotiation-based optimisation strategy to allocate container moves to Straddle Carriers.

A key feature that distinguishes this mechanism from the process used by *ContMAS* is that we develop a schedule of planned moves ahead of time, whereas in *ContMAS* until now container moves are put up for bids when the machine is ready to dispose of the container. Planning ahead and therefore negotiating over containers not yet held by a machine is a feature likely to be included in one of the next versions of *ContMAS*.

In our approach each machine agent, Quay Crane or Straddle Carrier, maintains a *schedule* of container moves. In essence this is a timeline: a list of container moves (each with associated source and destination locations) with associated timing information. The timing information is defined in terms of *processing* time and *setup* time. Processing time is the time taken to move a given container from its source location to its destination location. The processing time depends only on the container and the machine. The setup time is the time between finishing one container and being ready to pick up the next container. It depends on both containers.

The container move allocation problem is how to assign the needed container moves to machines (QCs and SCs) in a way that meets all constraints, while attempting to reduce the overall processing time. A *solution* to the container move allocation problem is a set of machines, each with a schedule of container moves. Taken collectively, the moves proposed must correctly unload the ship[4] while respecting the various constraints. The overall goal is to reduce the ship turnaround time, and thus the overall quality of a solution is given by its cost: how much time is taken? This is simply the completion time of the last machine to complete (i.e. the maximum of the finishing time over the machines).

The process for deriving a solution has two phases: initial allocation and optimisation, following the Tabu search meta-heuristic [9]. In the initial allocation phase each container is considered in turn and is put up for "auction", with each (relevant[5]) machine bidding. The container is allocated to the cheapest bidding machine, and is inserted into its schedule at the end of its schedule. In doing the initial allocation we need to ensure that each container is unloaded from the ship before it is scheduled to be moved to the yard. This is done by tracking the time at which a container reaches the apron (its "minTime") and ensuring that the Straddle Carrier does not move the container earlier than its minTime.

The second phase, optimisation, attempts to improve the initial solution by repeatedly modifying it. The modifications considered involve selecting a container and considering (a) moving it to a different position in its machine's schedule; or (b) moving it to a different machine. The possible reallocations are evaluated based on (an approximation) of the cost difference, and the cheapest one is chosen and applied to the current solution, in order to obtain a new solution. In proposing and applying container move reallocations, we need to ensure that we do not reallocate a container move in a way that violates the "unload before move" constraint. We also need to ensure that we do not propose to deal with containers in a non-viable sequence (e.g. unloading C1 before C2 if C1 is below C2 in the ship).

The process described (briefly) above is performed before machines begin performing moves, and develops a complete scheduled plan for unloading a ship. A strength of the approach is that should something go wrong, the schedule can be updated to reflect necessary changes, and the allocation process re-run in order to deal with the change. For example, should a Straddle Carrier break down, the solution is updated by removing the Straddle Carrier in question, and putting its allocated container moves back into the list of moves to be allocated. The allocation process is then re-run, using the existing solution as a starting point, to allocate these container moves to other Straddle Carriers. In order to support this style of usage the solution includes not just a set of machines (with their associated schedules), but also a list of unallocated container moves, and the "current time". The latter is used during the process of container move allocation and optimisation to ensure that container moves which have already been done (i.e. are in the past) do not get changed.

We have implemented this negotiation-based approach for container management. The implementation makes use of a Tabu Search framework (OpenTS[6]). The

---

[4] We have focused on unloading only in our work so far.

[5] A machine is relevant to a container move if it is able to perform that type of move. For example, a Quay Crane is relevant to a move which involves the apron and a ship.

[6] http://www.coin-or.org/Ots

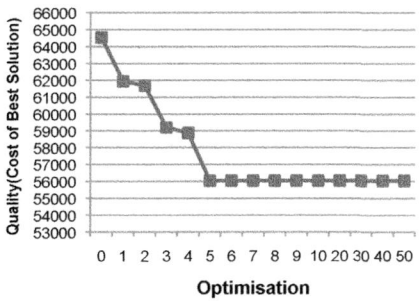

Fig. 3. Experimental Results

implementation has been integrated with *ContMAS* as an "advisor": when machines bid for container moves in *ContMAS*, they may consult the prepared schedule, and use this to guide whether they submit bids or not.

We now briefly present some (initial) experimental results. These were derived using real (anonymised) data from January 2009, extracted from the JMT system used by the local port, with only data fitting our simplified scenario being used (unloading only, using only one area in the yard, and with no yard-to-yard moves considered). We used data for a single ship being unloaded, which involved 82 containers, 3 Quay Cranes, and 8 straddle carriers. Figure 3 shows the solution quality (i.e. its cost: smaller is better) as the optimisation step is repeatedly applied. As can be seen, the initial solution resulting from the initial allocation phase (at x=0) is improved by the first few optimisation steps. Each point in Figure 3 is the average of ten runs.

6   Optimisation of Container Yard Allocation

The placement of containers in the yard can make a big difference to the cost of moving the container later to where it is needed. However, yard allocation is complicated in practice by various uncertainties. For instance, ships sometimes do not arrive at all and all of the containers scheduled for a particular voyage must then be rebooked on other vessels or returned (if that is possible.) More significantly for yard operations, those remaining containers may now be obstructing access to containers for later voyages. Additionally, tide or weather conditions may result in a ship being berthed with a reversed orientation — with the bow being where the stern was expected. As the loading sequence depends on the orientation this can create a significant problem of overstows. For these reasons most prior research (see Section 3) has addressed various sub-areas within the overall problem of optimising container locations within the yard. This prior research indicates that simplified variants of the Yard Allocation Problem are amenable to optimisation, however no single approach to date has addressed the complete problem. Note that this is a multi-objective problem with many, often conflicting, constraints to be satisfied. To try to tackle this task we have implemented an optimisation interface within *ContMAS* that allows a variety of approaches to be tried.

Agents that need a yard location in which to store an incoming container make a request of a *BayMapOptimiser* agent, which calls one of potentially several optimisers.

Each optimiser when called is given an ordered list of expected container moves (either from yard to ship or, as initially implemented, from ship to yard), and the current yard state, and must answer with a list of the optimal storage locations within the yard for each container.

Our initial module uses an Evolutionary Algorithm [10]. Given a sequence of expected container moves and a representation of the current yard state, an Evolutionary Algorithm (EA) is used to attempt to optimise the location for each container placement within the yard. Straddle Carriers, such as used within the yard we modelled, can only place or remove the uppermost container in a stack. Any time a Straddle Carrier needs to move a container that is part-way down in a stack, it must first remove all the over-stowed containers to a free location in the yard, and this is obviously expensive. This implies that the order of operations is important; containers should be loaded in a stack in the opposite order to which they will be removed. We therefore hypothesised that the sequence of container moves should be explicitly addressed by each component of the EA, and so our EA consists of an ordered genome representation, a fitness function that simulates the sequence of moves when assessing costs, and custom order-preserving crossover and mutation operators.

Genome Representation: The genome is made up of a sequence of (container id, yard location) genes, where each gene represents a move of a particular container to a [lane,bay,tier] location within the yard. Order is significant because the sequence in which containers are placed onto a stack determines the rehandle costs when they are extracted for loading onto a vessel. Containers usually appear more than once in the genome, to capture moves into and out of the yard; any additional entries for a given container signal potentially costly rehandles, or moves within the yard.

Fitness Function: The fitness of each entity is calculated by simulating the sequence of moves encoded in the genome to a simplified representation of the container terminal. Each move between yard and ship has a cost equal to the 'Manhattan' distance of the move. Any genome that encodes an invalid sequence of moves is given a high penalty cost. Invalid sequences include ones where a required move is missing from the genome, or falls out of sequence, or a move involves an overstowed container. A binary tournament is used to select a sample of the best (lowest cost) genomes for the next generation.

Mutation Operator: Mutation acts only on the location encoded within a specified proportion of genes in the genome; mutation does not affect the order of container moves. A random set of genes is selected, and each gene in the set gets its location adjusted to a random free location in the yard.

Crossover Operator: The order of genes in the genome is significant, so the crossover operator developed attempts to preserve the order of genes from each parent in the new child genome. It does this by identifying locations unique to the second parent, and then switching those for the locations of a random proportion of genes in the first parent, so leaving the order of moves untouched. This can result in invalid genomes, e.g., where the crossover results in a container to be in mid-air. Such invalid genomes are repaired by dropping mid-air containers down the stack to a supported position.

```
function Crossover(Genome A, Genome B):
    location_list = locations in Genome B that are not in Genome A
    new child Genome = copy of Genome A
    for 0 to some number_of_crossovers:
        randomly select a gene in the child Genome
        set that gene's location value to the next location in
                the location_list
    return child Genome
```

For example, if GenomeA = (AA12, [1,1,1]) (BB34, [2,2,2]) and GenomeB = (CC56, [1,1,1]) (AA12 ,[3,3,3]), the unique locations in Genome B would be simply [3,3,3], and one possible child genome would be (AA12, [3,3,3]) (BB34, [2,2,2,]). The effect is to construct a child genome that maintains the move ordering of Genome A, while incorporating location material from Genome B.

Figure 4 shows results from a single EA run of an example scenario involving the extraction of 20 containers from a $10 \times 3 \times 2$ yard. The containers are requested according to a fixed schedule and the EA is initialised with a population of 200 individuals. Termination is after a given number of generations. The figure shows the population converging on a lower (that is, better) fitness value, where the fitness value is proportional to the total distance of Straddle Carrier moves to complete the scenario.

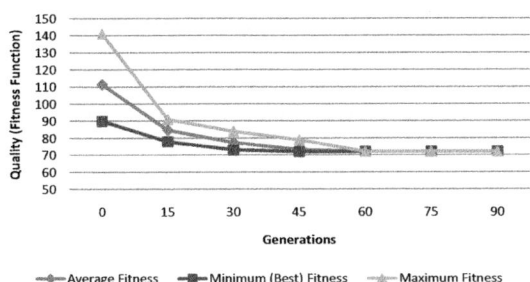

Fig. 4. Preliminary Experimental Results (minimal complexity problem)

7   Discussion and Conclusion

We have presented a port simulation platform (*ContMAS*) which has been implemented as a multi-agent system. The *ContMAS* platform can serve as an integrating framework for solutions to different aspects of the container terminal management and optimisation problem. *ContMAS* can be seen as a basic simulation tool which can be equipped with different optimisation strategies (called module agents). These module agents are easily replaceable, thus, allowing an easy integration of different optimisation strategies. This has been illustrated with the description of two specific aspects of the problems that we have tackled, namely yard allocation and straddle carrier move optimisation, which have been investigated, implemented, and integrated with *ContMAS*. Furthermore, we have conducted evaluations (some of which are covered in this paper) which have shown that our optimisations are effective, e.g. that the EA model is able to improve upon random yard allocations.

Overall, our conclusion is that taking an agent-based approach has proven to be a natural choice because of the nature of ports in which many actors work together with a high degree of autonomy. The agent paradigm supports the modeling of such an environment with a high level of detail, flexibility and consistency with the archetype by assuring as little transfer friction as possible. The use of a free and mature agent framework reduced development overhead and enabled access to easy exploitation of parallelization potential and advanced features like agent mobility for further development.

There is a range of directions for future work. One direction is to allow the replacement of the centralized module agents by a distributed solution. The challenge is, among others, that the optimisation phase currently considers a very large number of possible reallocations, and we need to reduce this for a distributed implementation to be practical. We are in the process of investigating heuristics for doing this reduction. Finally, regarding the EA-based yard allocation mechanism, our hypothesis that an order-based EA is required to optimise the complete yard allocation problem is as yet untested. We plan to conduct experimental tests against a control random allocation policy, and against the current 'block allocation' heuristic used by the local port.

References

1. Thurston, T., Hu, H.: Distributed agent architecture for port automation. In: Proceedings of the 26th Annual International Computer Software and Applications Conference (COMPSAC). IEEE Computer Society Press, Los Alamitos (2002)
2. Rebollo, M., Julian, V., Carrascosa, C., Botti, V.: A multi-agent system for the automation of a port container terminal. In: Workshop on Agents in Industry (2000)
3. Henesey, L., Davidsson, P., Persson, J.A.: Agent based simulation architecture for evaluating operational policies in transshipping containers. Autonomous Agents and Multi-Agent Systems 18, 220–238 (2009)
4. Steenken, D., Voß, S., Stahlbock, R.: Container terminal operation and operations research — a classification and literature review. OR Spectrum 26, 3–49 (2004)
5. Stahlbock, R., Voß, S.: Operations research at container terminals: a literature update. OR Spectrum 30, 1–52 (2008)
6. Chen, L., Bostel, N., Dejax, P., Cai, J., Xi, L.: A tabu search algorithm for the integrated scheduling problem of container handling systems in a maritime terminal. European Journal of Operational Research 181, 40–58 (2007)
7. Zhang, C., Liu, J., Wan, Y., Murty, K., Linn, R.: Storage space allocation in container terminals. Transportation Research Part B-Methodological 37(10), 883–903 (2003)
8. Preston, P., Kozan, E.: An approach to determine storage locations of containers at seaport terminals. Computers & Operations Research 28(10), 983–995 (2001)
9. Glover, F.: Future paths for integer programming and links to artificial intelligence. Computers & Operations Research 13(5), 533–549 (1986)
10. De Jong, K.A.: Evolutionary computation: a unified approach. MIT Press, Cambridge (2006)

HAI – A Human Agent Interface for JIAC

Sebastian Ahrndt, Marco Lützenberger, Axel Heßler, and Sahin Albayrak

DAI-Labor, Technische Universität Berlin, Germany
Ernst-Reuter-Platz 7
10587 Berlin, Germany
{sebastian.ahrndt,marco.luetzenberger,axel.hessler,
sahin.albayrak}@dai-labor.de

Abstract. There are many different application frameworks, which accelerate user interface development by simplifying repetitive and time consuming tasks. Most of these frameworks follow the widely accepted Model-View-Controller (MVC) architecture. Although, the existing frameworks are optimized for the implementation of object-oriented applications. The special features and possibilities offered by agent applications are not supported. Within this work, an architecture is designed, which allows the integration of any user interface in agent applications. As an extension of the MVC architecture, the advantages of agent-orientated software engineering will be combined with the advantages of the existing application frameworks. This structure provides the base for the Human Agent Interface, which allows the integration of any user interface in JIAC V agent systems.

Keywords: Human Agent Interaction, Interface, Agent to non-agent interoperability.

1 Introduction

The implementation of high-quality user interfaces (UI) is considered to be an essential phase of almost any software project. The importance of UIs and the complexity in developing them has been recognised long since. In an early work, *Myers* and *Rosson* [10] have analysed the implementation of user interfaces in detail and estimate the expenses on up to 50% of the total budget. In order to manage and accelerate the UI development, a large number of approaches and technologies have been presented so far. Support is mainly provided by so-called *Application Frameworks*, which simplify repetitive and time consuming tasks by providing tools, structures and reusable artefacts. Yet, as comprehensive and sophisticated these frameworks are, their principle is usually geared towards object-oriented structures and neglects support for other paradigms.

Due to their distributed nature, agent-based systems have an increased demand for user interfaces. Each involved agent usually requires an interface for configuration, management and observation purposes and, as the benefits of application frameworks are indisputable, we invented a way to extend common

F. Klügl and S. Ossowski (Eds.): MATES 2011, LNAI 6973, pp. 149–156, 2011.

agent-oriented software development with application framework concepts and exploit the advantages of both techniques.

In this paper, we present this approach. We start by describing our concept (see Section 2), which we evaluate afterwards (see Section 3). Subsequently, we compare our work to existing solutions (see Section 4) and finally, we wrap up with a conclusion (see Section 5). This paper is based on the diploma thesis of the first author [2].

2   Approach

The objective of our work was to facilitate interaction between user interfaces and multi-agent systems (MAS) by integrating application frameworks into the agent-oriented application development. When analysing related works, we were able to identify two main directions. On the one hand, agents were used in combination with existing frameworks. To make this approach work, the agents were geared towards the respective framework. On the other hand, we identified solutions with particular support for agent-oriented software development. These solutions were usually restricted by the applied technology. As an example, consider web-based approaches. Web orientation enables a standardised and easy distribution of UIs and supports a large number of different (mobile) devices, yet, the implementation is tied to web based programming languages as well as to the unflexible request-response model. The main intention of our work, was to counter such limitations.

We implemented our concept for the latest version of *JIAC V*, which we introduce in the following. Even though we made use of a particular agent framework for our implementation, our concept is not limited to it, but can be applied to many other agent platforms.

2.1   The Java Intelligent Agents Componentware (JIAC)

JIAC is a Java based agent framework which has been developed within industry- and government-funded projects at the *DAI-Labor* since 1998 [3]. In its latest incarnation, *JIAC V* [6] combines agent technology, scalability and performance and allows to execute hundreds of agents on a desktop computer. The modular architecture includes conformity to standards, extensibility, security mechanisms and combines service-oriented concepts with agent-oriented approaches. Agents can be implemented using Java or the *JIAC Agent Description Language* (*JADL++*), *JIAC*'s scripting language [6]. In *JIAC*, an agent's behaviour, its capabilities and its functions are encapsulated by so called "AgentBeans". The entire development process is supported by a comprehensive set of tools.

2.2   HAI in a Nutshell

The Human Agent Interface (HAI) has been developed with the objective to facilitate interaction between user interfaces and multi-agent systems. We derived the name "Human Agent Interface" directly from the purpose of our development. In order to remain independent from a specific UI technology or a particular agent framework, we arranged HAI to act as some kind of middle layer between the UI and the MAS. The advantage of this architecture lies with the clear separation between agent-specific parts and those from the user interface, such as JSPs, Silverlight pages or XUL, Flex components, to name but a few. Both, details and specific properties of the agent layer are hidden from the user interface. For the UI developer, the application appears as a monolithic system, whose functions are accessible via an API.

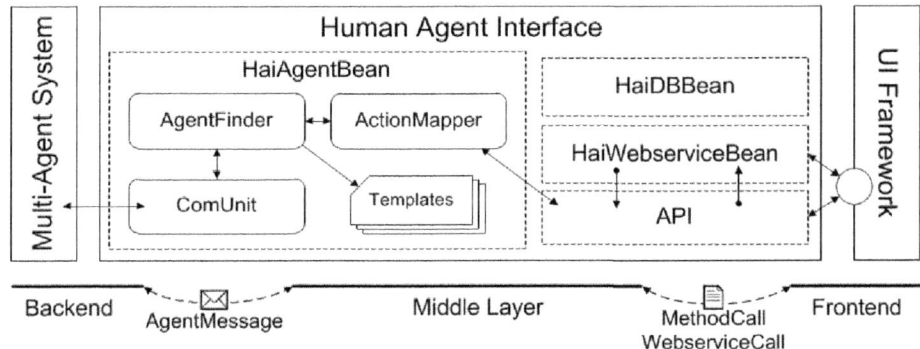

Fig. 1. The HAI as middle layer mediating between UI and MAS

Figure 1 emphasises the role as a middle layer and illustrates the HAI with some of its components. It also shows one of the main tasks: Converting UI request into agent messages and vice versa. In compliance with JIAC's principle of modularity, each capability is implemented as an AgentBean. Consequently, we implemented our HAI concept as JIAC V agent: The *HAI-Agent*. The loose coupling between capabilities and agent allows for custom and streamlined context adaptations, since unused features can be removed easily.

2.3   Integrating Agents into MVC

Using application frameworks to implement user interfaces offers many advantages for the development process. Nevertheless, as an objective of our work, we wanted to ensure, agent and UI developers do not influence each other. For this purpose, we made use of the MVC paradigm, since it logically separates an application on programming level.

In an MVC application the logic is implemented within the controller. When it comes to agent applications, the agents are usually dedicated to some application goal. The Human Agent Interface combines both principles and allows for the integration of agents into applications that comply with MVC. Since the application logic is hosted within the agents, a UI developer is not affected, when

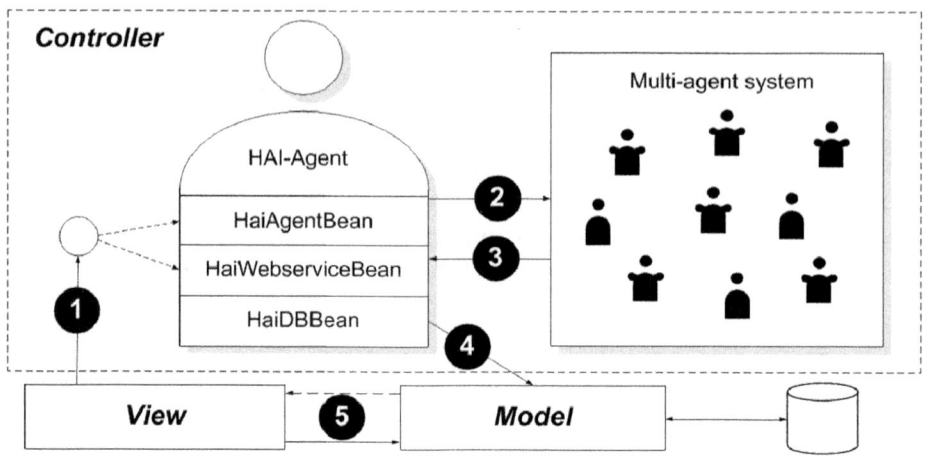

Fig. 2. MVC architecture with extended agent-based controller

the controlling components are changed. Figure 2 shows the MVC architecture
including Human Agent Interface and the MAS. The controller is modified in a
way, that the HAI-Agent can act as mediator and the application logic is realised
by the MAS. For this, incoming requests (1) are forwarded to the agent-system.
Requests are either triggered by method calls and directly sent to the HaiAgent-
Bean or triggered by web service calls and sent to the HaiWebserviceBean which
forwards them to the HaiAgentBean. If necessary the HaiDBBean is involved
to provide required data from a connected database. The request will then be
converted into an agent message, with additional data. The HAI-Agent proceeds
with the search for agents which are able to process the request. A definition of
the nature of a request is given by the user interface as parameter to the HaiA-
gentBean. If a fitting agent is located, the previously generated agent message
will be forwarded (2). Otherwise a failure code will be returned. The advantage
of this principle is the transparent communication between UI and the MAS for
the agent developers. Communication from the user interface can be handled
just as any other communication. The focus in implementing agent systems thus
remains on the agents themselves and does not additionally comprise user interface topics. After the agent has provided an answer to the redirected request,
the result is sent back to the HAI-Agent (3). The HAI-Agent then updates the
data model if necessary (4) and notifies the view on potential changes, which are
applied automatically (5).

For web interfaces the structure is slightly different since the underlying
request-response model does not support active views. The controller component has to specify a suitable view for the modified data — this structure is
commonly called: Model 2 paradigm [5]. If HAI is used in this context, incoming
data is stored in combination with an ID, which can be retrieved by a third
controller component (such as a servlet) which defines the associated view.

3   From Theory to Practice

We evaluated our work, within a government-funded project, in which we developed a complex graphical user interface and designed HAI to act as an interface between the UI layer and the MAS. The objective of the UI was to control and to visualise the results of an agent-based traffic simulation framework, which adds perceptions and attitudes of drivers to the simulation process [9]. To emphasise the operation principle of HAI, we describe some of the steps, done.

```
def initMap = {
  def i = new Invocation(name: "initMap", invocationId: null)
  i.invocationId = hai.invoke(MapServiceAgent.INIT, BERLIN)
  if(!i.save()){println "cannot save invocation id"}
}
```

Listing 1.1. Causing the HAI-Agent to search a spezific action.

For our work, we used *GRAILS* [12] as application framework. Since GRAILS is based on *Groovy* we had almost no trouble in using HAI for this project (`hai`). For the simulation framework, a simulation environment (city) had to be selected, first. Since different maps had different complexity and size, we were not able to define a suitable initialisation time-out. Instead, we applied asynchronous communication and realised the initialisation process by active waiting. Listing 1.1 illustrates our implementation, which causes the HAI-Agent to search for an agent which offers the `MapServiceAgent.INIT` action. The HAI-Agent converts the method call into an agent message, which is forwarded to the agent-system. After forwarding the message, an ID is generated, stored and returned to the UI as confirmation and in order to allow the UI actively check for answers. Since the simulation environment is vital for the simulation itself, the UI waits as long as an answer arrives or a time-out expired. Listing 1.2 shows the method which is called periodical to check for an answer.

```
def lookForAnswer = {
  def inv = Invocation.findByName("initMap")
  if(inv != null){
    if(timeout()){
       hai.deleteInvocation(inv.invocationId)
    }else{
      def res = hai.lookForInvocationResult(inv.invocationId)
      if(res != null){
        inv.delete(flush:true)
        render(view: "/settings/index", params:["map":res])
      }
    }
  }
}
```

Listing 1.2. Periodical check for an answer.

In order to support the many configuration parameters of the simulation framework, we made use of so called "configuration objects", which we stored within a database. Listing 1.3 shows a method (*findObject*) which uses the HaiDBBean to send data from the user interface to the agent-system. Since both, the agent-system and the user interface use the same data model, no translation was implemented.

```
def sendMapWeight = {
  hai.invoke(MapServiceAgent.SET_WEIGHT, hai.findObject("MapWeight", params.id))
  flash.message = "Preferences saved"
  render(view: "/settings/index")
}
```

Listing 1.3. Sending data from UI to MAS using the HaiDBBean

4   Related Work

To distinguish our work from others, we performed a comprehensive survey on existing approaches. We identified several approaches, but only two of them were generic and can be classified as frameworks: The *JACK WebBot* [1] and the *Jadex Webbridge Framework* [11]. Both of them support the development of web-based agent applications. The Jadex Webbridge Framework facilitates application development in compliance with the Model 2 paradigm. It allows the agent developer to do his work without knowledge on web development and by extending a provided controller component. The JACK WebBot is an extension of the JACK [7] framework and allows for the development of web applications by using JACK agents. JACK WebBot extends the Java Servlet API and thus requires a servlet container to provide user interfaces. To interact with the user interface JACK agents have to implement special interfaces.

Furthermore, we were able to identify several ad-hoc solutions. The *JADE* Framework [4], for instance, is equipped with the *JadeGateway* [8] and the *JADE GUI Agent* [15]. Both are concepts to furnish agent applications with servlet based web or SWING UIs. JIAC is equipped with the *Alter-Ego* [13] concept and the *MAMS* (Multi Access, Modular Services) [14] principle. Both concepts facilitate communication between UI and MAS, yet, most of the technical details have to be implemented by the agent developers.

4.1   Discussion

In our survey, we identified only two approaches capable of furnishing agent systems with user interfaces: The Jadex Webbridge Framework and the Jack WebBot. Both approaches facilitate the development of web-based agent applications. While the JACK WebBot has been tailored for JACK agent applications, the concept of the Jadex Webbridge Framework is a generic one and can also be realised with other agent frameworks. As a matter of fact, both solutions restrict the agents in their proactive behavior. Without an open request, an agent cannot start any interaction with the user. This function is provided by the Human Interface Agent. At the same HAI is not specialised to one type of user interface technology.

Nevertheless, there are other features that are not supported by HAI. The Webbridge Framework for instance allows to create agents for a request and also to withdraw them when they are no longer needed. This is an important feature, especially for resource management. The JACK WebBot is able to read and manipulate requests. This feature is used to increase the security of web sessions. The modular concept of HAI helps to solve some of these shortcomings in the future. This is one reason why we implemented HAI as JIAC V agent.

5   Conclusion

In this paper, we introduced a concept which enables and simplifies the development process of agent applications with user interfaces. Based on a survey similar approaches, we can say that there are a lot of ad-hoc but only a few generic solutions. These solutions were usually restricted by the applied technology. To counter such limitations and to bridge the gap between user interfaces and agent systems we introduced an extra layer: The Human Agent Interface (HAI). As a mediator, it performs all operations which are necessary to hide the details and specific properties of the agent layer from the user interface layer. To achieve the integration of this extra layer we introduced a concept which is based on MVC and integrates agents in applications. This approach allows developers to continue using application frameworks, which provide tools and functions that simplify repetitive and time consuming tasks to speed up the implementation of user interfaces. The agent-based MVC approach refines the controller component by splitting it up into the HAI and the agent system (for web interfaces there are three parts required: The servlet, which forwards request to HAI, the HAI itself and the agent system). The HAI is responsible for the conversion of user-requests into agent messages, inserting the required data and sending the message to a suitable agent in the multi-agent system. The actual program logic is performed by the agent system. User interface and MAS are kept separate. For this reason they can be implemented (mostly) independently from each other.

Further, a short insight into UI development with the Human Agent Interface has been given. The implemented HAI not only consists of the components described in the concept. We rather implemented a framework, which allows for monitoring, configuration and extensibility of the Human Agent Interface.

6   Future Work

A lot of research has been done in the domain of interface agents, to improve the interaction between humans and computers. But there are only a few approaches to equip agent applications with user interfaces. The Human Agent Interface is such a solution. However, it relates to the use of application frameworks, which are designed for object-oriented applications. To combine the advantages of agent-orientated software engineering with the advantages of application frameworks without an extra layer, we aspire a framework, which is geared towards agent systems.

References

1. Agent Oriented Software Pty. Ltd.: JACK Intelligent Agents – WebBot Manual. Agent Oriented Software Pty. Ltd (June 2005),
   http://www.aosgrp.com/documentation/jack/WebBot_Manual.pdf (July 9, 2011)
2. Ahrndt, S.: HAI – A Human Agent Interface for JIAC. Diploma thesis, Technische Universität Berlin, Berlin, Germany (May 2011)

3. Albayrak, S.: Intelligent Agents in Telecommunications Applications – Basics, Tools, Languages and Application. Frontiers in Artificial Intelligence and Applications, vol. 36. IOS Press, Amsterdam (1998)

4. Bellifemine, F., Poggi, A., Rimassa, G.: JADE - a fipa-compliant agent framework. In: Proceedings of the Fourth Practical Application of Intelligent Agents, pp. 97–108 (July 9, 2011), http://jmvidal.cse.sc.edu/library/jade.pdf

5. Ford, N.: Art of Java Web Development: Struts, Tapestry, Commons, Velocity, JUnit, Axis, Cocoon, InternetBeans, WebWork. Manning Publications (November 2003)

6. Hirsch, B., Konnerth, T., Heßler, A.: Merging agents and services – the JIAC agent platform. In: Bordini, R.H., Dastani, M., Dix, J., Amal, E.F.S. (eds.) Multi-Agent Programming: Languages, Tools and Applications, pp. 159–185. Springer, Heidelberg (2009)

7. Howden, N., Rönnquist, R., Hodgson, A., Lucas, A.: JACK intelligent agents – summary of an agent infrastructure. In: 5th International Conference on Autonomous Agents (2001)

8. Kelemen, V.: JADE tutorial – simple example for using the jadegateway class. MTA SZTAKI (October 2006), http://jade.tilab.com/doc/tutorials/JadeGateway.pdf (July 9, 2011)

9. Lützenberger, M., Masuch, N., Hirsch, B., Ahrndt, S., Heßler, A., Albayrak, S.: The BDI driver in the service city. In: Tumer, K., Yolum, P., Sonenberg, L., Stone, P. (eds.) Proceedings of the 10th International Conference on Autonomous Agents and Multiagent Systems. International Foundation for Autonomous Agents and Multiagent Systems, Taipei, Taiwan, pp. 1257–1258 (May 2011)

10. Myers, B.A., Rosson, M.B.: Survey on user interface programming. In: CHI 1992: Proceedings of the SIGCHI Conference on Human Factors in Computing Systems, pp. 195–202. ACM Press, New York (1992)

11. Pokahr, A., Braubach, L.: The webbridge framework for building web-based agent applications. In: Dastani, M.M., El Fallah Seghrouchni, A., Leite, J., Torroni, P. (eds.) LADS 2007. LNCS (LNAI), vol. 5118, pp. 173–190. Springer, Heidelberg (2008)

12. Rocher, G., Brown, J.: The Definitive Guide to Grails, 2nd edn. Apress Inc., New York (2009)

13. Schmidt, M., Többen, H., Keiser, J., Jentsch, O.: 4. abschlussbericht zum projekt MIATA (a management infrastructure for intelligent agent telecommunication applications). DAI Laboratory, Technical University of Berlin (2000)

14. Thiele, A., Konnerth, T., Kaiser, S., Hirsch, B.: Applying JIAC V to real world problems: The MAMS case. In: Braubach, L., van der Hoek, W., Petta, P., Pokahr, A. (eds.) MATES 2009. LNCS (LNAI), vol. 5774, pp. 268–277. Springer, Heidelberg (2009)

15. Vaucher, J., Ncho, A.: JADE tutorial and primer. Universite de Montreal (September 2003), http://www.iro.umontreal.ca/~vaucher/Agents/Jade/JadePrimer.html (July 9, 2011)

Agentification of Objects in Heterogeneous Dynamic Environments

Sebastian Bader

MMIS, University of Rostock, Germany
sebastian.bader@uni-rostock.de
http://mmis.informatik.uni-rostock.de

Abstract. In this article, we discuss an approach to build dynamic and heterogeneous ensembles of objects. The presented approach is based on a middleware for distributed systems and extends the deployment system such that ordinary objects are turned into agents without modifying the original object. By avoiding a direct connection between the different components, we obtain a highly dynamic and flexible system.

1   Introduction and Motivation

The design and implementation of smart environments is a challenging task. It includes, among other aspects, the connection of different components into a distributed system, and the definition of assistance functionalities. To complicate things further, such environments are usually heterogeneous and dynamic, that is, they consist of many different components from different vendors, which enter and leave the ensemble dynamically.

One approach to the design and implementation of such ensembles are multi-agent systems. They allow autonomous software components, called agents, to communicate and cooperate. Most multi-agent systems require a rather coordinated implementation of the single components. Usually, the type of agents and their interplay is known in advance. Adding new components might require some re-design. This is due to the fact, that most implementations do not allow on-line generation of plans, but require the plans to be constructed in advance.

The objective of this paper is three-fold. We propose an approach which (i) combines middleware systems as known from smart environment design and agent based modelling, (ii) allows for online construction of plans and (iii) decouples the ensemble by specifying environmental goals instead of object specific goals. Our work is based on the assumption that we can not make any assumption with respect to the configuration of the environment. Instead, all components may enter and leave dynamically. We furthermore believe that legacy code should be usable in such a system, in particular encapsulations of artefacts, like software adapters to physical objects, should be deployable into the ensemble and integrate seamlessly with it. For this, we combine the legacy code, formal specification and a deployment system to agentify objects. This results in a loose coupling between objects without modification of code.

F. Klügl and S. Ossowski (Eds.): MATES 2011, LNAI 6973, pp. 157–164, 2011.

2   Preliminaries and Related Work

Smart Environments. Smart environment should support their users by providing proactive assistance. That is, the environment should support its users as much as possible while achieving their usual tasks. Several such system have been proposed before. To name just a few, we refer to [6,11,13] and to [7] for a general introduction into the area. Assistance can be provided by controlling the environment to satisfy the users needs, like for example the lighting conditions. Designing such a system is a complex task, because such environments tend to be heterogeneous and dynamic with respect to their components.

Objects versus Agents. Objects and agents differ in particular with respect to the following aspects: While objects are passive in the sense that they only receive method calls, agents are active. That is, they are to some degree autonomous and can trigger actions and events on their own. Notions like believe and goal, are usually inadequate while talking about objects, but are fundamental to agents, which have intrinsic goals, and they are flexible to choose how to behave with respect to their beliefs. Multi-agent systems are inherently multithreaded and distributed. Therefore, most communication must be asynchronous, while method calls in object oriented programming are usually synchronous. Objects are usually characterised by their properties and methods. As mentioned above, agents have in addition a set of current beliefs and of current goals.

One multi-agent systems is Jason [2], based on the AgentSpeak language developed in [16]. It allows to specify rules of the form `event : context <- body`. Triggered by some event, the current context, that is the agents belief with respect to the state of the world is evaluated. If the specified context conditions hold, the body of the rule is executed. The body consists of actions to be executed. Those actions can either create new events, control objects directly, or send messages to other agents.

Publish / Subscribe Systems. Middleware systems within the area of ubiquitous computing are usually defined as an abstraction layer used to connect software components, running on different hosts within some network. The core services provided by such systems are look-up facilities to locate remote components, event distribution and remote procedure calls. Event distribution is often implemented as publish/subscribe system. The events are picked up by the middleware and distributed to every component which has registered itself. The registration is done by specifying a filter to be applied to the events. If the filter matches, the event is propagated. Many different middleware systems for distributed systems have been proposed [4,5,14,19], and the concept of publish / subscribe has for example been implemented in [3,8,15]. Most systems allow filters to be expressed at the level of events only, but some work has been done with respect to event aggregation [15].

Deployment System. Objects and agents are usually registered in a distributed environment using some deployment systems. Such a system is responsible to connect a given object with the middleware, thus, we obtain a separation between the objects functionality and the middleware itself. The systems are also responsible for object creation, startup and shutdown of communication channels and for event processing. In Section 3.3, we describe some aspects of our deployment system in detail.

Goal-Based Interaction. Normally, we interact with objects and devices by invoking single methods. That is to bring about a certain state, we perform a sequence of actions, hopefully leading to the goal state. In [12] *goal-based interaction* for dynamically changing heterogeneous environments has been discussed. Instead of invoking actions, a goal state is specified. Afterwards, some planning system computes an appropriate sequence of actions leading from the current to the desired state of the world. Goal-based interaction is thus a promising approach to decouple smart environments. As mentioned above, such environments are dynamic and heterogeneous. Therefore, it is not possible to hard-wire all possible action sequences in advance. Depending on the current state of the world, suitable actions need to be chosen. Furthermore, the goal-based interaction allows to decouple the environment, because it suffices to specify a goal to be achieved, instead of knowing the internals of the remote object, which allow to conclude the concrete sequence of actions.

Action Description Languages. To describe the capabilities of devices and their methods, action description languages are used. Here we use PDDL [10] as known from planning and shown in Ex. 3. Such operators have successfully been used in the area of automatic planning [10] as well as in the context of smart environments [17].

3   From Objects to Agents

In this section, we describe the agentification of objects. After discussing some general assumptions, we extend the simple event filtering presented above to allow filtering with respect to the current state of the whole world. As argued below, the perceived state of the world, coincides with the beliefs of the agent. Afterwards, we discuss goal-based interaction with objects – instead of interacting by method calls, we allow a new form interaction, namely by uttering goal states to be achieved by the object. Then, we describe how to turn simple objects into agents using the proposed mechanisms.

As already discussed in the introduction, the following approach is based on some assumptions: (a) Components of the system can be executed on different hosts. (b) Every component might encapsulate different functionality. (c) Components may enter and leave the ensemble at any point in time. (d) Interaction with objects / components should be goal-based. (e) Legacy code should be usable without (severe) modifications. Based on these assumptions we designed a system in which simple Java objects can be deployed as agents. That is, we agentify objects using our deployment system. To furthermore ease the development we support goal-based interaction with objects. This allows to decouple different objects further, because the plan chosen to achieve a given goal is only important for the object itself, not for the invoking agent.

3.1   State-Filtering in Publish / Subscribe Systems

As mentioned above, publish subscribe systems are used to enable indirect communication between publishers and subscribers of events. That is, the system sends messages to all registered subscribes on all events triggered by the publisher. Ex. 1 shows a simple scenario serving as running example.

Example 1. Assume a simple lamp, which can be turned on and off, and whose dim value can be changed. Those actions result in events of the following form, distributed via the publish / subscribe system: (Lamp3 (on true)) *or* (Lamp3 (on true) (dimValue 0.5)) *Subscribers can register for such events using for example the following filter:* ($on = true) || (dimValue >= 0.5) *with $ indicating event keys and* || *denoting a logical or.*   ○

By assuming a certain format of the event description, we are able to actually track the state of the producing objects. In our architecture we use events containing key-value pairs as shown in Ex. 1. We furthermore, assume that all keys represent state properties of the sender and that the corresponding values carry the value of that property at the time of the event. Finally, we assume that all events carry the unique ID of the sender (Lamp3 in the example above). These assumptions allow to track the state of the published objects.

Based on this state tracking mechanism, we are able to include the state of other objects into the filters specified in the publish/subscribe system. In our system, the state of other objects can be access using the following syntax: $on@Lamp2 = true stating that the property on of the object Lamp2 must be true. Unfortunately, there is no guarantee that the publisher actually is in the state perceived by some subscriber. This is due to the facts that there might be no guarantee of message delivery and there usually is a delay between sending and receiving the message. Nonetheless, the perceived state coincides with the subscribers belief of the publisher's state.

3.2   Goal-Based Interaction with Objects

In object orient programming, the world is modelled using objects, which are characterised by their attributes and methods. Interaction with objects usually means to invoke methods. As argued above, this paradigm is not necessarily adequate while developing heterogeneous and dynamic ensembles. We apply the idea of goal-based interaction to objects. Assume that every object knows how to bring about a certain internal state. Therefore, we should interact with such objects not by invoking methods, but by asking to achieve a certain goal.

Example 2. To set the dim value of a lamp to 0.5, we would normally invoke the following methods on it: (turnOn Lamp3) (dimLight Lamp3 0.5) *The lamp is first turned on and afterwards the dim value is set to 0.5. But, this sequence of actions can only be constructed knowing the internals of the lamp, namely that it must be switched on before dimming. As shown below, our system allows to specify the goal state as:* (dimValue Lamp3 0.5) *This will result in exactly the same sequence of actions, but this time, not the caller, but the lamp, needs to know its internals. To abstract things further, we can also specify goals with respect to properties of the environment:* (luminosity stage 0.5) *In this example* stage *is an abstract location and the goal is forwarded to all objects at the* stage.   ∘

Different types of goals are discussed in the literature. In [9], for example, the authors distinguish three types of goals: achieve, maintain and perform goals. An *achieve goal* is used to ask for a certain state, that is in our case to ask an object to achieve the given internal state. *Maintain goals* indicate the desire to keep the state, either for a given period of time, or until cancellation. *Perform goals* are used to indicate the request to perform a given sequence of actions.

As discussed below, other types of goals are needed as well. In particular while asking for optimised results. Therefore, we propose to extend the list of types to include *minimise, maximise* and *repeat* goals. *Minimise* and *maximise goals* are used to ask the object to optimise a given value function, mapping the internal state to some real value. *Repeat goals* ask the object to repeat a given goal in a given frequency. Before discussing a larger example, we describe the agentification of objects using our deployment system.

3.3   Agentification of Objects

After describing the conceptual ingredients of our approach in the previous sections, we discuss now the agentification of objects. We are currently working on an implementation of the proposed ideas, which already covers most of the aspects presented below. As argued above, most agent-specific functionality is embedded into the deployment system, not in the published objects. This allows to use existing legacy code without modification and to connect different components in a very flexible manner.

Object Creation and Initialisation. An object is created using some unique id and a specification of the object. For this, we rely on our middleware described in [1], which allows to create arbitrary Java objects using a simple format based on S-Expressions [18]. In addition to the creation of the object, we allow to annotate it with positions and additional properties, like a human readable name.

Publication of the Object. After creating the object, it is published using different options. Currently, we support the publication via publish/subscribe, plain sockets and http. The publish/subscribe system ensures that all events generated by the object are distributed to all interested subscribers. Such events are used to trigger reactions and to update the internal state of the object. The socket and HTTP-interface allow the invocation of methods as well as the specification of goals for the published object. In addition, all published objects are registered with a lookup-system allowing to locate objects in the network.

Connection of Objects. Often some objects within a given ensemble have some kind of strong and more or less static interconnection, even though the correct location of the objects is usually not fixed. For this, the system creates proxy objects of remote objects. Those can be used like local objects. This kind of dependency, or resulting functionality, could also be implemented within the publish/subscribe system, or any other message-passing protocol. But in situations requiring a rather fixed connection between objects the proposed approach has turned out to be better usable than purely event-based communication.

Declaration of Goals. To allow goal-based interaction with deployed objects, we need to define the goals achievable for a given object. For this, we employ a PDDL-like notion as known from planning. Every action provided by the object is annotated with its preconditions and effects as shown in Ex. 3. Usually, all proposition not being valid after executing a given action, need to be listed as so called negative effects. In object oriented programming, in contrast to planning in general, most of the properties are functional. That is, it can not be that the two propositions (dimValue Lamp true) and (dimValue Lamp false) hold at the same time. By convention, all properties declared by some object are assumed to be functional, which allows a shorter formalisation.

Example 3. The functionality of our lamp can be formalised as follows:

```
(:action dimLight                      (:action turnOn
 :parameters (?v - float)              :precondition (not isOn ?@)
 :precondition (isOn ?@)               :effect ((isOn ?@)
 :effect (dimValue ?@ ?v) )                     (dimValue ?@ 1)) )
```

The special variable ?@ refers to the deployed object itself, in our example a lamp. Asking a lamp which is turned off to achieve the state (dimValue Lamp3 0.5) would result in the following action sequence computed from the specification: (turnOn Lamp3) (dimValue Lamp3 0.5).   ∘

So far we have been concerned with effects on internal state properties only. In principle, two types of effects can be distinguished: those concerning internal and those for external parameters. But instead of annotating actions with external effects, we define a mapping between internal and external properties as shown in Ex. 4. Please note, that the specification of the objects functionality as shown in Ex. 3 is completely independent from the environment the object is deployed into. Both, the object and its environment are linked by specifying the property map shown in Ex. 4. To allow the goal based interaction with objects, they are deployed by providing the specification and the effect map.

Example 4. To link internal and external properties, all objects are annotated with mappings as follows: (dimValue ?@ ?v) => (luminosity @position ?v) This mapping connects the internal dimValue with the external luminosity property. Please note that the position, is only available within the deployment system, the lamp itself has no knowledge of it, and should not have.   ∘

Specification of Reactions to Events. Analogously to the specification of agentspeak rules, we allow to attach certain reactions to perceived events. This can be done as follows: `--subscribe ($sender = Button) && ($on@Lamp2 = true) (:achieve (luminosity state 0.4))`. Based on the state tracking described above and the event distribution by the publish subscribe system, we are able to specify rules as known from AgentSpeak. In our system, the context is specified using the @-constructs within the specification of filters. Thus we are able to specify basically arbitrary conditions with respect to events and the current believe with respect to the state of other objects.

4 Summary and Future Work

As mentioned above, the construction of smart environments is a challenging task. Here, we proposed a novel middleware which combines different aspects to allow the agentification of simple objects. For this we employ formal specification of the object's methods, which allow to interact with objects in a goal-based fashion. Instead of calling methods directly, we can interact with objects by specifying goal states to be reached. This results in a very loose coupling between the objects deployed into the system. Instead of hard-wiring action sequences, it suffices to specify goals. To abstract the interaction further, we map states with respect to environmental parameters with internal states of the objects. This allows to specify high level goals, like (`luminosity stage 0.5`) stating that there should be some light at the stage. This high-level goal is translated into an appropriate action sequence leading to the desired state of the world.

As mentioned above, there are some open problems. In particular, we would like to extend the approach to other goal types, specifying optimisation problems. So far no ontological reasoning has been added to the system. All goals are implicitly specified within the same ontology. Besides allowing a goal-based interaction, the formal action specification allows to construct unit test for the objects automatically. After specifying the PDDL-description of the object's actions, we can construct test-cases automatically.

Acknowledgement. The author would like to thank three anonymous reviewers whose comments on a previous version helped to improve the article.

References

1. Bader, S., Ruscher, G., Kirste, T.: A middleware for rapid prototyping smart environments. In: Proc. of Ubicomp 2010, pp. 355–356 (2010)
2. Bordini, R.H., Wooldridge, M., Hübner, J.F.: Programming Multi-Agent Systems in AgentSpeak using Jason. Wiley, Chichester (2007)
3. Carzaniga, A., Wolf, A.L.: Forwarding in a content-based network. In: Proc. of ACM SIGCOMM 2003, pp. 163–174 (2003)
4. Cheyer, A., Martin, D.: The open agent architecture. Journal of Autonomous Agents and Multi-Agent Systems 4(1), 143–148 (2001)

5. Coen, M.H., Phillips, B., Warshawsky, N., Weisman, L., Peters, S., Finin, P.: Meeting the computational needs of intelligent environments: The metaglue system. In: Proc. of MANSE 1999, pp. 201–212 (1999)
6. Cook, D.J., Youngblood, G.M., Das, S.K.: A multi-agent approach to controlling a smart environment. In: Augusto, J.C., Nugent, C.D. (eds.) Designing Smart Homes. LNCS (LNAI), vol. 4008, pp. 165–182. Springer, Heidelberg (2006)
7. Cook, D.J., Das, S.K.: Smart Environments. Wiley, Chichester (2005)
8. Cugola, G., Di Nitto, E., Fuggetta, A.: The jedi event-based infrastructure and its application to the development of the opss wfms. IEEE Transactions on Software Engineering 27(9), 827–850 (2001)
9. Dastani, M., Van Riemsdijk, M.B., Meyer, J.C.: Goal types in agent programming. In: In Proc. of ECAI 2006, pp. 220–224 (2006)
10. Gerevini, A., Haslum, P., Long, D., Saetti, A., Dimopoulos, Y.: Deterministic planning in the fifth international planning competition: PDDL3 and experimental evaluation of the planners. Artificial Intelligence 173(5-6), 619–668 (2009)
11. Hagras, H., Callaghan, V., Colley, M., Clarke, G., Pounds-Cornish, A., Duman, H.: Creating an ambient-intelligence environment using embedded agents. IEEE Intelligent Systems 19, 12–20 (2004)
12. Heider, T., Kirste, T.: Supporting goal-based interaction with dynamic intelligent environments. In: Proc. of the 15th European Conference on Artificial Intelligence, pp. 596–600 (2002)
13. Kidd, C.D., Orr, R., Abowd, G.D., Atkeson, C.G., Essa, I.A., MacIntyre, B., Mynatt, E.D., Starner, T., Newstetter, W.: The aware home: A living laboratory for ubiquitous computing research. In: Proc. of the Second International Workshop on Cooperative Buildings, Integrating Information, Organization, and Architecture, pp. 191–198. Springer, Heidelberg (1999)
14. Kirste, T., Herfet, T., Schnaider, M.: EMBASSI: mutimodal assistance for universal access to infotainment and service infrastructures. In: WUAUC 2001, pp. 41–50. ACM Press, New York (2001)
15. Parzyjegla, H., Graff, D., Schröter, A., Richling, J., Mühl, G.: Design and Implementation of the Rebeca Publish/Subscribe Middleware. In: Sachs, K., Petrov, I., Guerrero, P. (eds.) Buchmann Festschrift. LNCS, vol. 6462, pp. 124–140. Springer, Heidelberg (2010)
16. Rao, A.S.: Agentspeak(l): Bdi agents speak out in a logical computable language. In: Perram, J., Van de Velde, W. (eds.) MAAMAW 1996. LNCS, vol. 1038, pp. 42–55. Springer, Heidelberg (1996)
17. Reisse, C., Kirste, T.: A distributed mechanism for device cooperation in smart environments. In: Advances in Pervasive Computing. Adjunct Proc. of the 6th International Conference on Pervasive Computing, pp. 53–56 (2008)
18. Rivest, R.L.: S-expressions. CSAIL MIT website (1997)
19. Saffiotti, A., Broxvall, M., Gritti, M., LeBlanc, K., Lundh, R., Rashid, J., Seo, B.S., Cho, Y.: The peis-ecology project: Vision and results. In: IROS (2008)

Gateway Architecture
for Web-Based Agent Services

Tobias Betz, Lawrence Cabac, and Matthias Wester-Ebbinghaus

University of Hamburg
Faculty of Mathematics, Informatics and Natural Sciences
Department of Informatics
{betz,cabac,wester}@informatik.uni-hamburg.de
http://www.informatik.uni-hamburg.de/TGI

Abstract. Many publications in the last years point out the benefit
of combining software agents and Web services. These approaches are
mainly based on W3C compliant Web services and try to integrate them
into FIPA compliant agent systems. The major obstacles are mismatches
in service description and communication. This paper presents a Gateway
architecture for connecting software agents and RESTful Web services
based on JSON communication. To keep the communication transparent
the Gateway translates the message encodings in both ways without any
restrictions for the participating platforms. Instead of translating and
offering machine-readable service descriptions, this approach puts the
focus on human-machine interactions with software agent services. For
this purpose we provide a Javascript framework to support the developer
to create dynamic Web pages that act as human-readable service descriptions and also as service invocation application. Moreover, with the help
of this approach it is possible to create a Web-based and agent-oriented
graphical user interface.

Keywords: Web services, REST, WebSocket, Multi-Agent System,
MULAN, FIPA, WebGateway.

1 Introduction

The fusion of multi-agent systems and Web services tries to combine the best aspects of both technologies. On one hand, we have Web services with their advantages in terms of interoperability as well as flexibility in heterogeneous
systems and their ability to automate service invocations with the help of machine-
readable service descriptions. On the other hand, we have multi-agent systems
with their strengths in terms of autonomic and intelligent agent behavior. The
combination of both technologies results in hybrid systems that are able to act
in both worlds and offer a promising solution for the automation of service discovery, composition and invocation. From the perspective of multi-agent systems
these issues are addressed in many publications [4,6,11], which results in a variety
of solutions. In contrast to these approaches, we present an approach that does

F. Klügl and S. Ossowski (Eds.): MATES 2011, LNAI 6973, pp. 165–172, 2011.
© Springer-Verlag Berlin Heidelberg 2011

not rely on the W3C[1] Web service specification. This makes our approach more flexible since it is not restricted to the use of SOAP as communication and WSDL as service description language.

Section 2 describes our abstract architecture for the integration of Web services and multi-agent systems. It also discusses implementation matters. After that, Section 3 discusses the related work, before Section 4 concludes the paper and outlines future work.

2   Integrating Web Services into Multi-agent System

In this section, we present our proposal for the integration of Web services into multi-agent systems. We have implemented this proposal in the context of our MULAN multi-agent framework (www.paose.net, [7]) and our description will refer to this implementation. However, our proposal is abstract in the sense that it is rather neutral to the concrete multi-agent framework that is used. We exploit the FIPA-compliance of MULAN[2] but actually, any multi-agent framework with a notion of agent services would be equally compatible to our proposal. Consequently, what we present in this section is an abstract architecture that connects the Web service and the agent worlds such that a Web service is able to invoke agent services and vice versa.

2.1   WebGateway Architecture

The major challenge that has to be solved for a transparent, bidirectional communication between Web services and multi-agent systems is the difference and incompatibility of the used communication protocols and specifications of each technology. We close that gap by establishing a gateway with different communication interfaces to support the native communication of both Web service and agent platforms. We have implemented our proposed solution in the context of our multi-agent framework MULAN. MULAN allows to run multiple agent platforms in parallel on different hosts in a distributed environment.

As depicted in Figure 1, we encapsulate the functionality that is required for a gateway in an agent called *WebGateway*. A WebGateway-agent is able to communicate with other agents (both on the same platform as itself and on remote platforms) via the "ordinary" FIPA-compliant agent communication infrastructure of the MULAN framework. We call this the *internal interface* of a WebGateway-agent. In addition, a WebGateway-agent has what we call an *external interface* for communicating with Web service platforms. This external interface is realized using a Web server (Jetty[3] servlet container), which is integrated into the MULAN framework. As a default, we took the approach

---

[1] World Wide Web Consortium (W3C).

[2] Actually, MULAN comes in multiple variants and the FIPA-compliant variant is called CAPA, presented in [2].

[3] Jetty: http://www.eclipse.org/jetty

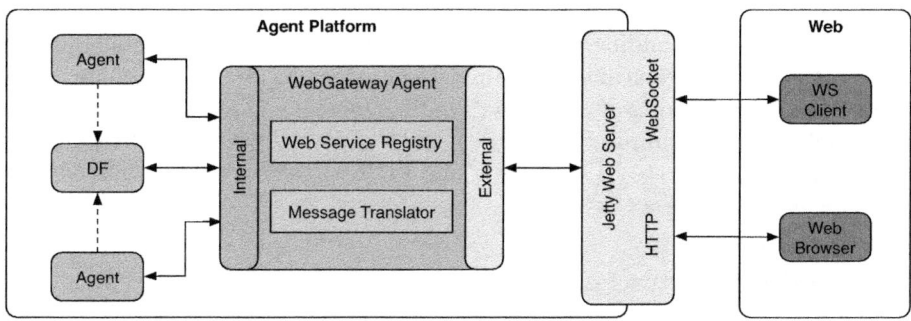

Fig. 1. The MULAN Gateway Architecture

to have one Web server for each MULAN host and to have one WebGateway-agent for each MULAN platform (it is possible to start multiple platforms on one host). When a WebGateway-agent is started on platform startup, it is automatically connected to the platform's associated Web server. The connection between a WebGateway-agent and its corresponding Web server features the standard HTTP protocol and also a second type of connection that uses the HTML5 WebSocket protocol [12], which enables bidirectional client/server communication.

One particular feature of our approach is the support for – and actually also a limitation to – RESTful Web services. The **RE**presentational **S**tate **T**ransfer (REST) architecture [3] gained increased attention because of its simplicity of publishing and consuming services over the Web. The architecture is based on resources that identify the participants of service interactions and that are addressed with globally unique URIs[4]. This resources can be manipulated over an uniform interface with a fixed set of operations (GET, POST, PUT, DELETE, etc.), which are part of the underling HTTP networking protocol. Resources are also decoupled from their representations so that their content can be accessed in a variety of formats e.g. HTML, JSON[5], XML or even JPEG images.

To fulfill the task of acting as a gateway between agents and Web services as communication partners, our proposed WebGateway-agent must have the following key features.

1. Registration and management of agent services that are published as Web services and vice versa (detailed description in Section 2.2).
2. A two-way translation of the supported message encodings (detailed description in section 2.3).
3. Routing and management of messages between the different interfaces.

The last mentioned feature has to combine the communication of both interfaces observing their characteristics: synchronous or asynchronous communication

---

[4] Uniform Resource Identifier.
[5] Javascript Object Notation (JSON).

depending on the used protocol (ACL, HTTP or WebSocket). Additionally, it has to handle the corresponding message performatives [8] in any possible interface combination. That means in fact the implementation of a cross-technological message tracking and routing mechanism (handling messages going in and out of each type of interface). To simplify the operation of the WebGateway-agent we limit the range of performatives to FIPA-Inform and FIPA-Request, which is sufficient for the invocation of Web services.

2.2   Service Registration

Referring to the FIPA specification underlying MULAN, agents have to register their services at the Directory Facilitator (DF). In order to publish such an agent service as a RESTful Web service, a second registration at the Web Service Registry (see Figure 2) has to be executed. This second registration differs from the one conforming to the FIPA specifications. In addition to the standard registration parameters (service name, service type, etc.), it is necessary to submit the representation of the related REST resource. This representation could, in fact, be any media type that is supported by the Jetty Web server but in our case, we have designed resource representations to be based on Java Server Pages[6] (JSP) together with supplementary source files as it is known from ordinary Web site development.

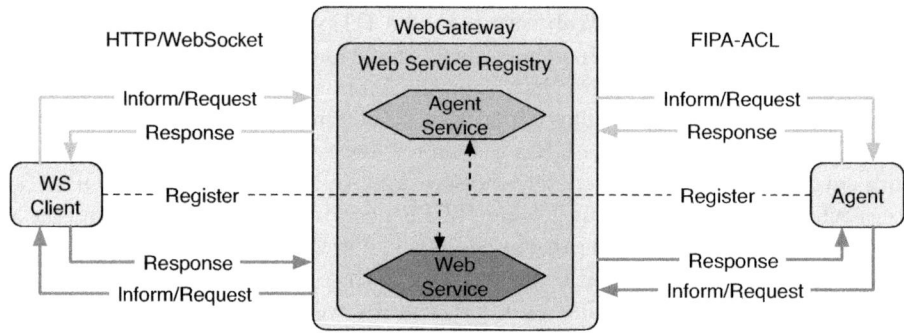

Fig. 2. Service Registration and Message Decoupling

After service registration on the agent side, the WebGateway-agent comes into play. It treats the agent service as a REST resource and assigns an address in the form of an URI to it. In addition, platforms and agents are also treated as REST resources and are assigned URIs. The composition schema of addresses is depicted in Figure 3 in terms of a 4-level naming hierarchy and the corresponding URI parts:

---

[6] Java Server Page (JSP): http://www.oracle.com/technetwork/java/javaee/jsp

1. Host: URI of the Web server inclusive port.
2. Platform: Name of the running MULAN platform.
3. Agent: Name of the agent that owns a service.
4. Service: Name of a specific service.

With this structure it is possible to provide a unique address even if several agent platforms and agents exist on the same host at the same time. The technical counterparts of the REST resources on the Web server side are implemented as Java Servlets[7] (interpreting the above mentioned JSPs). They are responsible for providing the resource representations. They also act as connection endpoints for HTTP and WebSocket connections and forward all incoming messages to the responsible WebGateway-agent. Each resource (see Figure 3) has its own Servlet. For once, we have default Servlets offering default representations in the form of lists of the respective nested resources (e.g. a platform resource displays a list of registered agents). But it is also possible to customize Servlets for resources.

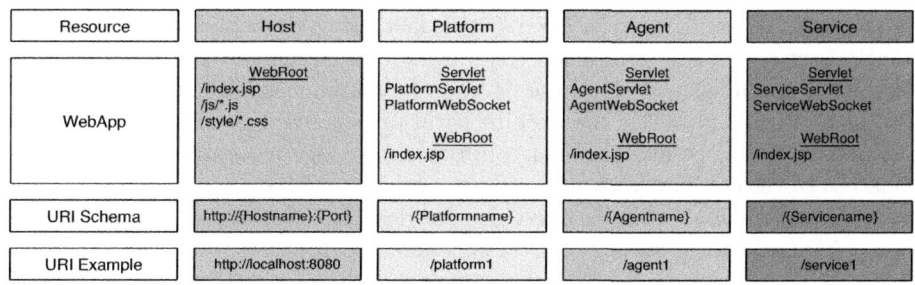

Fig. 3. Resource Addressing and Servlet Binding

2.3   Message Translation

Translation of messages is essential to ensure a transparent and loosely coupled interconnection. The gateway has to deal with different content languages and has to convert a received message to the corresponding encoding of the recipient. Actually, the WebGateway-agent supports a set of languages:

- JSON: The major language that is used to communicate with Web services. It has advantages over XML because of its simplicity and its perfect integration in Javascript applications.
- SL: The Semantic Language (SL) [9] is part of the FIPA specification and is used as a message content language for agent communication.
- Form Content: HTML FORM[8] content that is transferred by HTTP POST requests as *application/x-www-form-urlencoded* or *multipart/form-data* encoded message data.

---

[7] Java Servlets: http://www.oracle.com/technetwork/java/index-jsp-135475.html
[8] HTML forms: http://www.w3.org/TR/html4/interact/forms.html

The modular design of our message translator (depicted in Figure 1) makes it possible to extend the WebGateway-agent with any kind of content language. Listing 1 and Listing 2 illustrate the content translation from a JSON-encoded to an SL-encoded message.

```
{
  "frame": "web-event-action",
  "events": [
    {
      "frame": "web-event",
      "event-id": "id1",
      "value": "button_click"
    }
  ]
}
```

Listing 1. JSON

```
(
  web-event-action
  :events (sequence
    (
      web-event
      :event-id id1
      :data button_click
    )
  )
)
```

Listing 2. Semantic Language

3   Related Work

In the area of multi-agent systems, the field of Web service integration into multi-agent systems is well researched and yields in many interesting solutions. The work reported in this paper is therefore influenced by several directions but primarily inspired by the architectural design described in the publication of D. Greenwood et al. [4]. Their approach provides a intermediary processor called *Web Service Integration Gateway Service* (WSIGS) that is positioned on the communication path between the service participants. It is implemented as a JADE platform service and is accessible to internal platform agents and external Web services. A different solution with almost the same functionality was introduced by M. O. Shafiq et al. [11]. The authors interconnect both technologies, FIPA multi-agent systems and Web services, with the help of a middleware called *AgentWeb Gateway*, that provides appropriate transformation mechanisms to translate communication protocols and service description languages. The *WS2JADE* Approach from X. T. Nguyen et al. [6] is based on a two layer architecture. (1) The interconnection layer contains dynamic entities called *WSAG* (Web Service Agents), which are capable of communicating with and offering Web services as their own agent services. (2) The static management layer is responsible for active service discovery and registration. It also provides a deployment process that generates WSAGs and ontology mappings at runtime. A common feature of all these approaches is that they assume and are based on Web services that use the standard WSU[9] stack, i.e. they use an XML based communication language (SOAP) and service description language (WSDL). Another well established Web service implementation is the RESTful architecture [10]. It increasingly gained popularity because of its simplicity in terms of implementation and resource addressing. An approach which takes advantage of these features is proposed of E. L. Soto [5]. He implemented a *Web Service Message Transport Service* (WSMTS) for JADE platforms that is capable of handling FIPA-SL messages in XML representation. The open language

---

[9] WSDL, SOAP, UDDI (WSU).

specification allows to extend the message with additional information like Web service endpoint references (WS-Addressing[10]) to ensure an end-to-end communication with only one single message encoding. In this case, agents are able to register themselves with a specific address to publish their services as a REST service. The resulting advantage of this combined message format is the support of more complex interaction patterns beside request/response interactions.

A still problematic issue, concerning the use and composition of RESTful services, is the change of state of a resource and the corresponding update of clients. Especially Web clients have to constantly send *GET* requests to check if the state has changed, which will result in heavy traffic and unnecessarily high load of Javascript. For a bidirectional communication, as used for instance in a User Interface Framework S. Aghaee et al. [1, Section 5.2] recommend the use of W3C WebSockets [12]. The WebSocket API provides a mechanism to sent data in various representations (JSON, XML, etc.) to clients only when the resource has changed.

4 Conclusion and Future Works

In this paper, we presented a gateway architecture that makes it possible to interconnect multi-agent systems and Web services. In contrast to most other solutions in this area, we rely on a RESTful architecture where agents and their services are treated as resources. Our approach offers a very intuitive way of resource addressing and a very accessible way of resource representation. In our current work, we especially focus on the latter point. We work on a Javascript-based framework that assists the creation of Web-based graphical resource representations. We use this framework specifically to provide graphical user interfaces (GUI) for humans in order to gain access to agents and their services in the context of an agent-based collaboration platform. On this platform, so-called *Agentlet* applications are deployed where agents carry information about their graphical Web representation. For this purpose, we are developing a Web component catalogue, where the representation of each component can be switched between JSON and FIPA-SL in order to make it both readable on the agent and the Web service side. Thus, access to agents and their services is possible via any browser and is consequently very lightweight and nearly platform-independent.

Besides the large potential for further improvements of our Web component framework (new components, more extensive functionality) and WebGateway (support of additional content language encodings), the simplicity of the used service description is not always an advantage with respect to automation of service workflows. A possible improvement in this area could be the integration of WADL[11], which plays a similar role for RESTful Web service as WSDL for SOAP Web services. The further use of our approach in future student projects and the continuous advancement of our agent-based collaboration platform will help to improve the introduced components step by step.

---

[10] WS-Addressing: `http://www.w3.org/Submission/ws-addressing`
[11] Web Application Description Language (WADL): `http://java.net/projects/wadl`

References

1. Aghaee, S., Pautasso, C.: Mashup development with html5. In: Proceedings of the 3rd and 4th International Workshop on Web APIs and Services Mashups, Mashups 2009/2010, pp. 10:1–10:8. ACM, New York (2010)
2. Duvigneau, M., Moldt, D., Rölke, H.: Concurrent architecture for a multi-agent platform. In: Giunchiglia, F., Odell, J., Weiß, G. (eds.) Proceedings of Agent-Oriented Software Engineering. 3rd International Workshop, AOSE 2002, Bologna, pp. 147–159. ACM Press, New York (2002)
3. Fielding, R.T., Taylor, R.N.: Principled design of the modern web architecture. ACM Trans. Internet Technol. 2, 115–150 (2002)
4. Greenwood, D., Calisti, M.: Engineering web service - agent integration. In: 2004 IEEE International Conference on Systems, Man and Cybernetics, vol. 2, pp. 1918–1925 (October 2004)
5. Soto, E.L.: Agent Communication Using Web Services, a New FIPA Message Transport Service for Jade. In: Petta, P., Müller, J.P., Klusch, M., Georgeff, M. (eds.) MATES 2007. LNCS (LNAI), vol. 4687, pp. 73–84. Springer, Heidelberg (2007)
6. Nguyen, X., Kowalczyk, R.: WS2JADE: Integrating Web Service with Jade Agents. In: Huang, J., Kowalczyk, R., Maamar, Z., Martin, D., Müller, I., Stoutenburg, S., Sycara, K. (eds.) SOCASE 2007. LNCS, vol. 4504, pp. 147–159. Springer, Heidelberg (2007)
7. University of Hamburg Department of Informatics. Petri net-based agent-oriented software engineering. Website (2011), http://paose.net
8. Foundation of Intelligent Physical Agents. Fipa communicative act library specification. Website (2002), http://fipa.org/specs/fipa00037/SC00037J.html
9. Foundation of Intelligent Physical Agents. Fipa sl content language specification. Website (2002), http://fipa.org/specs/fipa00008/SC00008I.html
10. Pautasso, C., Zimmermann, O., Leymann, F.: Restful web services vs. "big" web services: making the right architectural decision. In: Proceeding of the 17th International Conference on World Wide Web, WWW 2008, pp. 805–814. ACM, New York (2008)
11. Omair Shafiq, M., Ding, Y., Fensel, D.: Bridging multi agent systems and web services: towards interoperability between software agents and semantic web services. In: 10th IEEE International on Enterprise Distributed Object Computing Conference, EDOC 2006, pp. 85–96 (October 2006)
12. World Wide Web Consortium (W3C). The websocket api editor's draft 6. Website (June 2011), http://dev.w3.org/html5/websockets

Self-organization of Roles Based on Multilateral Negotiation for Task Allocation

Florin Leon

Technical University "Gheorghe Asachi" of Iaşi
Bd. Mangeron 27, 700050 Iaşi, Romania
fleon@cs.tuiasi.ro

Abstract. An important issue in many multiagent systems is the way in which agents can be coordinated in order to perform different roles. This paper proposes a method by which the agents can self-organize based on the changes of their individual utilities. We assume that the tasks given to the agents have a number of attributes and complexity levels, and that the agents have different preferences regarding these features. The adaptive behaviour of the agents is based on the psychological theory of cognitive dissonance, where an agent working on a low-preference task gradually improves its attitude towards it. The agents go through personal learning curves and improve their performance by learning or decrease it by forgetting. A (near-)optimal assignment of tasks between agents is achieved by an evolutionary multilateral negotiation, as agents value the attributes of the tasks differently. Over repeated trials, the system is shown to stabilize, and the agents converge to specific roles, i.e. handling tasks mainly defined by particular attributes. The total productivity of the system increases as an emergent property of the system.

Keywords: multiagent system, self-organization, organizational roles, multilateral negotiation solutions, task allocation, evolutionary algorithm.

1 Introduction

The ability of a multiagent system to dynamically reorganize its structure and operation at run-time is highly valuable for many applications. Therefore, allocating tasks to agents in multiagent systems is a significant research issue.

A popular approach to task allocation is by using auction based mechanisms. Each agent computes a cost for completing a task and broadcasts the bid for it. The auctioneer agent decides the best available bid and the winning bidder attempts to perform the task. Following the classic contract-net protocol [3], several variations of this method have been more recently proposed for the control of unmanned space or aerial vehicles [11,9]. Also, an emergent allocation method for mobile robots was proposed, where each robot uses only the information obtained from its immediate neighbours [1].

The *Extended Generalized Assignment Problem* (E-GAP) [10] studies the assignment of tasks to agents, taking into account the agents' capacities in order

F. Klügl and S. Ossowski (Eds.): MATES 2011, LNAI 6973, pp. 173–180, 2011.

to maximize a total reward. It considers dynamic domains and interdependencies (possible constraints) among tasks. Beside the greedy centralized approach to solving such problems, approximate solutions have been proposed, e.g. algorithms modelling colonies of social insects, such as SWARM-GAP [5].

Since coordination and automatic adoption of roles are also important matters for multiagent systems, Campbell and Wu [2] provide an extensive review of multiagent role allocation.

In this paper, this problem is addressed by using negotiation outcomes for the allocation of tasks defined by attributes, where the process focuses on agent utility functions regarding these attributes, without an explicit transmission of agent potentials.

2   Description of the Proposed Model

The following subsections formalize the definition of tasks that the agents should negotiate for, the adaptation model of the agents, directly related to the adoption of roles and change in productivity, and present an evolutionary approach to find a "fair", (near-)optimal task allocation at a given time. The model can be used to simulate a self-organizing company, where employees are encouraged to accept tasks themselves, rather than being assigned, similar to the recommendations provided by the agile software developing methodologies or modern management practices.

2.1   Task Definition

The tasks are considered to be defined by a series of p attributes. A task has specific values of these attributes, considered to be *complexity levels*, each within a certain domain. Let T be the set of tasks $T = \{t_i\}$, $m = |T|$ and F the set of attributes or features $F = \{c_j\}$. Then: $t_i = \{c_1, ..., c_p\}$, with $c_j \in D_j, \forall j \in \{1, ..., p\}$ and $p = |F|$.

Agents have *competence levels* l_a^j associated with each attribute j, which describe how much knowledge an agent a has regarding a particular feature j of a task. These levels can increase or decrease according to the agent's experience. The complexity levels refer to only a certain moment in the evolution of technology. As technology evolves, one can consider that the competence level naturally decreases, unless a person keeps up with it by learning.

It is assumed that an agent has the greatest utility when the complexity level of an attribute c_j approximately matches the competence level of the agent on that attribute. The utilities of tasks are based on the valuation of individual attributes the task is composed of. For an agent $a \in A$ and a task $t \in T$:

$$u_a(t) = \sum_{j=1}^{p} u_a^j(c_j) \text{ with } u_a^j(c_j) = \begin{cases} 1 - \frac{l_a^j - c_j}{\mu_a^j}, & l_a^j - \mu_a^j \le c_j \le l_a^j \\ 1 - \frac{c_j - l_a^j}{\nu_a^j}, & l_a^j \le c_j \le l_a^j + \nu_a^j \\ 0, & \text{otherwise} \end{cases} \quad (1)$$

The equation for the utility of an individual attribute is adapted after the shape of a fuzzy triangular number with centre l_a^j, left width μ_a^j and right width ν_a^j. Thus, agents have non-monotonic utility functions. Although the shape of all utility functions is the same, the actual functions are different depending on parameters l_a^j, μ_a^j and ν_a^j which are unique for each agent.

If the task is too easy, the agent can solve it with no problems, but it has no "challenge" associated with it. If the task is too complex, the agent will have difficulty achieving it, although it can improve its own competence level.

This adapting behaviour of the agents is rooted in the classic psychological theory of *cognitive dissonance* [6], meaning that an agent working in a low-preference (or unpleasant) situation gradually improves its attitude toward it, in order to reduce the discrepancy (or dissonance) between the reality and its own "painful" perspective about it.

2.2   Evolutionary Approach to Determine Negotiation Outcomes

A negotiation problem is one where multiple agents try to come to an agreement or deal. Each agent is assumed to have a preference over all possible deals. Agents want to maximize their own utility but they also face the risk of a breakdown in negotiation [12]. A qualitative criterion to identify system states that are optimal from a social point of view is the identification of the Pareto optimal states, i.e. states where it is not possible to increase the utility of some agents without reducing that of any of the others. Commonly encountered quantitative solutions for the bargaining problem are, among others, the Nash solution (the deal that maximizes the product of the utilities) and the utilitarian solution (the deal that maximizes the sum of the utilities).

Let X be a finite set of potential agreements. In our case, X contains combinations of disjunct sets of tasks such that all the tasks are allocated, and each task is allocated to exactly one agent:

$$X = \{S_1 \times \ldots \times S_n | S_i \subset S, S_i \cap S_j = \phi, \forall i \neq j, i, j \in A, S_1 \cup \ldots \cup S_n = S\},$$
$$(2)$$

where $S = \wp(T)$ and $n = |A|$.

An evolutionary approach is considered for finding the negotiation outcomes that are usually believed to be fair or desirable: the Nash solution and the utilitarian solution. The encoding takes into account the specificity of the problem, i.e. each task must appear only once in a possible allocation. Therefore, a permutation-based encoding is used. The partition of the permutation between different agents is defined by $n - 1$ integer genes, with values from 1 to $m - 1$. Therefore, a hybrid representation is used: the first genes of the chromosome are the split points and the rest contains the actual permutation of tasks, as shown in Fig. 1.

The fitness function is the product or the sum of agent utilities for a given deal, i.e. a chromosome. The crossover and mutation operations are different for the first and the second part of the chromosome. A normal one-point crossover is applied to the split point section, while a modified crossover is applied to the

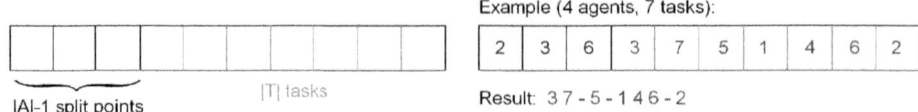

Example (4 agents, 7 tasks):

| | | | | | | | | 2 | 3 | 6 | 3 | 7 | 5 | 1 | 4 | 6 | 2 |

|A|-1 split points |T| tasks

Result: 3 7 - 5 - 1 4 6 - 2

Fig. 1. Chromosome encoding and example

permutation. The procedure for the latter is as follows: one crossover point is selected, the first part of the first parent is directly copied into the child and then the remaining distinct values are copied in order from the second parent into the remaining loci of the child.

Mutation by resetting a gene is performed to the split points part of the chromosome. In order to keep the chromosome valid, the split points are sorted in an ascending order. If two split points are equal, a new mutation is used to make them different, because each agent must be allocated at least one task. For the permutation part, the interchange mutation is used, i.e. two genes are randomly selected and interchanged. In this way, a new valid permutation is generated, because no duplicate values appear.

The chosen selection method is the tournament selection with two individuals, because it is fast and uses only local information. Elitism is used, i.e. the best individual is directly copied into the next generation, in order not to lose the best solution of the current generation. However, it was considered that copying more than one individual would decrease the genetic diversity needed to find a global optimal solution.

2.3   Agent Adaptation: Learning and Forgetting

It is considered that the knowledge of the agents traverses a sigmoid learning curve, defined by an equation inspired after a recent psychology study [8]:

$$L(x) = \frac{1}{1 + e^{-\alpha \cdot (x+\beta)}} \tag{3}$$

Here, parameter α controls the steepness of the sigmoid curve in its central part while parameter β translates the learning curve on the abscise in order to fit the domain of the task attributes.

The main feature of the proposed adaptation process is that it takes into account the effort of reaching different competence levels, as defined by the inverse of the sigmoid function from equation (3). Thus, the agents perform equal small steps on the ordinate, and these reflect into unequal steps on the abscise:

$$l_a^j(k+1) = \begin{cases} L^{-1}\left((1-\lambda) \cdot L(l_a^j(k)) + \lambda \cdot L(c_j)\right), l_a^j(k) \le c_j \\ L^{-1}\left((1-\varphi) \cdot L(l_a^j(k)) + \varphi \cdot L(c_j)\right), l_a^j(k) > c_j \end{cases} \tag{4}$$

When an agent receives a task above its competence level, it will learn using learning rate λ. The basic idea of moving a small distance towards the target, which is the complexity level of a task attribute in our case, is commonly encountered in adaptive methods such as Kohonen's self-organizing map or Q-Learning reinforcement learning algorithm. On the other hand, if the agent constantly receives tasks below its competence level, it starts to decrease its competence in that area with a small forgetting rate $\varphi \ll \lambda$.

2.4 Duration and Productivity

The *duration* of solving a task is defined as:

$$d_a^i = \sum_{j=1}^{|F|} d_a^{ij}, \forall i = 1..|T|. \tag{5}$$

The time taken for an agent to handle a specific task attribute with a certain complexity level is computed as follows:

$$d_a^{ij} = \begin{cases} 1, l_a^j \leq c_j \\ 1 + \delta \cdot \left(L(c_j) - L(l_a^j)\right), l_a^j > c_j \end{cases} \tag{6}$$

Thus, an agent with a sufficient competence level can solve a task in a time unit. However, if an agent with a high competence level does so, the system wastes its resources, because the highly specialized agent could be used to solve more difficult tasks. The time to solve tasks above one's competence level also takes into account the effort difference on sigmoid learning curve multiplied by an amplification factor δ.

Finally, *productivity* is defined as the number of tasks solved in a time period.

3 Case Studies

In order to demonstrate the behaviour of a system following the previously presented model, we will first consider a situation where 3 agents are given 10 tasks defined by 5 attributes. This scenario was useful to compare the results given by the evolutionary algorithm to the actual optimal solution computed by taking into account all 55,980 possible assignments in a task allocation epoch. The total number of possible assignments is: $n! \cdot S(m, n)$, where n is the number of agents, m is the number of tasks and $S(m, n)$ is the Stirling number of the second kind. The domain of all attributes is $D_j = [0, 9]$. The utility functions are given in such a way that the first two agents initially compete over the same type of tasks, and the third agent has different preferences. The learning curve used by the agents is a particularization of equation (3), where $\alpha = 1$ and $\beta = -4.5$, so that the curve should be positioned symmetrically in the definition domain of the task attributes. Other parameters used are the following: $\lambda = 0.1$, $\varphi = 0.001$, $\delta = 10$, the population size of the evolutionary algorithm is 50, and the number of generations for each task allocation epoch is 200.

The negotiation process for the same set of random tasks is repeated 100 times. The evolution of agent utilities is presented in Fig. 2. Both solutions cause

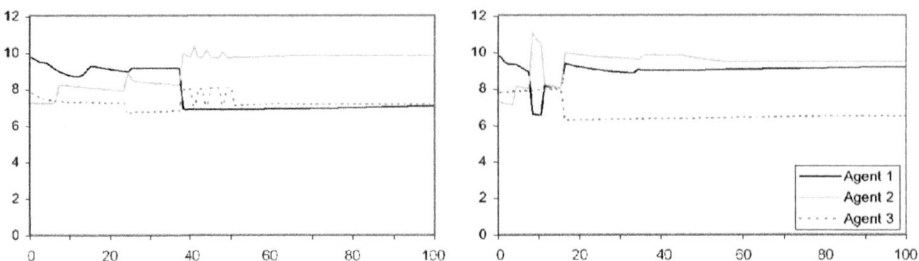

Fig. 2. The evolution of agent utilities over 100 repeated trials using as a negotiation outcome: a) the Nash solution; b) the utilitarian solution

fluctuations at the beginning, as agents adapt to their roles and go through non-equilibrium states. After a while, the total utilities eventually stabilize over some value. The solutions provided by the Nash and the utilitarian solution can be different, although usually close, and therefore the obtained equilibrium utilities are also different.

The evolution of attribute utilities of the agents over 100 repeated trials is displayed in Fig. 3. Since the first two agents have similar initial attribute preferences, it can be seen that the utility of *Attribute 1* is relatively equal at first and then decreases for *Agent 2* while it remains constant for *Agent 1*. Similarly, the utility of *Attribute 2* remains relatively constant for *Agent 1* and increases for *Agent 2*. Both agents find new equilibrium states where they can receive maximum utility by specializing for different types of tasks.

The total productivity of the system is displayed in Fig. 4. One important thing to underline is that the system productivity converges to similar values both when using the Nash solution and the utilitarian solution. The fluctuations in agent utilities over the learning trials are reflected in the system productivity. Although the figure shows only 100 epochs, further epochs were considered and the stable values were found to remain unchanged. While Fig. 4a shows the results for the simple case study with 3 agents and 10 tasks, Fig. 4b shows the corresponding productivity evolution with 100 agents and 1000 tasks. In this case, the search space is huge, but the evolutionary algorithm can be applied in a straightforward manner, while allowing more individuals (100) and generations

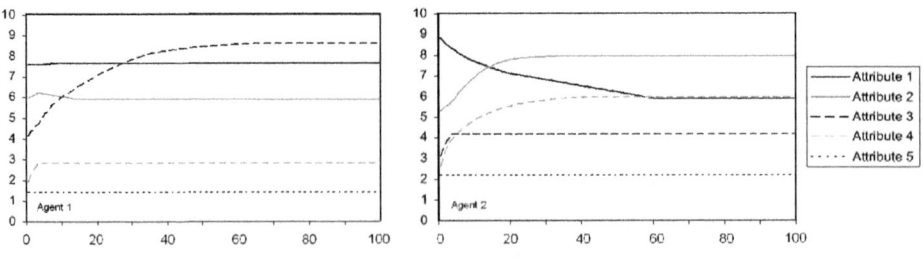

Fig. 3. The evolution of attribute utilities of two agents over 100 repeated trials

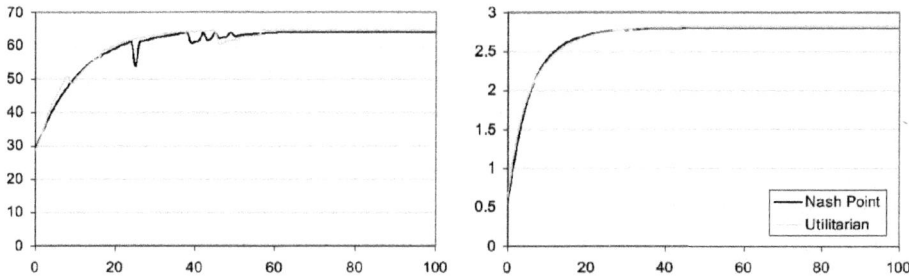

Fig. 4. The evolution of system productivity for different numbers of agents and tasks: a) 3 agents and 10 tasks; b) 100 agents and 1000 tasks

(1000), at the expense of a greater computing time. Therefore, the model can easily scale to any (reasonable) number of agents and tasks.

When dealing with more agents, it can be seen that the fluctuations are reduced, as there are far more possibilities to achieve a good allocation deal. When the number of agents is small, the initial variation is more apparent, as agents quickly shift from one role to another. As stated before, the difference between the Nash and the utilitarian solution also reflect in the overall system productivity converging to slightly different values.

The increase and stabilization of the total productivity is an emergent property of the system, because the explicit aim of the agents is to adapt and maximize their own individual utilities, not to solve tasks more quickly. The shape of the productivity evolution function is very similar to that of productivity evolution measured in actual human working environments [7].

4   Conclusions

The paper presents a method by which agents can self-organize their roles by changing their individual utilities to fit the particularities of task distributions. This is achieved by reaching a (near-)optimal negotiation outcome, computed by means of an evolutionary algorithm with hybrid encoding. The adaptive behaviour is based on the main idea of cognitive dissonance theory. Knowledge dynamic effects such as learning and forgetting are also taken into account. Over repeated trials, the system is shown to stabilize and the agents converge to specific roles by handling tasks defined by particular complexity levels of their attributes. As an emergent property of this behaviour, the overall system productivity increases and eventually stabilizes, following a typical shape also revealed by studies about the human worker performance.

Compared to E-GAP [10], the present method does not address roles explicitly, but implicitly, based on the changes of the agents' individual utilities. Also, rather than treating task allocation as a constraint optimization problem, it uses negotiation as a mechanism to achieve emergent coordination.

Several future directions of research have been identified. The investigation of using direct multilateral negotiation techniques (e.g. [4]) to reach the desired outcomes would be especially important in situations where the agents involved are not fully cooperative and do not reveal their private information regarding their utilities, not even to an external, impartial mediator. Another important aspect would be to consider tasks no longer independent and to take into account a more complex function for defining the utilities. Also, the model could be extended to include functional limitations of the agents, i.e. an agent might not reach an acceptable level of performance despite repeated learning trials. Finally, the dynamics of the environment could be explicitly modelled, so that to allow the complexity levels of tasks to evolve, instead of being restricted to a predefined domain.

Acknowledgments. This work was supported by CNCSIS-UEFISCSU, project number PNII-IDEI 316/2008, *Behavioural Patterns Library for Intelligent Agents Used in Engineering and Management.*

References

1. Atay, N., Bayazit, B.: Emergent Task Allocation for Mobile Robots. In: Proceedings of Robotics: Science and Systems Conference (2007)
2. Campbell, A., Wu, A.S.: Multi-agent role allocation: issues, approaches, and multiple perspectives. Autonomous Agents and Multi-Agent Systems 22(2), 317–355 (2010)
3. Davis, R., Smith, R.G.: Negotiation as a metaphor for distributed problem solving. Artificial Intelligence 20, 63–109 (1983)
4. Endriss, U.: Monotonic Concession Protocols for Multilateral Negotiation. In: Proceedings of the Fifth International Joint Conference on Autonomous Agents and Multiagent Systems, pp. 392–399. ACM Press, New York (2006)
5. Ferreira, P.R., Bazzan, A.L.C.: Swarm-GAP: A Swarm Based Approximation Algorithm for E-GAP. In: First International Workshop on Agent Technology for Disaster Management, pp. 49–55 (2006)
6. Festinger, L., Riecken, H. W., Schachter, S.: When Prophecy Fails: A Social and Psychological Study of A Modern Group that Predicted the Destruction of the World. Harper-Torchbooks (1956)
7. Jovanovic, B., Nyarko, Y.: A Bayesian Learning Model Fitted to a Variety of Empirical Learning Curves. Brookings Papers on Economic Activity, pp. 247–305 (1995)
8. Leibowitz, N., Baum, B., Enden, G., Karniel, A.: The exponential learning equation as a function of successful trials results in sigmoid performance. Journal of Mathematical Psychology 54, 338–340 (2010)
9. Lemaire, T., Alami, R., Lacroix, S.: A distributed task sallocation scheme in multi-uav context. In: Proc. IEEE Int. Conf. Robot. Autom (ICRA), pp. 3822–3827 (2004)
10. Scerri, P., Farinelli, A., Okamoto, S., Tambe, M.: Allocating tasks in extreme teams. In: Proceedings of the Fourth International Joint Conference on Autonomous Agents and Multiagent Systems, pp. 727–734. ACM Press, New York (2005)
11. Thomas, G., Howard, A.M., Williams, A.B., Moore-Alston, A.: Multi-robot task allocation in lunar mission construction scenarios. In: IEEE International Conference on Systems, Man and Cybernetics, Hawaii, vol. 1, pp. 518–523 (2005)
12. Vidal, J. M.: Fundamentals of Multiagent Systems with NetLogo Examples (2007), http://jmvidal.cse.sc.edu/papers/mas.pdf

Representing Emotion and Mood States for Virtual Agents

Luis Peña[1], Jose-María Peña[2], and Sascha Ossowski[1]

[1] Universidad Rey Juan Carlos*
{luis.pena,sascha.ossowski}@urjc.es
[2] Universidad Politecnica de Madrid
jmpena@fi.upm.es

Abstract. Emotional agents are an active research domain, with direct application in several industrial fields such as video games, interactive environments, or enhanced human computer interactions. Emotional behaviour should consider both the representation of the emotions and the mood states. The two most widely accepted and used models for this purpose, the OCC and the PAD models, are rooted in cognitive psychology. Upon this background, this paper puts forward two main contributions: firstly, it discusses the use of a common representation for both mood states and emotions; secondly, it introduces the concept of the Mood Vector Space and analyses its the properties.

Keywords: Emotional Model, OCC, PAD, Mood Vector Space.

1 Introduction

The creation of more believable agents for virtual environments and simulation scenarios is putting the problem of emotion synthesis and analysis into the spotlight. Many theories have been created for this purpose. Some are rather complex, based on numerous parameters derived from empirical data, but are inapplicable from an engineering perspective; others are tractable from a modelling and a computational point of view but have less psychological basis.

The main objectives that emotional synthesis has to deal with are (1) emotion creation based on environment analysis, (2) projection of these emotions into actions of the agent and (3) modelling of the influence of personality over the entire process. Setting out from the PAD Temperament and Emotional models created be Mehrabian [8,7] and their psychological foundations, in this paper we present an approach for the projection and representation of emotions within a continuous space. In particular, we define the Mood Vector Space to model emotions and transitions among them. Its target are architectures for agents acting in complex and dynamic environments such as video games, which require

* This work was supported in part by the Spanish Ministry of Science and Innovation through the projects *AT* (Grant CONSOLIDER CSD2007-0022, INGENIO 2010) and *OVAMAH* (Grant TIN2009-13839-C03-02).

F. Klügl and S. Ossowski (Eds.): MATES 2011, LNAI 6973, pp. 181–188, 2011.

computational efficiency at runtime and ease of configuration at design time. We also establish in this vector space the necessary functions to account for certain psychological characteristics that the emotional synthesis and analysis must have in order to grant the correct representation of emotions in computational agents.

The paper is organized as follows: In section 2 we shortly review models from cognitive psychology that we use throughout the paper and present related work regarding computational models of emotions. In section 3 we introduce and formally describe our MVS model for representing the dynamics of mood and emotions. Finally, in section 4 we present our conclusions and future work.

2   Background

In this section we briefly discuss some well-known psychological models of emotions and review some computational approaches that draw upon them.

2.1   OCC Model

Ortony et al. developed a computational emotion model, that is often referred to as the OCC model [9], which has established itself as the standard model for emotion synthesis. This model specifies 22 categories for emotions (JOY, HATE,...) based on valenced reactions to situations constructed either (i) as being goal-relevant events (they could be acts from an accountable agent, including itself), or (ii) as attractive or unattractive objects. It also offers a structure for the variables, such as likelihood of an event or the familiarity of an object, which determines the intensity of the emotion types.

We will use the emotional tag derived by the OCC model as input for the Mood Vector Space model outlined in section 3.

2.2   Pleasure–Arousal–Dominance Emotional and Temperament Models

The work on the use of the three parameters for classifying, measuring and applying emotions and temperament goes back to Mehrabian, who proposes a framework for the representation of emotional states and temperament of a person [8] [7]. Emotions can be represented in a three dimensional space and, in this space we can also present a more stable and lasting emotional states that we call moods.

The PAD Emotion Model. This model[8] is an extremely general, yet precise, system for the measurement and description of emotions. Three basic dimensions of emotion are used: Pleasure-Displeasure ($\pm P$) or estimation of the liking or disliking, Arousal-Nonarousal ($\pm A$) or general level of physical activity and mental alertness, and Dominance-Submissiveness ($\pm D$) or feelings of control vs. lack of control over one's activities and surroundings.

PAD Temperament Model. This model[7] is a very general descriptive system for the study of temperament and personality. It is based on same three dimensions of the PAD Emotion Model (*P-A-D*).

Temperament is distinguished from emotional states in that it refers to an individual's stable or lasting emotional characteristics (i.e., emotional traits or emotional predispositions). More precisely, temperament is an average of a person's emotional states across a representative variety of life situations. A set of three PAD temperament scales has been developed and shown to provide a reasonably general description of emotional traits or temperament.

2.3 PAD Space for Emotions and Temperament

The work of Mehrabian postulates that the PAD Space is suitable for representing emotions of a concrete and isolated event given at a specific instant, and emotional states (moods) as representing emotional information gathered along a period of time, thus more stable and persistent in time.

These two separated elements are relevant for the emotional behaviour of a person. The temperament of a person creates a tendency of the emotional states that must be achieved if the emotional stimuli are weak or inexistent. On the other hand, the emotions prompted by the consequences of the events perceived by a person are relevant by two aspects: the reactive behaviour derived by a particular strong emotion, and the aggregation of several emotions which change the emotional state (mood) of a person.

The present work, as we show in the Section 3, introduces this formalization and a mechanism to translate emotions and moods in the same space.

2.4 Computational Models

Computational models for emotional agents and emotional behaviour take different ways to model the dynamics of emotions and their influence on the behaviour of the agents. In the following, we focus on work that uses OCC as basis for the analysis and/or synthesis of the emotions, and the models that use PAD as projection/management system.

In FAtiMA [2], the OCC model is treated as initially conceived: each tag separates the type of emotion, and each emotion has associated an intensity derived from the concrete parameters attached to it (for example the desirability of a consequence can produce JOY or DISTRESS). Then, the emotions produced are evaluated against a set of rules trying to match some preconditions to trigger that rule and the actions derived by it.

Other approaches, like WASABI [1] or EBDI [5], use a projection of OCC emotions into a three dimensional PAD space. They consider the different emotions as a vectorial value of $\mathbb{R}^3$. In the case of WASABI the emotions are treated differently depending on whether they are primary or secondary: while the former are denoted by points, the latter are treated as regions of the space. Once an event is analysed, the agent is aware of which emotions are more likely to elicit according to the distance to the central point of each of the emotions, make the behaviour of the agent change according to this information. In EBDI, the projection of the OCC emotions into the PAD space makes the agent change its rational strategy into an emotional strategy according to the decomposition of the relationship that the three parameters (Pleasure, Arousal and Dominance) have among them. This decomposition is treated as a general estimation of the emotional state of the agent which influences the value of each strategy.

There are many other ways of analysing the emotional components of the events but almost all of them make some reference to the OCC model. For instance, the EMA model [6] uses a general decomposition of desirability, appealing and praiseworthy, and the FLAME [3] approach applies a fuzzy estimation of the desirability of an event and analyzes the possible emotions according a set of rules, etc.

In summary, while the OCC and PAD models are certainly interesting starting points for computational models of emotions, we notice a certain lack of formalism in present approaches. Within computational approaches the semantics and especially the dynamics of the model elements are not clearly defined. The Mood Vector Space introduced in the next section constitutes a homogeneous formal framework for modelling a software agent's emotional states and mood along time.

3   Mood Vector Space

In this section, we define the Mood Vector Space (MVS) as a formal structure that can represent in the same space the two major items of emotional behaviour models: emotions and emotional states (moods). This structure is conceived to accomplish the following requirements that are important for mood simulation:

- **R1:** to represent different moods and emotions in the space (according to the PAD representation, bounded in the range $[-1, 1]$).
- **R2:** to support the addition of emotions to the current mood (to represent the influence the perceived events over the mood).
- **R3:** to provide a mechanism to classify the continuous value of the mood into a discrete set of mood tags.
- **R4:** to account for the decay of the current mood along the time towards a default mood (usually extracted by the personality of the agent).

In the following we outline the different steps that lead to the definition of the MVS.

3.1   Mood Space

A Mood Space M is defined as an algebraic structure $M = (\mathcal{M}, \oplus)$ where the first element is a subset of the 3D real number space $\mathbb{R}^3$ bounded between -1 and 1, $\mathcal{M} = [-1, 1]^3$; and the second element is a binary operation in $\mathcal{M}, \oplus :$ $\mathcal{M} \times \mathcal{M} \longrightarrow \mathcal{M}$: $(\overrightarrow{u}, \overrightarrow{v}) \xrightarrow{\oplus} \overrightarrow{u} \oplus \overrightarrow{v}$. To meet requirements **R1** and **R2**, the Mood Space $M = (\mathcal{M}, \oplus)$ must obey the properties of an abelian group.

3.2   Mood Vector Space

If we include the scalar multiplication/division by a real number and the subtraction to the Mood space set $\mathcal{M}$, it represents a vector space. Thus, we have denoted the elements of $\mathcal{M}$ as vectors.

We want to create a vector space because of the interesting properties that we can implement, such as dynamics, tendencies or distances. In many cases, the representation of the emotions are well interpreted as "vectors", some kind of impulse with certain intensity that moves a person to do something, with some decay latency.

3.3   Extended Mood Space

An Extended Mood Space M is an algebraic structure $M = (\mathcal{M}, \oplus, \odot, \| \cdot \|)$, where $(\mathcal{M}, \oplus)$ is a Mood Space, presenting also the properties for being a Mood Vector Space (respecting the $\oplus$ operator and real number multiplication). If we add the $\odot$ operator as an inner product operator and the $\| \cdot \|$ operator as the norm, M is considered a normed vector space.

The norm, of course, enables us to calculate distances between two points in the MVS space. Usually, the distance between emotions or moods is necessary for the correct identification of the behaviour to use given a sequence of perceived event (requirement **R3**).

3.4   Topological Mood Space

The existence of a normed vector space M with the properties presented in Section 3.3, together with $\odot$ operation and the $\| \cdot \|$ operator, and the properties given by this norm operator, provide the possibility to define a topological field K, based on the element addition $\oplus$ and the scalar multiplication. If M is a vector space over a topological field K, M is a topological vector space. Indeed, all normed vector spaces are topological vector spaces. Additionally, if the inner product $\odot$ satisfies the properties of (1) symmetry over the product, (2) linearity with respect the product and (3) linearity with respect the addition, they make the inner product complete over the field $\mathbb{R}$, thus the Topological Mood Space defined with this operation is a Hilbert space.

3.5   Attenuated Mood Space

The dynamics of emotions requires the inclusion of a mechanism to express their decay or their transition to a basic temperament position in the PAD space. Therefore we define an Attenuated Mood Space M as an algebraic structure $M = (\mathcal{M}, \oplus, \odot, \| \cdot \|, A)$, where $(\mathcal{M}, \oplus, \odot, \| \cdot \|)$ is an Extended Mood Space and A is a family of functions indexed by $\mathcal{M}$ denoted as $A = \{a_{\vec{v}} : \vec{v} \in \mathcal{M}\} = \{a_{\vec{v}}\}_{\vec{v} \in \mathcal{M}}$, for which $\forall \vec{v} \in \mathcal{M}$ is possible to define an infinite sequence: $\langle \vec{u_n} : n \in \mathbb{N} \quad \vec{u_n} \in \mathcal{M} \rangle_{\vec{v}}$ such as:

$$\forall \overrightarrow{u} \in \mathcal{M} : \text{the sequence} \langle \overrightarrow{u_0}, \overrightarrow{u_1}, \cdots \rangle_{\overrightarrow{v}} \quad \text{starts with} \quad \overrightarrow{u_0} = \overrightarrow{u}$$

$$\text{generated by } a_{\overrightarrow{v}}(\cdot) \text{ as} \quad \overrightarrow{u_i} = a_{\overrightarrow{v}}(\overrightarrow{u_{i-1}}) \quad \text{such as} \quad \lim_{n \to \infty} \overrightarrow{u_n} = \overrightarrow{v} \quad (1)$$

The family of functions A represents a set of functions $\{a_{\overrightarrow{v}}\}_{\overrightarrow{v}}$ that converge to given values of $\overrightarrow{v}$ for all the elements $\overrightarrow{u} \in \mathcal{M}$.

In order to be complete, it is necessary to define how the limit of the sequence is computed (eq. 1). As M is a normed vector space according to the properties presented in Section 3.3:

$$\lim_{n \to \infty} \overrightarrow{u_n} = \overrightarrow{v} \implies \lim_{n \to \infty} \| \overrightarrow{u_n} \ominus \overrightarrow{v} \| = 0^1 \quad (2)$$

The creation of the Attenuated Mood Space is necessary to create the emotional dynamics required at **R4**.

3.6   Emotional Agent System in a Mood Vector Space

It is possible to define an Emotional Agent System $\mathcal{A}$ as an algebraic structure $\mathcal{A} = (M, A, E, m_0)$, where M is a Mood Vector Space, A a finite set of agents $A = \{A_0, A_1, \cdots, A_n\}$, and E is a set of elements defined as $E = \{(a, t, v, \alpha)/a \in A, t \in \mathbb{N}, v \in \mathcal{M}, \alpha \in \mathbb{R}\}$, named the emotion set, which represents the emotions elicited from all the agents, together with its intensity at a given point in time. Finally, m_0 is a function that represents the default mood state for the agents (the mood state in absence of any emotion, thus the initial state), $m_0 : A \longrightarrow \mathcal{M} \quad : \quad A_i \xrightarrow{m_0} \overrightarrow{u_i^0}$

The state of an Emotional Agent System, can be represented as the mood state of all its agents, and it is denoted as $M(\mathcal{A}, t) = \{\overrightarrow{u_0^t}, \overrightarrow{u_1^t}, \cdots, \overrightarrow{u_n^t}\}$, being $t \in \mathbb{N}$. This state can be defined as follows:

$$\forall i \in [0, n] : \text{if } t = 0 \quad \overrightarrow{u_i^0} = m_0(A_i) \quad \text{Initial mood state} \quad (3)$$

$$\text{if } t > 0 \quad \overrightarrow{u_i^t} = \overrightarrow{u_i^{t-1}} \oplus E_{(A_i, t)} \quad (4)$$

$$\text{where } E_{(A_i, t)} = \alpha_0 \overrightarrow{v_0} \oplus \cdots \oplus \alpha_m \overrightarrow{v_m} \quad \forall(A_i, t, v_j, \alpha_j) \in E \quad (5)$$

$E_{(A_i, t)}$ represents the aggregation of the emotions elicited from the agent A_i at time t scaled according to the intensities α_j and combined by means of the $\oplus$ operator.

If we want to include a mechanism that ensures that the mood state of the agents returns to their default state along time (and in absence of new emotions), we must assure that M is an Attenuated Mood Space and redefine the equation 4 as:

$$\text{if } t > 0 \quad \overrightarrow{u_i^t} = a_{\overrightarrow{v}}(\overrightarrow{u_i^{t-1}} \oplus E_{(A_i, t)}) \quad (6)$$

where $\overrightarrow{v} = m_0(A_i)$ is the default (initial) mood state and $a_{\overrightarrow{v}}(\cdot)$ is the function, from the family of function A in the Attenuated Mood Space, that defines an infinite sequence that converges to this default (initial) mood state $m_0(A_i)$.

---

[1] The $\ominus$ operator represents the addition operation $\oplus$ using the inverse element.

We can also include a mechanism to discretise the MVS in order to obtain a specific mood tag $M_i^\tau \in M^\tau$. To do so, we include a function of neighbourhood $f_\nu(A_i)$ (for instance a minimal norm distance function) that returns the mood tag from the current mood for a specific agent A_i, $f_\nu : \mathcal{M} \longrightarrow \mathcal{M}^\tau$:
$$\vec{u}_i^t \xrightarrow{\ f_\nu\ } M_i^\tau$$
We remark that an Emotional Agent System fulfils the requirements put forward at the beginning of the section for the representation of emotions and moods.

4   Conclusion and Discussion

This paper has put forward a formalism for representing emotions and moods, setting out from the psychological framework of the PAD space. Within our Mood Vector Space we can manage the emotional behaviour of an agent based on transitions and relations across a three dimensional space. The algebraic formulation of the properties and functions facilitates the application in a computational model.

Differently from many other approaches, the MVS approach allows for a homogeneous representation of emotional components in a well founded framework that goes beyond the traditional view of the OCC categories. In addition, the Mood Vector Space provides the ability to include in the same space emotions and moods, granting the mathematical tools to manipulate these elements. On this basis, it supports the transformation and manipulation of dynamically changing emotional elements, composition of emotions into emotional states, etc. Finally, the decay and threshold mechanism of the MVS model takes into account the requirements of psychological findings regarding emotional and temperament dynamics.

The ALMA model [4] is perhaps most similar to our approach. It uses the OCC model as reference for an agent's emotion prompted by the environment. These emotions are then transformed into PAD components. The main difference with our approach is that the ALMA model assumes that the mood movement is based on a pull-push strategy which takes the centre of the PAD space as reference and the centre of the emotions elicited as influence on the mood. In our approach, the PAD space is homogeneous for the transitions, supporting the psychological concept of accumulation of emotions in our mood. The relevance of a point in the mood space is according to the distance to the default mood point derived by the personality, and operations over the mood applied by the emotions or decay are supported.

MVS has been designed for application in different agent architectures and domains. It has already been used to model the emotional behaviour of software agents in a commercial video game [Neverwinter Nights[TM2]][10]. In future work, we plan to use it as part of an agent architecture for the online video game Diplomacy [DipGame[3]]. In particular, we aim at exploring the implementation of multilevel MVS to represent mood in different contexts, e.g. when dealing with different groups of agents (or "nations").

---

[2] http://nwn.bioware.com/

[3] http://www.dipgame.org/

References

1. Becker-Asano, C.: WASABI: Affect Simulation for Agents with Believable Interactivity. Ph.D. thesis, F. of Technology, Uni. of Bielefeld (2008)
2. Dias, J., Paiva, A.: Feeling and reasoning: A computational model for emotional characters. In: Bento, C., Cardoso, A., Dias, G. (eds.) EPIA 2005. LNCS (LNAI), vol. 3808, pp. 127–140. Springer, Heidelberg (2005)
3. El-Nasr, M.S., Yen, J., Ioerger, T.R.: Flame-fuzzy logic adaptive model of emotions. Autonomous Agents and Multi-Agent Systems 3, 219–257 (2000), http://portal.acm.org/citation.cfm?id=608604.608653
4. Gebhard, P.: Alma: a layered model of affect. In: AAMAS 2005: Proc. of the 4th Inter. J. Conf. on Autonomous Agents and MAS, pp. 29–36. ACM, New York (2005)
5. Jiang, H.: From Rational to Emotional Agents. Ph.D. thesis, University of South Carolina (2007)
6. Marsella, S.C., Gratch, J.: Ema: A process model of appraisal dynamics. Journal of Cognitive Systems Research 10, 70–90 (2009)
7. Mehrabian, A.: Pleasure-arousal-dominance: A general framework for describing and measuring individual differences in temperament. In: Current Psychology, vol. 14, pp. 261–292 (1996)
8. Mehrabian, A.: Framework for a comprehensive description and measurement of emotional states. Genetic, Social, and General Psychology Monographs 121, 339–361 (1995)
9. Ortony, A., Clore, G.L., Collins, A.: The Cognitive Structure of Emotions. Cambridge University Press, Cambridge (1988)
10. Peña, L., Peña, J.M., Ossowski, S., Sanchez, J.A.: Eep – a lightweight emotional model: Application to rpg video game characters. In: 2011 IEEE Conference on Computational Intelligence and Games (2011)

An Artificial Market for Efficient Allocation of Road Transport Networks

Matteo Vasirani and Sascha Ossowski

Centre for Intelligent Information Technology
University Rey Juan Carlos, Madrid, Spain
{matteo.vasirani,sascha.ossowski}@urjc.es

Abstract. The efficient utilisation of large and distributed socio-technical systems is a difficult problem. Centralised approaches can be computationally intractable, unresponsive to change and require extensive knowledge of the underlying system. In the last decade, distributed approaches based on artificial markets have been proposed as a paradigm for the design and the control of complex systems, such as group of robots or distributed computation environments. In this work we model an artificial market as a framework for the efficient allocation of a road transport network, where each network portion is controlled by a market agent that "produces mobility" on its links. We demonstrate that the collective behaviour of the market agents, if properly designed, lead to an optimised use of the road network.

1 Introduction

Achieving an efficient utilisation of large and distributed socio-technical systems is a difficult problem. In general, centralised approaches tends to be computationally intractable, unresponsive to change and require extensive knowledge of the underlying system. Distributed approaches are not as prone to these problems, but they can be highly sub-optimal. In the last decade, economic approaches based on artificial markets [1] have been proposed as a paradigm for the design and the control of complex socio-technical systems, such as group of robots [2] or distributed computation environments [3][5].

In this work we propose the application of an artificial market for the efficient allocation of a road transport network, where each network portion is controlled by a market agent that "produces mobility" on its links. We model the price selection strategy of the market agents in such a way that the overall outcome of the market is aligned with the minimisation of the social transportation cost. We analytically demonstrate that the collective behaviour of the market agents leads to an optimised use of the road network. Finally, we define a learning-based framework for the application of the artificial market in real-world road transport scenarios, when demand and cost are dynamic and uncertain functions.

This paper is structured as follows: in section 2 we introduce our notion of artificial market and its application to a simple road transport scenario. In section 3 we go beyond the pure economic analysis and we extend the artificial market to be applied to real-world road transport networks. In section 4 we perform an experimental evaluation. Finally we conclude in section 5.

F. Klügl and S. Ossowski (Eds.): MATES 2011, LNAI 6973, pp. 189–196, 2011.

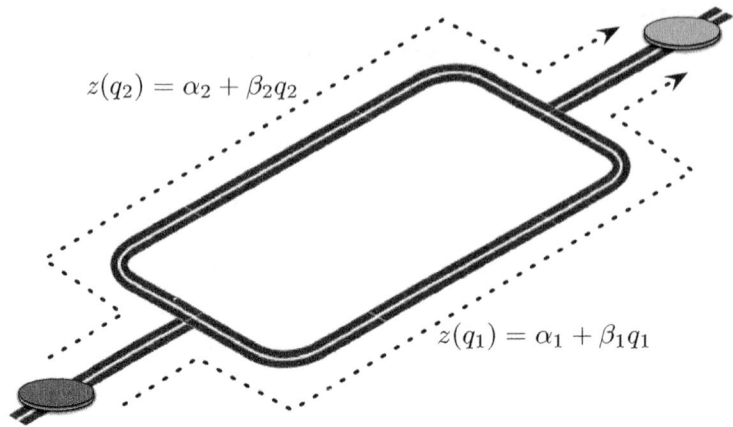

$$z(q_2) = \alpha_2 + \beta_2 q_2$$

$$z(q_1) = \alpha_1 + \beta_1 q_1$$

Fig. 1. Two congestible links in parallel

2   Road Transport Artificial Market

Let's consider the static situation in figure 1. The travel time z_i on each link is an increasing linear function of the number of road users that choose the link, with intercept α_i and slope β_i, such that time increases by β_i hours for each additional user on the road. Let's also assume that there are Q road users that want to travel along one of the two alternative roads. According to Wardrop's first principle [6], each user non-cooperatively seeks to minimise the cost of transportation (i.e., travel time). The result is that at equilibrium no road user can unilaterally reduce his transportation costs by shifting to another route. The equilibrium condition is expressed by Eq. 2

$$(\alpha_1 + \beta_1 q_1)v = (\alpha_2 + \beta_2 q_2)v$$
$$s.\, t. \tag{1}$$
$$q_1 + q_2 = Q$$

where v is the value of time, assumed to be homogeneous among road users. Solving Eq. 2, we obtain the number of users that will choose link 1 and 2 respectively:

$$q_1^u = \frac{\beta_2 Q}{\beta_1 + \beta_2} + \frac{\alpha_2 - \alpha_1}{\beta_1 + \beta_2} \qquad q_2^u = \frac{\beta_1 Q}{\beta_1 + \beta_2} - \frac{\alpha_2 - \alpha_1}{\beta_1 + \beta_2} \tag{2}$$

The above values q_1^u and q_2^u represent the *user equilibrium assignment*. In general the resulting user equilibrium is not socially efficient, that is, it does not minimise the overall transportation cost. On the other hand, the minimisation of the overall transportation cost Θ is the objective of the road transport system administrator (Eq. 4).

$$\Theta = q_1(\alpha_1 + \beta_1 q_1)v + q_2(\alpha_2 + \beta_2 q_2)v$$
$$s.\, t. \tag{3}$$
$$q_1 + q_2 = Q$$

If we replace $q_1 = Q - q_2$ in Eq. 4, we can calculate the derivative of Θ with respect to q_1 and equalling the derivative to 0 we obtain:

$$q_1^s = \frac{\beta_2 Q}{\beta_1 + \beta_2} + \frac{1}{2}\frac{\alpha_2 - \alpha_1}{\beta_1 + \beta_2} \qquad q_2^s = \frac{\beta_1 Q}{\beta_1 + \beta_2} - \frac{1}{2}\frac{\alpha_2 - \alpha_1}{\beta_1 + \beta_2} \tag{4}$$

The above values q_1^s and q_2^s represent the *system optimum assignment*, based on Wardrop's second principle [6], which states that road users cooperate with one another in order to minimise the social transportation cost.

In order to force the attainment of a socially optimal user equilibrium we conceive the entire urban road network as a market of competitive agents that "produce mobility" on a portion of the network. Following this metaphor, for each market agent the output q is the number of road users that the agent can accommodate in its controlled area. The price p is the price charged for the "production" of a road user that travels in the area controlled by the agent. Since producing mobility is costly for the society, we assume that each agent is characterised by a cost function c. If the cost function takes into account exclusively the impact of congestion, it can be modelled as the delay caused by the presence of road users:

$$c(q) = v(z(q) - z(0)) \tag{5}$$

where $z(q)$ is the travel time when q road users travel on the link, $z(0)$ is the travel time at free flow, and v is the value of time.

For agent 1, the cost function becomes:

$$c_1(q_1) = v(z(q_1) - z(0)) = v(\alpha_1 + \beta_1 q_1 - \alpha_1) = \beta_1 v q_1 \tag{6}$$

If agent 1 produces mobility for q_1 road users, the total production cost TC_1 is:

$$TC_1 = \beta_1 v q_1 \cdot q_1 = \beta_1 v q_1^2 \tag{7}$$

Since agent 1 is operating in a market, it charges a price $p_1(q_1)$ to the q_1 road users that travel on its link. The goal is raising a total revenue TR_1 which covers the total cost and generates an arbitrary profit π_1:

$$TR_1 = p_1(q_1) \cdot q_1 = TC_1 + \pi_1 = \beta_1 v q_1^2 + \pi_1 \tag{8}$$

The profit maximising price is therefore:

$$p_1(q_1) = \beta_1 v q_1 + \pi_1/q_1 \tag{9}$$

Similarly, for agent 2, the profit maximising price is:

$$p_2(q_2) = \beta_2 v q_2 + \pi_2/q_2 \tag{10}$$

Given that the links are now priced, the transportation cost for road users is now the travel time cost plus the mobility cost. At equilibrium, the cost of travelling on link 1 equals the cost of travelling on link 2:

$$(\alpha_1 + \beta_1 q_1)v + \beta_1 v q_1 + \pi_1/q_1 = (\alpha_2 + \beta_2 q_2)v + \beta_2 v q_2 + \pi_2/q_2$$
$$s.\,t. \tag{11}$$
$$q_1 + q_2 = Q$$

It is interesting to notice that if $\pi_1 = \pi_2 = 0$, the number of road users that will choose link 1 and 2 respectively is:

$$q_1^m = \frac{\beta_2 Q}{\beta_1 + \beta_2} + \frac{1}{2}\frac{\alpha_2 - \alpha_1}{\beta_1 + \beta_2} = q_1^s \qquad q_2^m = \frac{\beta_1 Q}{\beta_1 + \beta_2} - \frac{1}{2}\frac{\alpha_2 - \alpha_1}{\beta_1 + \beta_2} = q_2^s \qquad (12)$$

Setting a price that simply covers productions costs induce a user equilibrium that is equivalent to the system optimum. In this way, the social transportation cost is minimised by two independent market agents that compete in the market to accommodate the road users, rather than by a centralised regulator with full knowledge. Indeed, for the two links in parallel, the selected price is equivalent to the social welfare maximising toll that derives from a first-best marginal external cost analysis [4].

3 Beyond Economic Analysis

In the previous section we analytically demonstrated how the collective behaviour of well-designed market agents minimises the social transportation cost. This fact validates the artificial market as an allocation technique for a road transport system with many advantages over centralised control, such as the complete distribution and the computational tractability. However, in general it is not always possible to have perfect knowledge of the demand functions (i.e., the quantity Q in the previous example) or the cost function $c(q)$. For this reason, it is necessary to go beyond static economic analysis, and using AI techniques to compensate the impossibility of deriving analytical solutions. In this section we extend the artificial market notion for a more realistic road transport network. We identify an approximation of the cost function, based on realistic assumptions and minimal *a priori* knowledge. We then define the state and action space of each agent that operates in the market. Finally we outline possible learning algorithms that are suitable for the production price selection problem that each agent faces.

3.1 State Space

Let $W = \{w_1, w_2, \ldots, w_m\}$ be a set of $m = 24/\tau$ time windows that composes a day, each of them of τ hours. Let $P = \{p_1 = p_{\min}, p_2, \ldots, p_n = p_{\max}\}$ be the set of n possible prices applied by the agent that governs the link, where $p_{\min}$ and $p_{\max}$ are the minimum and maximum price respectively. Let $u_{\text{in}}(t)$ be the average speed of the road users that enter the link at time t, and $u_{\text{out}}(t)$ be the average speed of the road users that exit the link at time t. Let $u(t) = (u_{\text{in}}(t) + u_{\text{out}}(t))/2$ be the average of the two speeds at time t. Let $\bar{u}$ be the average speed over a time window $w_j \in W$, calculated as:

$$\bar{u} = \frac{\displaystyle\int_{w_{j-1}}^{w_j} u(t)dt}{w_j - w_{j-1}} \qquad (13)$$

Finally, let $U = \{\bar{u}_1, \bar{u}_2, \ldots, \bar{u}_r\}$ be a discretisation of the image of the function $\bar{u}$. The state space is therefore defined as $S = W \times P \times U$

3.2 Action Space

The production price selection problem that each agent is aiming to solve consists in setting a price $p \in \mathcal{P}$ that equals the experienced cost. Given that the price p is part of the state space, the action space $\mathcal{A}$ is then defined as:

$$\mathcal{A} = \{\oplus, \ominus, \odot\} \tag{14}$$

where $\oplus$ corresponds to the action of increasing the current price, $\ominus$ corresponds to the action of decreasing the current price, while $\odot$ corresponds to the action of leaving the price unchanged.

3.3 Setting the Production Price

From the analysis conducted in section 2, we derived that the social transportation cost is minimised when each market agent sets a price p that is equal to the production cost c. If we consider only congestion, the cost function is proportional to the delay caused by a certain quantity of road users in a given time window $w \in \mathcal{W}$, and therefore the cost c can be approximated as:

$$c = v\left(\frac{\ell}{\bar{u}} - \frac{\ell}{u_{\text{ff}}}\right) \tag{15}$$

where v is the value of time (assumed to be constant among road users), ℓ is the length of the link, $\bar{u}$ is the average speed detected over the time window w, and u_{ff} is the speed at free flow on the link, i.e., the speed of a single road user travelling on the link.

Given that the agent is producing mobility at price p, we can compute the absolute difference between the price p and the cost c:

$$\omega = \left|p - v\left(\frac{\ell}{\bar{u}} - \frac{\ell}{u_{\text{ff}}}\right)\right| \tag{16}$$

The value ω can be used by the market agent as feedback information to adjust p and approximate it to the cost c, by using some learning algorithm.

4 Experimental Evaluation: Two Congestible Links in Parallel

The aim of this experimental evaluation is replicating the situation depicted in figure 1, to evaluate whether the two market agents are able to minimise the social transportation cost as in the analysis derived in section 2.

Let's assume that the speed at free flow on the two links is 50 km/h and 30 km/h respectively, and that both links are 1 km long. Let's also assume that for both links each additional road user causes a travel time increase of 1 sec. Therefore, the travel time (expressed in hours) on link 1 and 2 respectively is:

$$z_1(q_1) = \frac{1}{50} + 0.0003q_1 \qquad z_2(q_2) = \frac{1}{30} + 0.0003q_2 \tag{17}$$

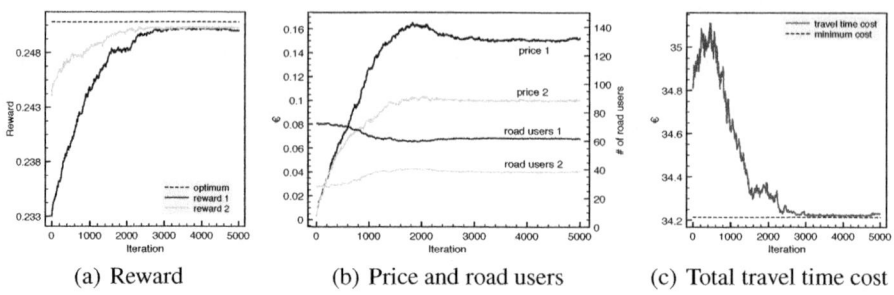

(a) Reward   (b) Price and road users   (c) Total travel time cost

Fig. 2. Experimental results

For the price set, it is reasonable to assume $p_{\min} = 0$, while to set $p_{\max}$ we rely on the following reasoning. In general, a link in a road network is characterised by the maximum number of road users that the link can accommodate, $\mu_{\max}$, expressed in road users per km. In these experiments, we assume that a 1 km link cannot accommodate more than 100 road users, and therefore $\mu_{\max} = 100$. Given that, the maximum price is set to $p_{\max} = \ell\beta_1 v\mu_{\max} = \ell\beta_2 v\mu_{\max} = 0.03v$.

In these experiments, we assume a value of time v of 8.36€/h, which is the average hourly salary in Spain[1], and therefore the maximum price for each link is $p_{\max} = 0.25€$. Finally, we discretise the two price sets every cent of Euro, obtaining $\mathcal{P}_1 = \mathcal{P}_2 = \{0.00, 0.01, 0.02, \ldots, 0.25\}$.

For the average speed set, we discretise every 10 km/h, obtaining $\mathcal{U}_1 = \{0-10, 10-20, 20-30, 30-40, 40-50\}$ and $\mathcal{U}_2 = \{0-10, 10-20, 20-30\}$ respectively. Given that we generate a static quantity of road users, the sets $\mathcal{W}_1$ and $\mathcal{W}_2$ only comprise a single time window, and therefore they can be removed from the state spaces of the two market agents.

4.1 Results

For the evaluation, we run 50 experimental trials and we plotted the average of the following metrics: reward received by each agent, the price selected by each agent and the corresponding number of road users that select each link, and the social cost incurred by the whole system. In these experiments, each agent uses Q-learning with ϵ-greedy action selection [7] as learning method. After observing state s, the agent executes an action a and it observes again the environment state s' and the reward r. The agent uses these quantities to update the current action-value function $Q(s, a)$, using the formula:

$$Q(s, a) \leftarrow Q(s, a) + \alpha \cdot [r + \gamma \cdot \max_{b \in \mathcal{A}} Q(s', b) - Q(s, a)] \qquad (18)$$

where $\gamma \in [0, 1)$ is the discount rate, and $\alpha \in (0, 1]$ is the learning rate. In the experiments, we set $\alpha = 0.8$, $\gamma = 0.1$ and $\epsilon = 0.1$. These values have been experimentally selected as those that gave the best results. For each state s, the learning agent selects

---

[1] http://ec.europa.eu/eurostat

the greedy action (i.e., the action with the highest $Q(s, a)$ value) with probability $1 - \epsilon$, and one of the other possible actions with probability ϵ.

As reward function $r(s, a)$ we use:

$$r(s, a) = K - \omega \tag{19}$$

where ω is the absolute difference between price and cost, defined in Eq. 16, and K is a constant such that $K \geq \omega$.

Figure 2(a) plots the reward that on average each agent receives after every learning iteration[2]. It is possible to appreciate how each agent converges to a reward quite close to the highest possible reward after 2000 iterations.

Figure 2(b) plots the evolution of the price of the two links. After roughly 2000 iteration, the price of link 1 and 2 settles around 0.15€ and 0.1€ respectively. The dynamics of the prices affect the road users' route choice. At the unpriced equilibrium, roughly 70 road users select link 1, and the remaining 30 select link 2. The evolution of prices forces a new equilibrium, where roughly 60 road users select link 1 and 40 road users select link 2.

This new equilibrium of course affects the total travel time cost paid by the whole population of road users (see Figure 2(c)). Again, it is possible to appreciate how the competitive market equilibrium minimises the social transportation cost, which very closely approaches the minimum social cost.

5   Conclusions

In this paper, we proposed the application of an artificial market for the efficient allocation of a road transport network. We modelled each network portion as a competitive market agent that produces mobility. By defining appropriate production price selection strategies, the outcome of the market turned out to be aligned with the minimisation of the social transportation cost. This fact has been demonstrated both analytically and experimentally: the distributed and independent price selection was equivalent, from a social welfare point of view, to the optimal pricing performed by an omniscient, centralised, regulator.

For tractability reasons, we evaluated the artificial market with a simple two-link problem, in order to compare the solution reached by the two learning-based market agents with the optimal solution that we analytically derived. As future work, we need to model a more complex scenario, with several possible routes to choose from, and a traffic demand that varies with the time of the day.

Furthermore, this work could be evaluated using a traffic simulator to compute the resulting traffic assignment, rather than computing the equilibrium assignment according to Wardrop's first principle. In this way it is possible to model more precisely the route choice of each individual road user.

---

[2] A learning iteration is a single update of the $Q(s, a)$ function.

References

1. Clearwater, S.H.: Market-based Control: a Paradigm for Distributed Resource Allocation. World Scientific, Singapore (1996)
2. Dias, M.B., Stentz, A.: A free market architecture for distributed control of a multirobot system. In: 6th International Conference on Intelligent Autonomous Systems, pp. 115–122 (2000)
3. Ferguson, D.F., Nikolaou, C., Sairamesh, J., Yemini, Y.: Economic Models for Allocating Resources in Computer Systems. In: Market-based Control: a Paradigm for Distributed Resource Allocation, pp. 156–183. World Scientific, Singapore (1996)
4. Small, K., Verhoef, E.T.: The Economics of Urban Transportation. Routledge, New York (2007)
5. Waldspurger, C.A., Hogg, T., Huberman, B.A., Kephart, J.O., Stornetta, W.S.: Spawn: a distributed computational economy. IEEE Transactions on Software Engineering 18(2), 103–117 (1992)
6. Wardrop, J.G.: Some theoretical aspects of road traffic research. Institute of Civil Engineers, Part II 1(36), 325–378 (1952)
7. Watkins, C., Dayan, P.: Technical note: Q-learning. Machine Learning 8(3-4), 279–292 (1992)

Author Index

GPSR Compliance

*The European Union's (EU) General Product Safety Regulation (GPSR)
is a set of rules that requires consumer products to be safe and our
obligations to ensure this.*

*If you have any concerns about our products, you can contact us on
ProductSafety@springernature.com*

In case Publisher is established outside the EU, the EU authorized
representative is:

Springer Nature Customer Service Center GmbH
Europaplatz 3
69115 Heidelberg, Germany

Batch number: 09478804

Printed by Printforce, the Netherlands